OXFORD STUDIES IN AFRICAN AFFAIRS

MUSLIMS AND CHIEFS IN WEST AFRICA

MUSLIMS AND CHIEFS IN WEST AFRICA

A STUDY OF ISLAM IN THE
MIDDLE VOLTA BASIN
IN THE
PRE-COLONIAL PERIOD

BY

NEHEMIA LEVTZION

Lecturer in African History
The Hebrew University of
Jerusalem

OXFORD
AT THE CLARENDON PRESS
1968

Oxford University Press, Ely House, London W. I
GLASGOW NEW YORK TORONTO MELBOURNE WELLINGTON
CAPE TOWN SALISBURY IBADAN NAIROBI LUSAKA ADDIS ABABA
BOMBAY CALCUTTA MADRAS KARACHI LAHORE DACCA
KUALA LUMPUR HONG KONG TOKYO

PRINTED IN GREAT BRITAIN

TO MY PARENTS

ACKNOWLEDGEMENTS

I WISH to express my gratitude to those who made this study possible. The Friends of the Hebrew University of Jerusalem in Great Britain awarded grants enabling me to pursue my studies in London and my field-work in Africa. Dr. W. Zander, its secretary, showed keen interest in this work during all its stages. The Hebrew University of Jerusalem gave a supplementary grant for field-work, and the Central Research Fund of the University of London helped with the cost of travels in Africa.

While in Africa I was attached to the Institute of African Studies at the University of Ghana, which accorded me its kind hospitality. I am grateful to Mr. Thomas Hodgkin, then Director of the Institute, and to Professor Ivor Wilks, who first invited me to study the history of Islam in Ghana, and inspired me with their enthusiasm.

Mr. D. H. Jones and Dr. H. J. Fisher supervised this study as a Ph.D. thesis at the School of Oriental and African Studies, University of London. To them and all the scholars in whose steps I follow I wish to express my deep indebtedness.

My interpreter al-ḥājj 'Umar Muhammad of Tamale was a most pleasant companion. He was of invaluable help in introducing me to his brethren, the Muslims, and in winning their confidence. To him and to the Muslims and chiefs who have been my informants go my sincere thanks.

My wife, Tirtza, has her own share of this book. When working in the field or at the study, she has always been near for advice and encouragement.

N. L.

Institute of Asian and African Studies
The Hebrew University of Jerusalem
November 1967

CONTENTS

LIST OF MAPS

INTRODUCTION

(*a*) *The Geographical Setting*

WITHIN the great bend of the Niger the Volta river system drains an extensive area, covering most of the republics of Upper Volta and Ghana, as well as parts of Togo and the Ivory Coast.

The vegetation of the Volta Basin changes gradually, from north to south, with the increase of rainfall and the lengthening of the wet season. In the upper reaches of the Volta Basin the Sahel gives way to the Sudan savannah, and a predominantly nomad population is replaced by agricultural communities. Cereal crops, mainly millet, form the staple food, and as the area is relatively free of the tsetse fly, cattle breeding is still important. The Upper Volta Basin, dominated by the two Mossi states of Yatenga and Wagadugu, is densely populated, reaching about 130 inhabitants per square mile.[1] The density of this area, compared with that of the drier country to the north, goes some way to explain the important historical fact that the Mossi states blocked the expansion of the northern Sudanese empire.

Further to the south the nucleated villages of the Mossi disappear, and their place is taken by individual compounds scattered widely, without any clear boundary between one settlement and the other. Here live several stateless tribes which occupy the country on each side of the border between the republics of Upper Volta and Ghana. The annual rainfall rises from about thirty inches north of Wagadugu to about forty inches at the northern end of Ghana. Figures for 1921 (the first census which covered the whole Northern Territories, and therefore closer to the pre-colonial period) show an average density of 82·2 inhabitants per square mile in the north-eastern section (between Navrongo and Bawku), and 53·6 in the north-west (Lawra district). In between, the district of Tumu is sparsely populated, with only 9·3 inhabitants per square mile.[2] Compared with the long-established population to the east and west, many of the Isala clans

[1] Ilboudo, 1966, p. 13; figures from *Rapport économique de 1958*.

[2] Figures for density of population in Ghana are taken from Hilton's atlas (1960). The 1921 census was less accurate than the more recent ones; but as its figures are reckoned as too low and the population has steadily increased during the colonial period, the 1921 figures seem to be the nearest to the late nineteenth-century situation.

in the region of Tumu entered the area as migrants only a few centuries ago.[1] This suggests that the area has always been thinly populated. The Zaberma raids during the last quarter of the nineteenth century contributed to the depopulation of Tumu and its environs. In spite of the lack of elaborate political organization, the density of population in other parts of the far north added to the security of the peoples there.

The stateless tribes separate the Mossi states from the kindred Mamprusi and Dagomba states. These are already in the Guinea savannah, or the 'orchard bush' country. The Gambaga scarp marks an ecological division; south of the scarp, yam is grown on a large scale together with millet, maize, and Guinea corn.[2] As the Guinea savannah approaches the forest, both crops of the dry north and the wet south may be grown. Yet the apparent advantage proves false, because this area lacks the optimal conditions of both, and neither cereal nor root crops are very successful. A considerable decrease in the population density is noticed: Mamprusi, Dagomba, and Wa had between ten and fifteen inhabitants per square mile in 1921, whereas Gonja, still further to the south, had between about two and five inhabitants per square mile only.

Just south of the Black Volta conditions are even worse, with a tract of scarcely inhabited country, a kind of *cordon sanitaire*. This is the 'desert of Ghofan' mentioned by Dupuis, which separates the savannah kingdoms from the forest states. The population increases again as the woodland changes into forest, and one enters the land of the Akan peoples.

The present study is concerned mainly with the middle part of the Volta Basin: the area which is bounded by the Akan states to the south and the Mossi states to the north, by the Kotokoli and Bassari of Togo to the east and the Lobi, Kulanga, and Brong of the Ivory Coast to the west.

(*b*) *Historical Outlines*

The majority of the peoples in the Middle Volta Basin speak Voltaic languages. It is likely that peoples speaking these languages were the early inhabitants of the area, living in stateless societies. The segmentary political system is still represented among peoples counting

[1] Cf. Rattray, 1932, ii. 468–74.

[2] Manoukian, 1951, pp. 16–17.

more than two-thirds of the population in the Northern and Upper Regions of Ghana, but occupying less than one-third of the area only. The rest of this country consists of the organized states, which dominate not only the tribal map but also the political history.

The area under study is part of a middle belt running across the width of West Africa. It forms a second tier south of the northern belt of the western and central Sudan, where early Sudanese states emerged towards the end of the first millennium. The political evolution in the north extended southward some centuries later with the formation of states in that second tier. Nupe in Nigeria, Borgu in Dahomey, as well as Mamprusi, Dagomba, and Mossi in the Volta Basin are often referred to as neo-Sudanese states. The traditions of these states suggest that they are the creation of groups of invaders, horsemen from the north-east. In the north they became acquainted with the idea of chieftainship as opposed to the politico-ritual organization of the indigenous population, where the authority of the Earth-priest depended not on physical but on moral and religious sanctions. Because of their political and military superiority the invaders imposed their authority over the acephalous peoples, but being inferior in numbers they adopted the language of the indigenous population.[1]

A collation of the traditions of Mamprusi, Dagomba, and Mossi, who claim a common origin, indicates that their ancestors came from the direction of Hausaland or Bornu. On their way to the Middle Volta Basin they may have absorbed some elements of Mande culture from peoples speaking southern Mande dialects in the regions of Illo and Busa (on the Nigerian-Dahomean border) or in Busanga (on the Voltaic-Ghanian border).[2] They entered the Volta Basin in the north-eastern corner of Ghana, where they came into contact with local people speaking a Mole-Dagbane dialect, which the foreigners later adopted. This contact is represented in the tradition by the marriage of the future chiefs' ancestor to the daughter of the *tengdana*, the Earth-priest. In these terms the tradition explains the political revolution; the newcomer murdered his father-in-law, the *tengdana*, and imposed himself as a ruler over the people of the land.[3]

[1] Fage, 1964, pp. 177–8; Lombard, 1965, pp. 67–77, 89–95.

[2] According to a tradition recorded by Tamakloe (1931), the ancestor of the Dagomba rendered military aid to 'Malle—a country adjacent to Hausaland'. On the southern Mande dialects, see Prost, 1945; Lombard, 1965, pp. 44–45.

[3] Tamakloe, 1931. Other variants of Dagomba traditions: Duncan-Johnstone and Blair, 1932; Tait's manuscripts; Rattray, 1932, ii. 463–4. Mamprusi traditions:

The subsequent history is that of the consolidation of the political power in the hands of the new rulers, and the splitting up of the single dynasty into four. Na Gbewa or Na Bawa, son of the usurper Kpogonumbo, is acknowledged as the legendary founder of the kingdom by both Dagomba and Mamprusi traditions. Na Gbewa's 'sons' quarrelled over the chieftaincy, and separated. Tusogu continued the main line as the ruler of Mamprusi, the father-state. His 'brother' Sitobu moved down from the Gambaga scarp to lay the foundation of the Dagomba state. Na Nyaghse, Sitobu's son, is said to have killed all the *tengdanas* in western Dagomba, where the kingdom had first been consolidated. This explains the homogeneity of western Dagomba compared with eastern Dagomba, where Konkomba, the former inhabitants, still live under the jurisdiction of Dagomba chiefs.

Another 'son' of Na Gbewa, Ngmantambu, established a third kingdom, Nanumba, south of Dagomba. At first it extended as far as Salaga, but retracted under the pressure of the Gonja to its present frontiers around Bimbila. Nanumba has always been under the shadow of its more powerful neighbour, Dagomba, to the extent that it is sometimes regarded as an offshoot of Dagomba, rather than an independent state tracing its origin back to the common ancestor, Na Gbewa.

The Mossi traditions tell of a daughter of Nedega, the king of Gambaga, who ran away from her father and married a Busanga hunter. Their son, Widraogo, established a principality in the region of Tenkodugu, out of which the Mossi kingdoms developed. The expansion of the Mossi in a north-western direction resulted in a confrontation with the Sudanese empires of Mali and Songhay.

According to a revised chronology, the Mossi-Dagomba states were given their present form in the fifteenth century.[1] In the late sixteenth century the political monopoly of these sister states, north of the Black Volta river, was challenged by warriors of Mande origin, the Gbanya founders of the Gonja state. The Gbanya warriors exerted pressure over the Dagomba. The latter were forced to remove their capital from Yendi-Dabari in western Dagomba to present Yendi in eastern Dagomba. Early in the eighteenth century the Dagomba finally checked the Gonja expansion.

Rattray, 1932, ii. 547–9; Mackay, unpublished manuscript. Mossi traditions: Marc, 1909; Delafosse, 1912; Tauxier, 1912, 1917, and 1924; Dim Delbosom, 1932; Prost, 1953; Tiendrebeogo, 1963.

[1] Fage, 1964. See Appendix on the chronology, below pp. 194–203.

During the seventeenth century, shortly before the Gonja conquest of Daboya put an end to Dagomba's influence west of the White Volta, rulers claiming Dagomba origin founded two kingdoms: Buna on the western bank of the Black Volta, and Wa on the eastern bank of that river. Whereas the chiefs of Wa still speak a Mole-Dagbane dialect, the chiefs of Buna adopted the language of their Kulanga subjects.

In the middle of the eighteenth century the Chokossi state, centred on Sansanne-Mango (north-west Togo), was founded by warriors of Mande origin commanding Akan troops. They came into the Volta Basin from Grumania (Anno) in the Ivory Coast as mercenaries of the Gonja and later of the Mamprusi. The chiefs abandoned their Mande language and speak *Anufo*, the Akan dialect of their troops.

South of the Black Volta river, on the fringes of the forest, Bono-Mansu emerged as the first Akan state, probably in the fifteenth century, at about the same period as the Mossi-Dagomba states. In 1723 Bono-Mansu was conquered by Ashanti which rose as the powerful state of the forest. The possession of fire-arms gave Ashanti a decisive superiority over its northern neighbours, and the musketeers of the forest defeated the horsemen of the savannah. In the second quarter of the eighteenth century Gonja and Dagomba became tributaries to Ashanti. Ashanti domination lasted until 1874, when the Ashanti defeat by the British was a sign for a general revolt of all the tributary states. Independence, however, was short because the rival European powers—Britain, Germany, and France—were already pushing north to incorporate pieces of the 'hinterland' into their respective spheres of influence.

(*c*) *Sources*

(1) *Travellers, Administrators, Anthropologists, and Historians*

Contemporary evidence for the pre-colonial history of the Middle Volta Basin is rare. The first European visited this area in 1876 only,[1] but some information about it reached European travellers, along the trade-routes. Lucas in Fezzan, Clapperton and the brothers Lander in Hausaland and Borgu, Barth in Hausaland and Timbuktu, Bowdich and Dupuis in Kumasi—all met Muslim traders who were

[1] Gouldsbury's report, 1876.

acquainted with the kingdoms of Dagomba and Gonja.[1] As expected, these Muslim traders could tell more about trade and Islam than about the local peoples, and their social and political life. Indeed, the Europeans themselves, interested mainly in trade, directed their questions to this subject.

More information is available about the last quarter of the nineteenth century, when representatives of the European powers came to the area, first to explore its economic resources and the political set-up, and soon later to sign treaties of 'trade and friendship'. Muslims played a leading role in this phase, as hosts to European travellers, as spokesmen of the chiefs, and signatories on treaties.[2] During the actual occupation of the country the French and the British encountered resistance from Muslim warriors who operated in this area, with Babatu in the north, and with Samori in the north-west.

Hence, Muslims were in the first line of communication with the Europeans, whether on friendly or hostile terms. It is not surprising, therefore, that the importance of the Muslim element in the Middle Volta Basin was sometimes exaggerated by the early European observers. This had undoubtedly influenced the British administration, which for about two decades inclined to regard the Northern Territories of the Gold Coast as an islamized area, like Northern Nigeria, where missionary activities should be restricted.[3] In the late 1920s and early 1930s the administration contemplated the introduction of the 'Indirect Rule' system to this region. Before the new policy could be launched a survey of the social and political structure of the peoples and their history was needed. Captain R. S. Rattray was sent to undertake such a survey. In the introduction to his report, Rattray was anxious to underline the difference between the political system and the religious distribution of Northern Nigeria and that of the Northern Territories of the Gold Coast. He tried to remove the misconception that Hausa was a *lingua franca* in the Northern Territories, and that the population was overwhelmingly Muslim.[4] But Rattray, an experienced observer, did note the important role of Muslims in the

[1] Lucas in *Proceedings*, 1790; Denham and Clapperton, 1826; Clapperton, 1829; R. L. Lander, 1830; R. L. and J. Lander, 1832; Barth, 1857; Bowdich, 1819; Dupuis, 1824.

[2] Cf. *Bull. du Comité de l'Afrique Française*, 1895, p. 349; Treaties signed by Ferguson: encl. 1 in No. 31, *African* (*West*), No. 448, and encl. in No. 68, *African* (*West*), No. 479. On the imam as host to the Europeans in Mossi, see below, pp. 171–2.

[3] D. Kimble, 1963, pp. 79–83.

[4] Rattray, 1932, vol. 1, preface, p. x.

kingdom of Wa, the part taken by Muslims in the state ceremonies of Dagomba and Mamprusi, as well as the influence of Islam on funeral customs.[1]

In preparing for the introduction of 'Indirect Rule', district commissioners were invited to study the peoples under their administration. C. F. Mackay compiled a history of Mamprusi, supplemented by a history of the tributary Kusasi tribe by J. K. G. Syme. The constitution and history of Gonja and Dagomba were discussed in two conferences organized by A. Duncan-Johnstone and H. A. Blair. In 1931 Tamakole published his *Brief History of the Dagbamba People*, a product of over two decades of study, wherein outlines of the oral traditions of Gonja were also incorporated.[2]

During their short rule over Togoland, the Germans produced some important contributions on history and ethnography. The French in the Ivory Coast and the Upper Volta were even more prolific. Works by Delafosse, Marc, Tauxier, Marty, Labouret, and others are rich mines of information for the study of the Volta Basin. French authors, more than the British, paid attention to Islam, reflecting the awareness of the French authorities of 'the danger of Islam'.[3]

Back in the Gold Coast, the general anthropological survey of Rattray was followed by an intensive study of the Tallensi, a stateless society north of Mamprusi, by M. Fortes. The works of Rattray and Fortes served Madeline Manoukian in compiling her *Tribes of the Northern Territories of the Gold Coast* (1951). Islam is very poorly represented in this work, far below its relative importance in the area.[4] This may be due to the emphasis laid on the acephalous societies, where Islam is less significant than in the organized states.

The study of the Middle Volta states entered a new phase as interest in African history captured both professional historians and anthropologists. An example of the co-operation between an anthropologist and a historian was the project of recording the traditional history of Dagomba, undertaken by the late Dr. David Tait and Professor J. D. Fage. This has unfortunately been interrupted by the death of Dr. Tait, and the departure of Fage from Ghana. The material collected

[1] Ibid., vol. ii, pp. 452–4, 462–3, 559, 579, 584, 586.

[2] Tamakole prepared also an account of the traditional history of the Nanumba. His manuscript, obtained from a teacher at Yendi, is deposited at IAS, Legon.

[3] Cf. L. G. Binger, *Le péril de l'Islam*, Paris, 1906.

[4] The only reference to Islam deals with marriage procedure in Dagomba (Manoukian, 1951, p. 41).

is deposited at the Institute of African Studies of the University of Ghana, and I am grateful to Professor Fage for his kind permission to use it. The traditions were recorded by assistants and written down in the vernacular with an English translation.[1] The texts, referred to in the present study as *Tait's manuscripts*, include systematic recording of two versions of the Dagomba Drum History (texts A and B), a more casual recording of the histories of titled offices at Yendi (text C), and of Nanumba traditions (text D).

J. Goody, an anthropologist with a keen interest in history, has opened wide the study of the Gonja state in his clear analysis of its social and political structure. He was followed by a historian, D. H. Jones, who endeavoured to collect oral traditions in the various political divisions of Gonja. These were critically evaluated in his article 'Jakpa and the foundation of Gonja' (1963).[2]

'A Note on the Penetration of Islam into the West of the Northern Territories of the Gold Coast' by J. Goody (1953) was the first study of Islam in this area as a subject in its own right. The most important contribution, however, to the study of Islam in Ghana is that of Ivor Wilks. He first called attention to the importance of Islam in his small book *The Northern Factor in Ashanti History* (1961) and thus added a new dimension to the history of Ghana, by indicating its focal position, facing both south and north.

(2) *Arabic Manuscripts*

Early in the 1930s the provincial commissioner, A. Duncan-Johnstone, received an Arabic manuscript on the history of Gonja. This manuscript was translated into English with the aid of a Mallam, before it was returned, and the English translation was published by J. Goody in 1954. The existence of such a chronicle, written in the middle of the eighteenth century, drew attention to the prospects of finding Arabic material bearing on the history of this area.

These hopes proved true when a project to collect Arabic manuscripts was launched by the Institute of African Studies at Legon. It was carried out by Ivor Wilks, encouraged by the enthusiasm and inspiration of Thomas Hodgkin, the director of the Institute. A tactful approach, which gained the confidence of Muslims throughout Ghana, made the project successful beyond expectation. Within two

[1] The method is described in Fage, 1956.

[2] I am grateful to Mr. Jones for allowing me to consult his field-notes, which proved valuable preparation for my own field-work in the same area.

years (from the summer of 1962 to July 1964) 350 manuscripts were collected, and more have since been added each month.

Preliminary surveys of the collection have been presented by Ivor Wilks ('The growth of Islamic learning in Ghana', 1964) and Thomas Hodgkin ('The Islamic literary tradition in Ghana', 1966). Both point out interesting topics for further investigation in using this Arabic material.

The present study is mainly concerned with histories written in Arabic and Hausa. Only two of them were certainly composed before the late nineteenth century: the Gonja Chronicle, of which at least ten copies (including fragments) are available,[1] and the 'History of Sansanne-Mango', probably from the late eighteenth or early nineteenth century.[2]

The Civil War of Salaga in 1892 was recorded by two contemporary authors: Maḥmūd b. 'Abdallāh of the Lampur Ward at Salaga,[3] and al-ḥājj 'Umar b. Abī-Bakr, the most prolific among Muslim scholars in Ghana.[4] The latter composed also three poems (two in Arabic and one in Hausa) about the crisis which overcame the peoples of Africa with the European conquest.[3]

Chief-lists are the core of African traditional histories. Such lists, taken from oral traditions, have been recorded by Muslims for Daboya (IAS/AR-41 and 42), Wa (IAS/AR-151 and 152), Dagomba (IAS/AR-241 and 250), Mamprusi (IAS/AR-249), and other states and political divisions. It was probably under this influence that Muslims preserved lists of their own leaders, the imams. Lists of imams are available from Yendi (in possession of the Friday imam of Yendi), Djougou (in possession of al-ḥājj Nuḥu of Djougou), Namasa (IAS/AR–340i), and others. The lists of imams from Wa (of which there are many versions and copies) are of special interest, because the names are arranged in the form of a litany or an invocation, and are recited by the Muslims in times of need.

The student of Islam in Africa who is interested in tracing the development of schools of Islamic learning will find most valuable material in the *ijāza*, a certificate given to the student by his master,

[1] IAS/AR-10, 11, 12, 13, 14, 62, 248/i, 263, 272, and ff. 236–7 in vol. iii of the Copenhagen manuscripts.

[2] IAS/AR-346; see below, pp. 78–79.

[3] IAS/AR-1, 6, 15. Arabic text and English translation in *GNQ*, iii, 1961 and iv, 1962.

[4] IAS/AR-27; see below, p. 44 n. 2.

[5] IAS/AR-3, 4, 43.

sanctioned by the *silsila*, a scholastic genealogy, of the master. There are at least fifteen *ijāzāt* in the IAS collection; certificates for the study of the Koran and exegesis (*tafsīr*), and for the study of Mālikī law (*muwaṭṭa'*, after Mālik's treatise).[1]

From the very beginning of the colonial period, administrators encouraged Muslims to write down histories. Tamakloe says that when he collected information about the history of Gonja, Dagomba, Hausa, and Mossi for the Germans, von Zech and Mischlich (in 1897–1907), 'these histories had been written down by an Hausa Mallam'.[2] There is reason to suppose that Tamakloe refers to Mallam Alḥassan, who wrote the histories of these peoples in Hausa.[3] In all probability Mallam Alḥassan was encouraged by the Germans to undertake this task.

A manuscript of about 300 folios has the following title: 'Histories of Samory, Babatu, and others, written in Hausa about 1914 by Mallam Abu (who is said to have been with them) *for Dr. J. F. Corson* in the Northern Territories of the Gold Coast.'[4]

During his inquiries at Wa in 1954, Mr. D. H. Jones noted that the imam consulted a bound volume, inscribed on the fly-leaf as presented in 1922 by Colonel Whittle to Mallam Issaka on condition that he wrote on it the histories of the Walas in Hausa.[5] This manuscript seems to be related to the manuscript copied for Dr. Goody, entitled: 'The History of the Walas as written in 1922 A.D.'[6]

These three works, all commissioned by Europeans, were written in Hausa, not in Arabic, probably in accordance with the demand of the Europeans, because Hausa was more accessible to administrators in West Africa than Arabic.[7]

The late Friday imam of Yendi, Mallam Khālidu, wrote the history

[1] IAS/AR-49, 50, 126, 141, 142, 147, 162, 163, 175, 190, 232, 237, 295, 338, 339.

[2] Tamakloe, 1931, preface, p. xi.

[3] Mallam Alhasan's works have been translated into English by J. Withers-Gill. Among them, *A Short History of Salaga* (1924) is a translation of a Hausa version of the Arabic *Qiṣṣat Salagha Ta'rīkh Ghunjā* mentioned above (p. xix). Cf. a note by I. Wilks in *GNQ*, iii, 1961, p. 9.

[4] SOAS, London Library: acc. No. Hausa 98017. My italics.

[5] D. H. Jones, personal communication.

[6] IAS/AR-152, Hausa and Arabic versions.

[7] At least two of the authors of these Hausa manuscripts could write Arabic. Mallam Alḥasan translated the 'History of Salaga' from the Arabic. Also, there are Arabic letters from and to Mallam Alḥasan (IAS/AR-283 and 284). The 'History of Wa' has also an Arabic translation of the Hausa text. Had it not been for the administrator's request, the original may have been written in Arabic, the literary language of the Muslims.

of Dagomba in Arabic in the early 1930s.[1] This is an account of the Dagomba Drum History, almost unbiased by the author's Muslim faith. It is likely that Mallam Khālidu was stimulated to write this history following the inquiries into Dagomba history made by H. A. Blair, to whom Mallam Khālidu himself was an informant.[2]

Recently, two histories have been composed by Muslims at the request of the IAS: a history of the kings of Wa and its Muslims (IAS/AR–151) by Mallam Fante Ṣiḍḍīq, and a sketch of the history of Islam in West Africa by al-ḥājj Muḥammad Marḥaba Saghanogho of Bobo-Dyulasso.[3]

In his work al-ḥājj Marḥaba quotes from Ibn-Baṭṭūṭa, Ibn Khaldūn, Aḥmad Bābā, Muḥammad Bello, and others. He read historical works extensively and he is concerned with historical traditions. His remarkable erudition and command of Arabic make his work, though hastily written, a worthy example of modern Muslim historiography in West Africa. The writing of history among Muslims is, therefore, a living tradition, influenced by Muslim classical historiography, by the African traditional history, and recently by the growing interest in African history.

Among the most important manuscripts bearing on the history of Islam in the Volta Basin are those found at the Royal Library in Copenhagen. The three bundles of this collection hold about a thousand folios. All are magical or cabalistic formulae, save about a score of folios scattered throughout the bundles. Among these is a fragment of the Gonja Chronicle, which I incline to regard as a copy of the prototype of the Chronicle.[4] Colophons on a number of manuscripts suggest identification of individuals from Kumasi and the north. About fifteen letters of correspondence between Muslims in Kumasi and their co-religionists in Gonja, Dagomba, and Mamprusi throw new light on the Muslims in the Ashanti capital at the beginning of the nineteenth century. The date of these letters, and by inference also of other manuscripts in the collection, is suggested by the identification of the correspondents' names with those of the Muslims whom Bowdich and Dupuis met in Kumasi in 1817 and 1820. An

[1] IAS/AR-241 and 250. The date of writing may be inferred from marginal notes added by Mallam Khālidu himself.

[2] Duncan-Johnstone and Blair, 1932, p. 39.

[3] IAS/AR-246: *Al-jawāhir wa'l-yawāqīt fī dukhūl al-Islām fī'l-Maghrib ma'a 'l-tawāqīt* ('Jewels and rubies of a dated chronicle on the introduction of Islam to the Western parts'). Provisional translation by Salah Ibrahim.

[4] See the Introduction in the forthcoming edition of the Gonja Chronicle.

independent examination of the paper used in these manuscripts indicated that it should be ascribed to the period *c.* 1795–*c.* 1820. These are the oldest original manuscripts yet known from the Volta Basin.[1]

(3) *The Field Study*

During eleven months, from September 1963 to July 1964, I visited over a hundred Muslim communities in four African states (Ghana, Togo, Upper Volta, and Dahomey), where about a thousand informants were interviewed.[2] These figures indicate that I have chosen to cover a wide area, rather than to concentrate on a limited number of communities. It is through the study of this region—the Middle Volta Basin—as a whole that one can get nearer to the understanding of the spread of Islam. The social relationships of a Muslim community operate in two circles; within the local state on one hand, and within the network of the Muslim communities, spread along the trade-routes, on the other. The latter represents the process of *dispersion* of Muslims, the former their *integration* into local political systems. These are two principal themes in the history of Islam in this region.

An extensive study over a wide area is important not only for tracing lines of dispersion and for comparing patterns of integration, but also for a critical approach to the information collected. Interviews are usually held in the presence of all the leading members of the group (a family or a community). A version of the tradition pronounced in such an interview is unlikely to be contradicted later by any of those present, unless the group is torn by conflicting interests.[3] Muslims of the same origin, or ex-members of the same community, can be found in other places, where it is possible to hear the same tradition or its variants, independently of previous interviews.

For the traditional histories of the states concerned I had to rely on past recording of the official traditions. I have concentrated mainly on collecting histories of Muslim communities. In doing this one is not presented with a coherent official history, such as that transmitted

[1] N. Levtzion, 'Arabic manuscripts from Kumasi of the early nineteenth century', *THSG*, viii, 1965. I. Wilks guided me to this collection (cf. Wilks, communication to the *Research Bulletin*, Centre of Arabic Documentation, Ibadan, I, 1 July 1964, p. 12). I am grateful to Mr. O. K. Nordstrand, Conservator at the Royal Library, Copenhagen, who examined the paper.

[2] I have reduced to a minimum names of informants in footnotes. Readers interested in further details about informants may either consult the Ph.D. thesis, or write to the author.

[3] Cf. Vansina, 1965, p. 28.

by drummers, but one has to explore family histories and private genealogies.[1] Hence, one is spared the task of overcoming the sacred character of the Drum History, because history is profane among Muslims. Yet one has to be careful of the social etiquette while intruding into private domains. In this delicate task I had the invaluable guidance of my interpreter.

In most cases Muslim informants were very careful not to give any information about other families, even if they were acquainted with their history. A respectable elder would give such information only if a member of the other family was present. Only the imams' list is regarded as a common property of the community, but any further details about individual imams had to be collected from his own descendants. Indeed, a history of a family is best preserved by its own members, and imams with no descendants in that community are hardly remembered, except by name.

The history of a Muslim family in the Middle Volta Basin usually begins with its ancestor who had migrated to this area, not necessarily to that locality.[2] In most cases his country of origin is known, but not always the name of the town or even the region. It is interesting to note some stereotyped replies given as the reason for the migration: 'he was on his way to Mecca', 'he was a chief's son who had been deprived of his right to the chieftaincy', 'there was war in his country', etc. While trade is not often mentioned as a reason for migration, an explanation like, 'he was a Mallam, and used to wander about' is quite common.

For chronology one is heavily dependent on genealogies. Private genealogies are liable to distortion, but these may be checked by genealogies of other individuals who trace back to the same ancestor. Lists of imams may be collated with private genealogies, or it is sometimes possible to tie up a private genealogy with a chiefly one. The latter is not only more reliable, but may also offer some approximate dates. With this kind of evidence it is safer to speak of a period ('beginning', 'second half', or 'third quarter' of a century) rather than to give a definite date.

My interpreter, al-ḥājj 'Umar Muḥammad of Tamale, a Dagomba Muslim, speaks fluent Arabic, which he acquired in his extensive travels in Arab countries, having been on pilgrimage several times. Arabic is highly esteemed among Muslims, who were delighted to hear it spoken in their homes. Although most of my informants

[1] Ibid., pp. 156–7.

[2] Cf. Person, 1962, p. 468.

could not speak Arabic, they were acquainted with this language. I found them more drawn into the conversation when Arabic was used than when I tried English-speaking interpreters.

The Muslim informants were always very helpful and co-operative. Yet seldom had they a ready historical narration to tell, and most of the information had to be collected by putting leading questions. The line of investigation I followed has, therefore, conditioned the type of information obtained. But, in fact, my programme itself was worked out only after I had tried quite a number of alternatives. Also, the sort of material collected, genealogies and fragmentary family tales, could be analysed only after I left Ghana. The conclusions of this study have, therefore, emerged at the very last stage, that of the writing itself, and could not influence the inquiries during the field-work.

(*d*) *The Theme: the Process of Islamization*

Islam in West Africa is one of the better-known topics in African history. The earliest kingdoms in the northern belt of the western and central Sudan became known to the Arabs, and were recorded in Arabic geographical and historical works, at a time when Islam first penetrated tropical Africa. Much attention has, therefore, been paid to the spread of Islam in that golden age of African history, and to the place of Islam in the Sudanese state system.

As late as 1960 Professor H. F. C. Smith could complain of the nineteenth-century *jihād* movements as 'a neglected theme of West African history'.[1] But since then many scholars have been engaged in studying the ample Arabic material available for this revivalist phase in the history of Islam in Africa.

Hence, the study of Islam in West Africa is concerned with two decisive periods: eleventh to sixteenth centuries, and the nineteenth century. It is also limited to those parts of West Africa where Islam is both old and widespread. The sources for reconstructing the spread of Islam and for evaluating its position are Arabic, representing a puritan Islamic outlook. Indeed, traditional histories of Mali and Songhay, of Bornu and the Hausa states do help in obtaining a more balanced view of Muslim and non-Muslim elements in the history of these states. This has been done, in a most stimulating way, by Jean Rouch in his *Contribution à l'histoire des Songhay* (1953). But Rouch's study of current traditions was able to reveal the Muslim–Pagan

[1] H. F. C. Smith, 1961.

dichotomy because the area he was concerned with is an exception in the northern belt of the Sudan. From the Atlantic Ocean to Lake Chad only the country between the Niger bend and Hausaland was not overrun by the nineteenth-century *jihād* movements.

The present study is concerned with an area, where the spread of Islam began some centuries later than in the northern belt, and where the process of islamization, not revolutionized by a *jihād*, is still going on. The paucity of documentary evidence bearing on this process is compensated by the fact that present informants are in many cases direct descendants of those early Muslims who carried out the propagation of Islam in this part of Africa.

Because of its intermediate position between the Sahel and the forest, the Volta Basin was intersected by trade-routes linking the termini of the trans-Saharan trails with the gold and kola sources of the forest. Along these routes Muslim traders reached the area, and settled in market towns and under the auspices of the chiefs. The extension of the trade-routes and the establishment of Muslim communities—which will be dealt with in the first part—represent the first phase. At that stage Islam had been confined to foreign immigrants, and the process may be described as *the dispersion of Muslims*, rather than *the spread of Islam*. The second phase began with the building up of communication between the hospitable chiefs and their Muslim guests. Three aspects of the subsequent development of Islam in the Middle Volta states will be dealt with:

(*a*) the incorporation of Islamic elements in the culture of the states;
(*b*) the integration of the foreign Muslims into the socio-political system of the state;
(*c*) the conversion of members of the local society, mainly from the chiefly estate.

Each state had its own experience in this process, and the nuances in the patterns of islamization will emerge from the comparative study. One common feature, however, may be mentioned here, because it is relevant to the definition of the Middle Volta Basin as a distinct zone of Islam. In all the states of this area Muslims speak the local language as their first language, and regard themselves as members, not residents only, of the state. They refer to themselves as Dagombas, Walas, or Gonjas. In this respect they differ from their co-religionists west of the Black Volta river, where Muslims (Dyula) speak their own Mande dialect and keep their own ethnic identity.

The same is true of the Muslims in Borgu, to the east, who speak Dendi, not the language of the Bariba. This one feature already indicates a higher degree of integration of Muslims in the Middle Volta states than in the adjacent countries to the west and east.

The present study deals with the history of social groups (the Muslim communities) of different ethnic origins (but mainly Mande and Hausa) in several separate political units (Gonja, Chokossi, Dagomba, Mamprusi, Wa, as well as Mossi, Borgu, Kotokoli, and Ashanti) over a period of more than four centuries (from the fifteenth to the nineteenth centuries). Traditions of origin, family relationships, bonds of religion, and trade association link members of these groups with the northern belt of the Sudan.

In such a study, closer to social history than to any other branch of history, one has to treat as background material aspects of the subject which merit an equally detailed study. One is tempted to draw a fuller description of the development of trade, or to follow more thoroughly the history of the local states. Readers may find that the study of Muslim customs and beliefs or of Islamic scholarship falls short of their expectations. Yet all these aspects, important as they are, had to be subjected to the main theme of this study: the process of islamization as outlined above.

I must admit at least one lacuna in the present study, namely the history of the Qādirīya and the Tijānīya orders. This is due mainly to a difficulty which I encountered in my field-work. The spread of the Tijānīya since the late nineteenth century covered earlier traces of the Qādirīya in northern Ghana. This is the more pronounced because Muslims now affiliated to the Tijānīya had nothing to say about their ancestors' affiliation. I hope that future studies will do more justice to this subject, and it will be interesting to weigh the contribution of the religious orders, and in particular the Qādirīya, to the process of islamization.

PART I

THE TRADE PATTERNS

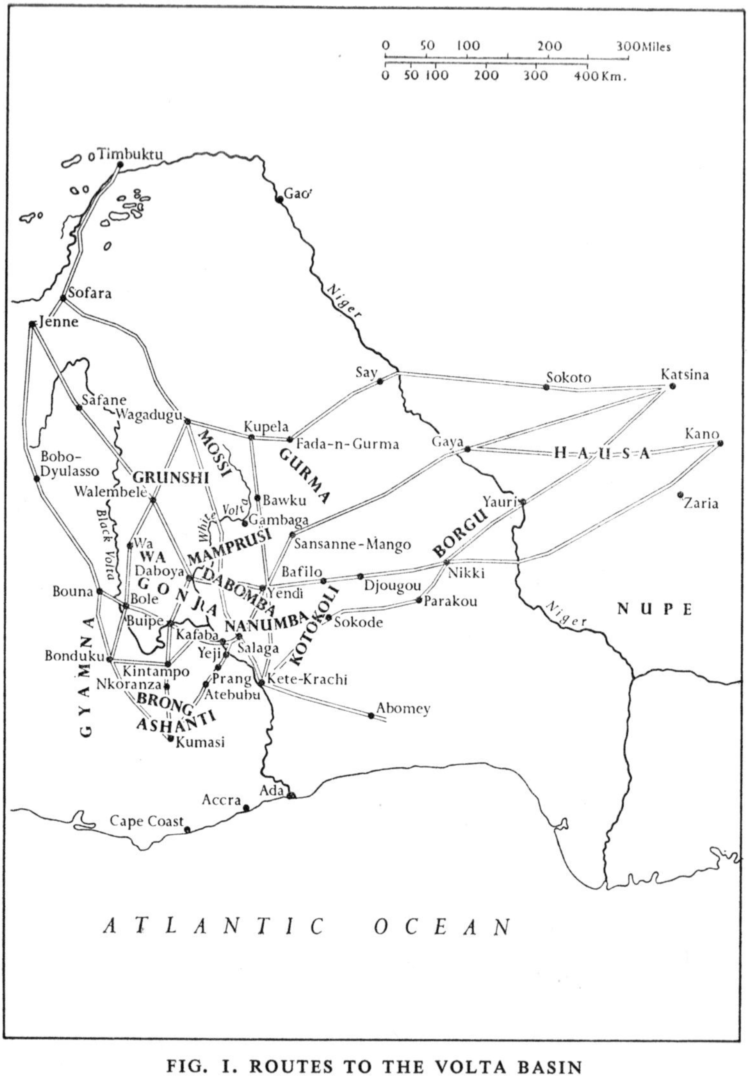

FIG. I. ROUTES TO THE VOLTA BASIN

CHAPTER I

The Mande Trade

MUSLIMS of North Africa carried the trans-Saharan trade to the Sahel, 'the shore' of the desert sea. There, in the termini of the caravans' trails, they met Sudanese traders, members of the great family of the Mande tribes, who brought the gold from the interior. Through their trade these Mande traders became detached from the agricultural and tribal ways of life, in which the traditional African religions are anchored. Under the influence of the North Africans they adopted Islam, and in their wanderings found hospitality and a sense of community among Muslims in the new trading centres which developed along the trade-routes. In this way a new social group, distinguished by trade and Islam, was dispersed throughout the Sudan. Muslim traders of Mande origin operated in a vast area: from the Sahel in the north to the fringes of the forest in the south, from the Atlantic Ocean in the west to Hausaland in the east.

These groups of Muslim traders are known by different names among various tribes. They are called Dyula among the Malinke of the Upper Niger, Marka by the Bambara in the region of Segu and Jenne, Dafing in the bend of the Upper Black Volta river, and Yarse by the peoples speaking the Mole–Dagbane languages. In Arabic sources the Mande traders are called Wangara.[1] By this name they are known to the Fulani and the Hausa. Under the influence of the Hausa the name Wangara, both for the various Mande peoples and their country, is widely used in the Middle Volta Basin.

These enterprising traders carried Islam into the interior as they extended the trade-routes southward in search of new and richer sources of gold. The first gold-fields exploited for the trans-Saharan trade were those of Bambuk, enclosed by the Senegal and the Faleme rivers at their confluence. The ancient kingdom of Ghana controlled the gold trade from these sources and owed its prosperity to it.

In the eleventh and twelfth centuries the traders reached the rich gold-fields of Bure on the Upper Niger river. The Arab geographers,

[1] Ibn-Baṭṭūṭa, 1922, iv. 394. The author of *Ta'rīkh al-Fattāsh* (1913, p. 38; trans., p. 65) says that Malinke and Wangara are of the same origin, but the former are warriors whereas the latter are traders.

al-Bakrī and al-Idrīsī, whose information suggests this development of the gold trade, allude also to the emergence of several principalities among the Malinke.[1] One of these had been the nucleus of the empire of Mali, which rose to hegemony in the western Sudan early in the thirteenth century. The political development of Mali may be associated with the control its rulers gained over the trade in the gold of Bure.

In their efforts to find more gold, the Sudanese traders were stimulated by the growing demand for African gold in the Muslim world and in Europe.[2] Trade in African gold was exclusively in the hands of Muslims, and it was in order to break this monopoly that the Portuguese opened the maritime route to the Guinea coast. In several factories along the coast the Portuguese succeeded in obtaining some gold, but nowhere else did the gold flow in such quantity as in Elmina, on the Gold Coast, discovered in 1471.[3] This gold came from the forest of the Akan in the hinterland of Elmina. The immediate flow of gold to the coast suggests that these fields had already been exploited commercially. The Portuguese only diverted part of the gold, which had previously been exported to the north. Mande traders engaged in this trade reached Elmina soon after its establishment by the Portuguese.[4]

The opening up of the trade between the Sahel and the gold-fields of the forest may be linked with the development of Jenne as a commercial centre. Located in the south-eastern end of the inner Niger delta, Jenne is the starting-point of several routes to the Volta Basin.

Early in the sixteenth century V. Fernandes heard from a Moorish trader that part of the Saharan salt was sent by canoes from Timbuktu to Jenne. In Jenne the salt bars were taken by the 'ungaros' (i.e. the Wangara) and carried on porters' heads to the gold-mines.[5] Raymond Mauny rightly suggests that salt for the gold-fields of Bure had no reason to be unloaded at Jenne, as it could be carried by boats up the main course of the Niger, as far as the river is navigable. It is, therefore, very likely that the salt that reached Jenne was carried further south to the Akan forest.[6] If this is accepted, al-Saʿdī may refer to the same trade pattern: 'Jenne is one of the greatest Muslim markets, where

[1] Al-Bakrī, 1911, p. 178; trans., 1913, p. 333; al-Idrīsī, 1866, p. 4; trans., p. 4.
[2] Wilks, 1961, pp. 5–6.
[3] Mauny, 1961, p. 298, quoting Pacheco Pereira, who visited the coast in 1506–8.
[4] V. Fernandes, 1951, p. 47; visited the coast in 1506–10.
[5] V. Fernandes, 1938, pp. 85–87.
[6] Mauny, 1961, pp. 359–60.

traders with salt from the mine of Taghāza meet traders with the gold of Bīṭu. . . . It is because of this blessed town [Jenne] that caravans come to Timbuktu from all points of the horizon: east and west, south and north.'[1]

The Niger waterway between Timbuktu and Jenne linked two overland routes: from Teghaza to Timbuktu and from Jenne to the forest. In 1512–14 Leo Africanus described the merchants of Timbuktu carrying their goods in small boats to Jenne.[2] It is very likely, therefore, that the commercial centres of Jenne and Timbuktu developed simultaneously.

The early termini of the trans-Saharan trade—Ghana, Awdaghost, and Walata—had overland routes only. Timbuktu, on the other hand, was accessible both by overland routes and by the Niger waterway. It was owing to this advantage that Timbuktu grew at the expense of Walata. 'The prosperity of Timbuktu', says al-Saʿdī, 'was the ruin of Bīru.'[3]

In 1352 Ibn-Baṭṭūṭa joined a caravan which took the old route: Sijilmasa–Teghaza–Walata. The description of this traveller leaves the impression that Walata was a busier commercial centre than Timbuktu.[4] Yet, a quarter of a century later, in the map of A. Cresques dated 1375, the trans-Saharan route is marked: 'Sigilmasa–Tagaza–Tenbuch [Timbuktu]'.[5] Hence, towards the end of the fourteenth century Timbuktu superseded Walata as the main terminus of the caravans' trade.[6]

At that period, it may be inferred, the Niger waterway gained importance, and Jenne could assume its commercial function as the port for the gold trade with the Akan forest.[7]

The fifteenth century saw a significant political development in the Volta Basin with the consolidation of the Mossi-Dagomba states and of Bono-Mansu, the earliest Akan state. All these states were associated with the trade-route from the Niger to the forest. The states

[1] Al-Saʿdī, 1900, pp. 11–12; trans., pp. 22–23.

[2] Leo Africanus, 1956, vol. ii, p. 465.

[3] Al-Saʿdī, 1900, p. 21; trans., p. 37. Bīru is the Songhay name of Walata.

[4] Ibn-Baṭṭūṭa, 1921, iv. 385–7 (Walata), pp. 430–1 (Timbuktu).

[5] Mauny, 1961, p. 432.

[6] In 1455 Ca da Mosto (1895, pp. 56–58) noted that the salt of Teghaza was carried over Timbuktu to Mali. In 1512 Leo Africanus (1956, pp. 463–5) took the route Sijilmasa–Teghaza–Timbuktu.

[7] According to al-Saʿdī (1900, p. 12; trans., p. 23), Jenne developed as an important trading centre in the twelfth and thirteenth centuries, a date which seems to be too early.

offered security to the trade, and the benefit their rulers derived from controlling the routes helped them in consolidating their authority.

The first group of Yarse, traders of Mande origin, settled in Mossi (Wagadugu) about the beginning of the sixteenth century.[1] Further to the south, excavations at Yendi-Dabari ('Ruined Yendi'), the old Dagomba capital abandoned *c.* 1700, revealed 'a large, rectangular, and possibly two-storied building, and a walled and carefully floored enclosure'. This building is markedly different from the typical Dagomba compound, where circular mud huts are built round a central courtyard. The building, the archaeologists suggest, may well have been a kind of caravanserai. As surface indications suggest that there are more structures like this, 'it may well be that the area so far excavated was a strangers' and merchants' quarter'.[2] Yendi-Dabari is about two miles east of the White Volta river. On the other side of this river a route from Kumasi to Jenne was recorded early in the nineteenth century.[3] Such a route had probably passed over the pre-eighteenth-century Dagomba capital. There are also traces of Wangara Muslims of that period in Dagomba.[4]

South of Dagomba, the area in the vicinity of the Black Volta bears marks of early habitation.[5] Buipe, Mpaha, and Kafaba preceded Salaga as markets on the northern bank of the Volta.[6] As in nineteenth-century Salaga, traders from the north preferred to transact their business in these centres to avoid the journey southward into the forest, where the climate was less favourable for the savannah people, and where beasts of burden could not survive.[7] Muslim groups in these centres claim to have come there from Hausa or Bornu before the Gonja invasion, i.e. before the end of the sixteenth century. The existence of early Muslims of Mande origin is attested by such patronymics as Dabo and Jabaghte.[8] The predominance of Hausa traders during the last two centuries might have covered more traces of Wangara Muslims of the pre-Gonja period.

The early trading centres on the Volta river were established for trade with Bono-Mansu, the first Akan state. Mrs. Meyerowitz proposed the late thirteenth century for the foundation of this state, but a revised chronology, based on Meyerowitz's own material, suggests

[1] See below, p. 201. [2] Shinnie and Ozanne, 1963, p. 118.
[3] Dupuis, 1824, manuscript pp. cxxxi–cxxxii. [4] See below, pp. 86–87.
[5] Goody, 1964, p. 201.
[6] 'The Story of Salaga, etc.', *GNQ*, iii, 1961, pp. 16–17, 26–27.
[7] Lonsdale, 1882. Quoted below, p. 41. [8] See below, pp. 61, 63.

a date about a hundred and fifty years later, probably in the middle of the fifteenth century.[1] This coincided with the development of the gold trade of the forest. Indeed, Bono-Mansu controlled some of the gold and kola sources of the forest, and a central theme in the recorded traditions is the trade, on which 'its prosperity and advanced civilization depended'.[2]

According to these traditions Muslim traders frequented the state, established their own quarters in the capital, and had social intercourse with the ruling class, in particular with the royal princesses.[3] At the time of the conquest of Bono-Mansu by the Ashanti in 1723, all the Muslim population of Bono is said to have fled across the frontiers.[4] Indeed, all the Muslims now in the area of the old Bono-Mansu state have come there since the last quarter of the nineteenth century.[5] It is possible, however, to recall two Muslim groups which might have been part of the Muslim population of Bono-Mansu.

In the Bole division of Gonja a group of Muslims is known as *Mbontisua*, a word which may be translated as 'the Muslims of the Akan'. According to their traditions Ndewura Jakpa, the legendary founder of the Gonja state, found their ancestors in the village of Ayiiwa (unidentified), between Nkoranza and Takyiman, from where they followed the Gonja warriors.[6] These Muslims are of the Timite patronymic group, and therefore of Mande origin. They had been in the region of Takyiman before the end of the sixteenth century (the Gonja invasion), probably for quite a long time, sufficient for allowing them to be given the appellation 'Muslims of the Akan'. If so, they could well have been one of the Mande Muslim groups, which through their trade came to live in Bono-Mansu. An attack of the Gonja on Bono-Mansu is recorded by the traditions.[7]

In 1820 Dupuis heard of Muslim communities living in the area, which had been in the past part of the Bono-Mansu state. In Takima (Takyiman), he says, the Muslims 'live in distinct societies under the jurisdiction of their own law', but in subordination to local chiefs.[8] He further mentions 'Moslem Mandings called Salkoh' in Coransah (Nkoranza).[9] Is it not possible that these communities, of Mande origin, were remnants of the Muslim population of Bono Mansu?

[1] See below, pp. 194–5.
[2] Meyerowitz, 1951, p. 198.
[3] Meyerowitz, 1958, pp. 106–22.
[4] Ibid., p. 126.
[5] Goody, 1965, p. 49.
[6] Goody, 1964, p. 198.
[7] Meyerowitz, 1958 ,p. 115.
[8] Dupuis, 1824, p. lviii.
[9] Ibid., p. 124.

The region of Takyiman-Nkoranza is important in the kola trade,[1] and Muslims might have remained there after the liquidation of the Bono-Mansu state. Did these early Muslims disappear only in the second and third quarters of the nineteenth century, before the present Muslim communities settled in that area?[2]

Muslim traders frequented the market of Bono-Mansu, and probably had their own section in the capital. Yet Islam left little impression on the religion and customs of the Akan people of Bono. Nor is there evidence for any contribution of Muslims from Bono to the spread of Islam in the Middle Volta Basin. An important centre for the diffusion of Islam in this part of Africa was Beʿo, which rivalled Bono in the gold trade.

Beʿo, twenty-five miles south-east of Bonduku, preceded the latter as a commercial centre and as an outpost of Islam.[3] The relationship between the two flourishing centres of Bono-Mansu and Beʿo is not clear, but the existence of both suggests two trade systems. While the route from Bono-Mansu passed along the White Volta river, the trade of Beʿo was carried either east or west of the Black Volta river, over the Wa–Bole route or the Buna–Dyulaso track. Generally speaking, the trade of Bono and Beʿo followed patterns similar to those of the two towns' successors, Kumasi and Bonduku respectively.

The market of Beʿo developed with the arrival of two important Mande groups, the Ligby and the Dyula. The Ligby, defined by linguists as proto-Dyula, had migrated from the Upper Niger to the fringes of the forest, towards the region where the modern frontiers of the Ivory Coast, Guinea, and Liberia meet. Thence, separated from such kindred groups as the Vai and the Kono, they moved eastwards, along the edge of the forest to Beʿo, where they arrived, according to Y. Person, in the fifteenth century.[4] In the Ivory Coast the Ligby may

[1] A. Freeman, 1898, pp. 351–2; Binger, 1892, ii. 137.

[2] J. Goody (1965, p. 49) suggests that the withdrawal of the Muslims from this area might have been a result of the extension of the Ashanti dominions.

[3] This old town had first been known as Begho, according to information collected by the French at Bonduku (cf. Delafosse, 1908, and Tauxier, 1921). The people in the area around the site of the old town pronounce the name as Beʿo or Biʿu. In two English manuscripts from the area—one from Namasa and the other from Nsawkaw—the name is spelled as Bew. Mrs. Meyerowitz calls the town Beeo (1952, p. 46). In the fragment of the Gonja Chronicle (Copenhagen manuscripts, vol. iii, ff. 236–7) the name is written بيع, which may be read as Biʿu or Beʿo. In three copies of the Chronicle (IAS/AR-11, 12, 62) the name may be read as BeKo (بيك).

[4] Person, 1964, pp. 326–9, 336. His study is based on linguistic and genealogical evidence.

have been engaged in the kola trade.[1] They were attracted to Beʻo by the prospects of gold, probably that of the region of Banda. The Ligby were accompanied by the Numu blacksmiths, members of another proto-Dyula group. In Beʻo they were joined by Dyula traders.

Ligby and Dyula made Beʻo a prosperous town, but they were strangers. They left after its decline, carrying with them the memory of Beʻo's glorious days. Other traditions of the old town are remembered by people still living in the area. They show the site of Beʻo between the villages of Namasa and Hani. The people of Namasa are Hwela, and those of Hani are Brong.

The traditions of Namasa tell of their ancestor Jasa Kala, who descended from heaven to a nearby hill. His son, Wuram Kwasi, is regarded as the first chief of Beʻo-Namasa. He was a hunter, and during his wanderings he came across people who had come out from a hole in the ground. These were the Brong, who became subjects of the chiefs of Beʻo. Wuram Kwasi was succeeded by his brother Beʻo-Kofi, during whose reign Mande Muslims are said to have settled in great numbers and Beʻo became a prosperous town. The traditions record the passing of 'the Daboya horsemen', i.e. the Gbanya founders of Gonja, who fought against 'the cave people', namely, the Brong. The chief of Beʻo helped his Brong subjects and 'the Daboya horsemen' were driven away. According to these traditions, the people of Beʻo scattered far and wide during the reign of the third and fourth chiefs after Beʻo-Kofi.[2] The chief-list is undoubtedly contracted, but the traditions do record the main landmarks in the history of Beʻo.

Whereas the Hwela speak of Beʻo-Namasa, the Brong keep the traditions of Beʻo-Nsawkaw. It is said, as in the former traditions, that the Brong came out of a hole near the present village of Hani, from where they scattered throughout many villages in the region. The foundation of the trading town is not recorded, but it is said that during the reign of the third chief 'there arose a quarrel between the Mohammedans and the Densos known as "Nomata". This quarrel scattered them, and the Densos and Mohammedans

[1] Worodugu in the Ivory Coast is 'the land of the kola'. Kola nuts had already been known in the western Sudan in the fourteenth century, or even earlier. This is suggested by Arabic (al-ʻUmarī and al-Maqqarī) and Portuguese (Ca da Mosto, Pacheco Pereira, and V. Fernandes) sources. See Mauny, 1961, pp. 248–50.

[2] Information at Namasa, supplemented by an Arabic manuscript (IAS/AR-340/ii) and an English manuscript, 'The History of Namasa' by the Namasahene Sumayila II (consulted at IAS, Legon).

migrated from Beʻo-Nsawkaw and settled at Kong and Bonduku respectively.'[1]

Beʻo accommodated, therefore, two autochthonous groups: Hwela and Brong. The Earth-priest of the ritual area around Namasa is a Hwela.[2] This suggests that the Hwela were the earlier residents in the area. It is likely that the chiefs of old Beʻo were Hwela because the Hwela, rather than the Brong, came under the religious and cultural influence of the Ligby. Generally speaking, when Muslims come to settle in a pagan state their close relations are with the chiefly estate rather than with the commoners; the chiefs adopt Islamic customs and beliefs while the subjects remain far longer untouched by Islam.

The Ligby must have lived in Beʻo for quite a long time to allow the decisive impact they had over the Hwela. About half of the Hwela adopted Islam and the Ligby language. This led early observers to regard the Hwela as proto-Dyula of the same migration as the Ligby.[3] The Muslim Hwela are said to be more fervent Muslims than the Dyula.[4] The islamization of the Hwela may, therefore, be underlined as one of the earliest contributions to the spread of Islam in the Middle Volta Basin.

The imams of Namasa belong to the Kamaghte patronymic group. They may have been Dyula who remained among the Hwela, or otherwise, Hwela who adopted the Dyula patronymic. It is claimed, however, that they continue the line of imams of Beʻo who had also been Kamaghte.[5] A Muslim of the Kamaghte group of Beʻo was instrumental in the introduction of Islam to Gonja.[6] Considering the impact of the Gonja Islam on neighbouring states, in particular Dagomba,[7] one should underline the significance of Beʻo in initiating the process of islamization in this region.

Different traditions of Beʻo agree that the people of the trading town dispersed as a result of an internal dispute. Internal disputes as

[1] 'A Short History of Bew-Nsawkaw', an English manuscript in possession of the Nsawkawhene. The 'Densos' may be the Donzo-Wattara mentioned by Tauxier (1921, pp. 67–69) as one of the Dyula groups who came from Beʻo to Bonduku. The 'Nomata' may be the Numu blacksmiths.

[2] Goody, 1964, p. 196.

[3] Delafosse, 1908, p. 226, and all subsequent writers until J. Goody and Y. Person.

[4] Tauxier, 1921, pp. 382–3.

[5] A list of the imams of Namasa (IAS/AR-340/1), with sixteen names, is said to go back to the period of the old town. It is unlikely that sixteen imams officiated for about four hundred years; either the list is deficient or it records only the imams of Namasa since the collapse of Beʻo.

[6] See below, pp. 51–52, 62.

[7] See below, pp. 90–91.

a reason for the dispersion of people who claim the same origin, is quite a common theme in African traditions.[1] But even if one accepts that a dispute did occur, it was probably only the last blow to a declining town, bringing to an end a longer process of dispersion. An internal dispute alone would not destroy a prosperous market town, and the escalation of a dispute up to a devastating war is more likely in a demoralized society, as the Civil War of Salaga in the last decade of the nineteenth century may suggest.[2]

The decline of Beʿo was due to a change in the trade patterns during the second half of the seventeenth century. The Moroccan conquest of Songhay and the failure of the Pashas to establish their authority wrought chaos on the middle Niger, and did much harm to the trade. At that period Danish, Dutch, and English traders overthrew the Portuguese trading monopoly on the Gold Coast, creating competitive conditions. In these circumstances an increasing part of the gold turned southward to the coast. Beʿo adjusted itself to this diversion of the trade, as the European merchants were somewhat perplexed by the growing supplies which reached the coast.[3] But the rise of Ashanti, and the control it was building up over the trade with the coast, could only deprive Beʿo of its commercial function. The trading town declined and its population scattered.

The Ligby probably began their migration to Banda before the final dispersion of the population of Beʿo. The Ligby, specializing in the gold trade, became closely associated with the Nafana of Banda, who specialized in extracting gold. The first Muslims are said to have come to Banda at the time of the first chief who led the Nafana migration to Banda.[4] With the decline of Beʿo the rest of the Ligby moved to Banda. The Ligby became engaged also in the kola trade and to a large extent in the slave trade.[5] Through their trade the Ligby settled in other commercial centres in the Middle Volta Basin. There is hardly any important Muslim community without at least one Ligby house, commonly known by the patronymic Bamba. The Ligby settled at Wenchi and Kintampo about 1882, after their villages in Banda had been devastated by the Abron of Gyaman. At that time many of the Ligby fugitives settled north of the Black Volta at Taslima and

[1] Cf. Rattray, 1932, ii. 515–16.

[2] See below, pp. 44–45.

[3] Wilks, 1961, p. 11.

[4] Information at Banda, corroborated by an unpublished manuscript by J. E. Fell, 'Notes on the History of Banda', dated 5 July 1913 (NAG, Kumasi, file No. D. 216).

[5] Information from Ligby elders at Yendi, Sansanne-Mango, and Salaga.

Banda-Nkwanta. They returned to Banda as soon as peace had been restored.[1]

Following the decline of Beʿo, its Dyula inhabitants sought their fortune in the country west of the Black Volta river. Muslim groups in Buna, Bonduku, and Kong claim to have come there from Beʿo.[2] In Bonduku the Dyula from Beʿo claim that they settled there soon after the foundation of the Gyaman kingdom by the Abron.[3] Person dates the foundation of Gyaman and that of the Dyula state of Kong at the end of the seventeenth century.[4] The migration of the Dyula from Beʿo may have taken place at the turn of the seventeenth century. Beʿo was later overrun by the Ashanti forces, in their drive to gain control over the trade to the north.

Since the beginning of the eighteenth century Ashanti has traded mainly with Hausaland to the north-east, and with the European factories on the coast to the south. The trade with the Western Sudan, formerly the most important outlet for the forest's products, has diminished. In 1817 Bowdich noted that the route northward, from Kumasi to Jenne and Timbuktu, 'is much less frequented by the Moors than that from Dagomba through Hausa'. This, he adds, is because 'the people northward are neither so commercial, so civilized or so wealthy as those north-eastward'.[5] But only a few years later, R. Caillié, passing through the territory of the Mande trade system, found active trade everywhere, an impression conveyed also by Binger at the end of the century.[6] It appears, therefore, that the Mande trade-route to Kumasi was disturbed on the limits of Ashanti's effective authority, while the trade west of the Black Volta continued.

The limits of Ashanti jurisdiction to the north-west, says Bowdich, reached the Comoe river.[7] Gyaman was conquered by Ashanti, but Ashanti rule over this kingdom was not firmly established, as the successive revolts prove.[8] Dupuis reports a revolt in the north-west at the very end of the eighteenth century, in which Gyaman was in alliance with Kong against Ashanti. This revolt, according to Dupuis, was at the instigation of Kong as a reaction against the deposition of

[1] Information from the Ligby elders at Banda, Wenchi, and Kintampo. See also Binger, 1892, ii. 145–6; Lonsdale's mission to Bonduku, *Parliamentary Papers*, 1883, xlviii, C. 3687.

[2] Tauxier, 1921, pp. 101, 439–40; Bernus, 1960, p. 265.

[3] Tauxier, loc. cit.

[4] Person, 1964, pp. 332–3.

[5] Bowdich, 1819, pp. 181–2.

[6] Caillié, 1830, *passim*; Binger, 1892, *passim*.

[7] Bowdich, loc. cit.

[8] Dupuis, 1824, pp. 241–9.

the pro-Muslim Asantehene Osei Kwame.[1] The Muslim informants of Dupuis, in Kumasi, deliberately over-stressed the Muslim character of the northern hinterland, and presented Ashanti's wars in the north as a confrontation with Muslim powers. Yet Gyaman was a pagan kingdom, as much as Ashanti itself, in spite of the important Muslim community of Bonduku. The rulers of Kong—though Islamized—were not fighting a Muslim holy war.[2] This revolt was probably not an intervention in Ashanti's internal politics in favour of a deposed ruler with some sympathy towards Muslims, but rather one of a series of wars of independence that occurred at the beginning of each reign.[3] This was another attempt to keep Ashanti off the north-west, where the trade system was dominated by Kong and Gyaman. There is no evidence that Kong suffered from the disruption of communications with Ashanti. In contrast, it prospered within another trade system.

The Black Volta river marks not only the Mande trade system to the west, but also a distinct zone of islamization to the east of that river. There, Muslims of Mande origin contributed to the spread of Islam until the seventeenth century. Since the beginning of the eighteenth century it has been the turn of the Hausa Muslims to leave their impact. The early Muslim communities of Mande origin east of the Black Volta—in Mossi, Dagomba, Wa, and Gonja—abandoned their Mande dialects and adopted the language of the rulers of their respective states. To the west of the Black Volta, the Muslim communities still speak their Mande dialect as the first language. They built up their communal autonomy and cultural identity. This occurred not only among stateless peoples, like the Senufo, but also in organized states, like Buna and Bonduku. These Dyula communities kept their identity, among other reasons, because they operated within the Mande trade system, keeping in constant communication with other regions of Mande peoples.

For Muslims in the Middle Volta Basin the Black Volta river, in its flow from north to south, marks the border of Mande land, or Wangara; Buna and Bonduku are in Wangara, but Wa and Bole on the other side of the river are not, although their Muslim communities are of Mande (Wangara) origin.

[1] Ibid., pp. 245–7; cf. Wilks, 1961, p. 22.

[2] After all, the Wattara rulers of Kong did not enforce Islam nearer to home. For a critical view of the Islamic character of the Wattara of Kong, see Binger, 1892, i. 56, quoted below, p. 81.

[3] Cf. Goody, 1965, pp. 30–31.

The two trade systems, however, were by no means completely separated. Dupuis described an important route from Kumasi to Jenne through Gonja, Grunshi, and Dafina.[1] Buna traded with Hausaland.[2] The more important south–north routes were intersected by lesser east–west routes. Hausa traders operated also west of the Black Volta river: in Bobo-Dyulaso, Bonduku, and even as far west as Tengrela.[3] Wenchi is mentioned both by Bowdich and Dupuis on the north-western route, and its orientation is towards the Mande trade.[4] Yet its new *zongo* was established by a Hausa Muslim at the end of the last century. This Hausa, Mallam Muʿādh, like another Hausa who followed him to Wenchi, came there from previous engagements in Mande land, in Sikasso and Mopti.[5] On the other hand, Muslims of Mande origin, representing important patronymic groups, are prominent in the Muslim communities of northern Togo and Dahomey, that is the area between the Middle Volta Basin and Hausaland.[6] Indeed, the interrelation between the Mande and the Hausa trade systems is well illustrated by the historical fact that the enterprising Wangara traders opened up both of them.

[1] Dupuis, 1824, pp. cxxxi–cxxxii.

[2] Renouard, 1836, pp. 103–4, 110–11.

[3] Binger, 1892, i. 187–8, 370; ii. 162. The complexity of the network of trade-routes at the end of the nineteenth century is well documented by Binger, both in his account and in his maps.

[4] Bowdich, 1819, p. 483, route No. 8 ('Weaki'); Dupuis, 1824, p. lviii ('Waraki').

[5] Information at the Zongo of Wenchi from descendants of the early Hausa residents.

[6] Fofana, Kulibali, Taraore, Wattara, etc. Information at Sokode, Tchamba, Parakou, etc.

CHAPTER II

The Hausa Trade

INFORMATION about towns and kingdoms in the Sudan reached the Arab geographers in North Africa through the trans-Saharan trade-routes. Kanem, Gao, and Ghana were known to Arab geographers as early as the ninth century (al-Yaʿqūbī). On the other hand, no town or kingdom in Hausaland is mentioned in the Arabic sources until the fourteenth century, when Ibn-Baṭṭūṭa visited Takedda and heard of 'Gobir, in the land of the unbelievers'.[1] Hausaland, it may be inferred, had not been linked by direct routes to North Africa before that period.

This situation is reflected also in the introduction of Islam: Gao in the west and Kanem in the east were islamized through their trans-Saharan contacts, in the ninth or tenth century. To Hausaland, lying in between these two regions, Islamic influence reached later, and it came not directly from North Africa but from other parts of the Sudan, which had been islamized earlier. On linguistic evidence, Professor Greenberg suggested an early Islamic influence on the Hausa by the Kanuri of Bornu.[2] Hausa traditions, however, associate the introduction of Islam with the arrival of the Wangara from the west.

'The Wangarawa', says the Kano Chronicle, 'came from Mele, bringing with them the Mohammedan religion' during the reign of the king of Kano Yeji, probably in the second half of the fourteenth century.[3] About the same time Islam is said to have been introduced to Katsina.[4] At that period Mali was at its peak, and the Wangara, Muslim traders of Mande origin, were expanding the sphere of their commercial activities.

Economic and cultural relations developed between Mali and

[1] Ibn-Baṭṭūṭa, 1922, iv. 441.

[2] Greenberg, 1960.

[3] Palmer, 1908, p. 70. The chronology, as reconstructed from the number of years assigned for each reign in the Kano Chronicle, stood up to a test controlled by external evidence (ibid., pp. 58–60). Until a new critical study of the Chronicle is undertaken in the light of new material, the chronology as suggested by Palmer may, provisionally, be retained.

[4] Palmer, 1928, iii. 77; Urvoy, 1936, p. 235.

Hausaland, but Mali's political authority probably did not reach the Hausa states.[1] It was only after the rise of Songhay as the dominant power that Hausaland became subject to political and military pressure from the west. In 1513–14 Askiyā al-ḥājj Muḥammad led an expedition against Katsina.[2] A short time later Leo Africanus visited the Sudan and passed through Hausaland on his way from Gao to Egypt via Bornu. Leo noticed the results of the Songhay expedition; Katsina was half ruined and its people were extremely poor. Zegzeg (Zaria) and Kano also suffered from the Songhay, but their people were richer as traders and artisans. Of all the Hausa states, the richest and most powerful was Guangara:

Guangara is a region situated to the south-east of Zamfara. It has a powerful ruler who commands 7,000 archers and 500 horsemen. He has a considerable revenue from tolls on trade. The inhabitants of the kingdom are very rich, as they go with their merchandise to remote countries. To the south of their country there is a land with vast quantities of gold. On their way to the country of the gold, the traders of Guangara have to cross high mountains, where beasts of burden cannot pass. Slave porters carry the goods and the provisions on their heads, while armed slaves protect the traders.[3]

The problem of identifying Guangara of Leo Africanus with any historical place in Hausaland will occupy historians for some time.[4] It is likely, however, that the name 'Guangara' is associated with the term 'Wangara'.[5] Wangara may have been an important element in the population of Guangara; they were the traders described by Leo. The importance of the Wangara as traders and Muslims is attested not only by the Kano traditions mentioned above, but also by Barth, saying: 'almost all the more considerable native merchants in Katsena are Wangarawa (Eastern Mandingoes)'.[6] Katsina succeeded Guangara as the great commercial centre of Hausaland.

The trade of Guangara to the gold country in the south may well refer to the gold trade with the forest in the hinterland of the Gold

[1] The domination of Mali over Hausaland was suggested by earlier writers (cf. Urvoy, 1936, p. 29). H. Lhote (1955 and 1956) proves that the authority of Mali did not extend as far as that.

[2] Al-Sa'dī, 1900, p. 78; trans., p. 129; Ka'ti, 1913, p. 71; trans., p. 147.

[3] Leo Africanus, 1956, pp. 477–9.

[4] Palmer (1928, iii. 75–77) identified Guangara with Katsina-Laka (north of Zaria, in the Chafi district), which is said to have been a famous centre of trade and Islamic learning. This is not convincing beyond doubt, and the present author hopes to deal with this subject in a forthcoming paper.

[5] Compare the name 'Gualata' in Leo Africanus (1956, p. 463) for 'Walata'.

[6] Barth, 1857, ii. 82.

Coast. The people of Zaria and Kano, says Leo, were also engaged in trade. His information renders support to the Kano Chronicle which describes the development of another branch of the trade, that of kola, in the same direction.

Queen Amina of Zaria, a contemporary of King Dawūda of Kano (1421–38), was the first to obtain kola nuts in Hausa. The chief of Nupe sent her a tribute of 40,000 kola nuts. 'In her time the whole products of the west were brought to Hausa.' The king of Kano, Abdulai Burja (1438–52), 'opened roads from Bornu to Gwanja'. During the following reign, that of Yaqqūba (1452–63), 'the Asbenawa came to Gobir, and salt became common in Hausaland . . . Merchants from Gwanja began coming to Katsina. . . . Beriberi [Bornu people] came in large numbers, and a colony of Arabs arrived. Some of the Arabs settled in Kano, and some in Katsina.'[1]

The Chronicle conveys the impression of a commercial revolution in Hausaland during the fifteenth century. Indeed, the foundation of Agades in the middle of that century,[2] indicates the growing importance of the trans-Saharan route to Hausaland. In the late fourteenth century the centre of the Bornu state had moved to the west of Lake Chad, and this power became involved in the trade and politics of Hausaland.[3]

It is likely that the first contact with the gold and kola sources of the Akan forest was made by Wangara traders from the Middle Niger, for a long time engaged in the gold trade. The route between the Middle Niger and Hausaland served as means of communication. Once the new sources had been known, the Wangara of Hausaland ventured to open a direct route to the forest, from which gold (as described by Leo Africanus) and kola (referred to in the Kano Chronicle) were brought to Hausaland. From there part of the products of the forest were taken on to Bornu and North Africa, which together made up the complex of the north-eastern trade-routes, starting from the Middle Volta Basin.

Evidence of trade between Hausaland and our region before the end of the sixteenth century is furnished by the claim of Muslim groups in the trading centres on the northern bank of the Volta river that their ancestors had been there before the Gonja invasion. The Muslim headman of Kafaba, who made peace with Jakpa, is said to

[1] Palmer, 1908, pp. 75–77.
[2] Mauny, 1961, p. 489.
[3] Urvoy, 1949, p. 61.

have been a Beriberi.[1] A Muslim of Salaga claims that his ancestor, of Hausa origin, helped Jakpa to overcome the Nanumba.[2] In Buipe the Kante patronymic group are said to have come before the Gonja. Their claim to be of Hausa origin, says Goody, receives recognition in the greetings which they are accorded.[3]

The trading centres on the northern bank of the Volta river were the meeting-point for traders from Mande and Hausa. Until the end of the seventeenth century the Mande trade seems to have been more important than the Hausa one. At that period the flow of gold to the north was affected by the intervention of the European factories on the coast. Kola nuts instead of gold became the main export product of the forest to the north.

Kola is chewed; its liquid, acting as stimulant, helps to overcome thirst. Being valuable, kola comprises a most appropriate present; it is given by a host to his guests and by subjects to their chiefs. Grown in the forest, it is consumed mainly by people of the savannah and the Sahel. Hence its importance in the West African inter-regional trade. Jenne and Timbuktu obtained most of their kola supplies from Worodugu, 'the kola country', in the Ivory Coast. Hausa and Bornu, on the other hand, depended almost exclusively on the kola nuts of the Ashanti forest.

The fall of the Songhay empire, the subsequent chaos on the Middle Niger, and the deterioration of security in the western Sahara all contributed to the shifting of the political and commercial centre of gravity from Timbuktu and Gao to Bornu and Hausaland.[4] The trans-Saharan routes moved eastward, and the main stream of trade from the Middle Volta Basin turned to the north-east.

Katsina, the northern gate to Hausaland, emerged as one of the most important commercial centres of the Sudan in the eighteenth century. This is evident from the information of *Sharīf* Imhammed to Lucas in 1788–9.[5] But in 1824, when the first Europeans visited Hausaland, Katsina had already been on the decline, its place having been taken by Kano.[6] The reason for this shift is to be found in the harm done to Katsina's trade by the Fulani *jihād*. For, while Kano immediately surrendered, a step that restored to it a calm atmosphere

[1] 'The History of Salaga, etc.', *GNQ*, iii, 1961, pp. 22–23.
[2] Information from Mallam Gani Zakariyā' of Salaga.
[3] Goody, 1964, p. 203.
[4] See Boahen, 1964, pp. 104–8.
[5] *Proceedings*, 1790, pp. 167–8.
[6] Denham and Clapperton, 1826, Clapperton's narrative, p. 121.

conducive to the resumption of trade, the rulers of Katsina and Gobir resisted, with the result that the ensuing continuous warfare wrought havoc to Katsina's trade. Barth relates that 'from this time [*c.* 1807] the town [Katsina] declined rapidly, and all the principal foreign merchants migrated to Kano, where they were beyond the reach of this constant struggle'.[1]

The caravans from Gonja, which until the early nineteenth century headed for Katsina,[2] now changed their course to Kano. Indeed, most of the Muslims of Hausa origin, who had come to the Middle Volta Basin during the eighteenth century, claim to have come from Katsina, whereas during the nineteenth century Muslims came from Kano, Sokoto, Nupe, and other centres, which gained importance after the Fulani *jihād*. It is also significant that the earlier Muslims had settled under the auspices of the chiefs and built up the Muslim communities of Dagomba and Mamprusi, whereas Muslims who came later were concentrated mainly in Muslim trading towns, such as Salaga and its successors. This, it seems, indicates two important developments: (*a*) an increase in the volume of the trade during the nineteenth century, and (*b*) a more puritan attitude under the influence of the Fulani *jihād*, as evinced by the tendency to settle apart from the native pagans.

Many of the Hausa from Katsina in the Middle Volta Basin have the patronymic Ture.[3] Ture is a well-known Mande patronymic, yet the word *bature* in Hausa means 'a white man'.[4] 'I have only to mention', says Barth about the word *bature*, 'that it never refers to any but Arabs and Europeans.'[5] Ture as a patronymic seems to be extinct in Katsina, but it is cherished by Muslims who left Katsina in the eighteenth century for an area where patronymics are significant among fellow Muslims of Mande origin. Indeed, it is very likely that the Hausa patronymic Ture is of Mande origin; has not Barth him-

[1] Barth, 1857, ii. 81.

[2] Lucas's information as presented in Rennel's map, *Proceedings*, appendix. The trade patterns of the pre-*jihād* period are still reflected in the routes described by Bowdich and Dupuis in 1817 and 1820, respectively.

[3] Among the many informants who said so, I will mention only Sulaymān Ture, the imam of Walwale. His grandfather, Seydou Touré, officiated during Binger's visit to Walwale in 1888 (1892, ii. 31).

[4] *Sura* in Malinke (Delafosse, 1955, ii. 700), and *wasuri* in Kanuri (Palmer, 1936, pp. 15, 46) have also the meaning of a white man. The origin of the Ture patronymic group is discussed by Person (1963), who underlines the early association of the Ture (of the Mande) with white elements in the Sahel.

[5] Barth, 1857, i. 471 n.

self said that 'almost all the more considerable native merchants in Katsena were Wangarawa'?[1]

This hypothesis gains some support from the fact that Muslims who came from Bornu in the eighteenth century have the patronymic Mande.[2] Information about the participation of Bornu Muslims in the trade to our area is scanty. A Muslim from Bornu ('a Beriberi') was the headman of Kafaba who met Jakpa, and the Kano Chronicle explicitly says that Abdulai Burja of Kano (1438–52?) 'opened roads from Bornu to Gwanja'. Yet Lucas noted in 1788/9:

> Among the few circumstances which characterise the trade of Cashna [Katsina], as distinguished from that of Bornou, the most remarkable is that the merchants of the former kingdom are the sole carriers, to the other nations, of a scarce and most valuable commodity, which is only obtained from the inhabitants of the latter. For though the salt of Bornou supplies the consumption of Cashna, and of the Negro kingdoms to the south, yet its owners have abandoned it to the commercial activity of the merchants of Agadez, the whole of that profitable trade.[3]

This evidence suggests that the activities of Bornu traders had been limited even before the Fulani *jihād*. The picture did not change after the upheaval at the beginning of the nineteenth century, as we learn from Barth: 'Gummel [about eighty miles north-east of Kano] is the chief market for the very extensive trade in natron, which is carried between Kukawa and Muniyo on one side and Nupe or Nyffe on the other; for this trade passes from one hand into another, and the Bornu people very rarely carry their merchandise further than Gummel.'[4]

In Gummel and Kukawa Barth met traders who had visited Yoruba, Gonja, and Mossi. All were foreigners, and not one a native of Bornu.[5] A quarter of a century earlier, in 1826, Clapperton reported from Kulfu in Nupe: 'Bornu caravans never go further than this place, though generally some of their number accompany the Haoussa merchants to Agolly in Yoruba, to Gonja and Borgoo.'[6]

One is led to the conclusion that there was no autonomous trade

[1] Barth, 1857, ii. 82.

[2] Information from many Muslims of Bornu origin. In Djougou one family of imams, whose ancestor came from Bornu, is known as 'Limam Mande'. At Walwale one of the gates to the imamship is Bawa-yiri, of Bornu origin. Their patronymic is Mande. Mande is one of the patronymics at Walwale, mentioned by Binger (1892, ii. 40).

[3] *Proceedings*, 1790, p. 167.

[4] Barth, 1857.

[5] Ibid.

[6] Clapperton, 1829, p. 137.

between Bornu and the Middle Volta Basin, and those Bornu Muslims who settled in our region must have come along with the Hausa caravans. The association between those traders from Hausa and Bornu may, presumably, be pushed further back in time; both groups could have been dominated by traders of Mande origin, as the patronymics Ture and Mande suggest.

Further evidence of the activity of Hausa traders of Mande origin on the route to the Middle Volta Basin is the name Wangara of the Muslim section at Djougou. Djougou comprises two main sections: Kilir, the residence of the chief, and Wangara, the Muslim quarters. The ruling dynasty of Djougou is of Gurma origin, and it was established at the expense of the 'Chief of Sassiru', who retained the Earth-priesthood.

One tradition tells of a weaver from Gurma who married a daughter of the Sassiru family. After the death of the chief a soothsayer advised the appointment of a stranger. In order to avoid the intrusion of a complete stranger, the son of their sister by the Gurma weaver was installed. Another tradition tells that the chiefs of Sassiru died one after the other. Before the whole chiefly family was extinguished, that son of the Gurma weaver and the chief's daughter was made a chief.[1]

The two traditions serve to promote a close relationship between the chief of foreign origin and the local Earth-priest. Hence the voluntary transfer of the chieftaincy to a son of the stranger from a daughter of the old dynasty. Indeed, these traditions regard the event as a change of dynasty rather than the emergence of a new political institution, that of a chief replacing an Earth-priest. The latter case is suggested by a third tradition.

Caravans from Hausaland passed near the residence of the chief of Sassiru, who created a toll-post on the route. At that time a weaver from Gurma settled among the people of that country. Because of his contacts with the foreign traders, he was appointed to supervise the toll-post, and to represent the chief of Sassiru before the strangers. He married the daughter of that chief, and the son born from this marriage—Kurugu—succeeded his father in the same office. Being more ambitious than his father, the son used his position in charge of the toll-post to make himself the chief of the region.[2]

[1] Both versions are quoted by Cornevin (1962*b*, pp. 191–2). I recorded a tale, similar to the second version, from al-ḥājj Mai-Suna of Salaga, whose ancestor had come from Djougou.

[2] 'Notes sur les "Pila-Pila" et les Tameka', *Études Dahoméennes*, 1956, iii, p. 55.

Kpetoni III, who died in 1899, was the tenth chief of Kilir, of the fourth generation after Kurugu, the founder of the dynasty. If about forty years is calculated as an average length of reign, a date in the middle of the eighteenth century may be suggested for the establishment of the dynasty.[1] This is indeed the period when the trade increased on that route. Djougou ('Zeggo') is mentioned on the route to Gonja in Rennel's map, based on information collected by Lucas in 1788–9.[2] In 1820 the king of Kilinga (i.e. Kilir) was described as very powerful.[3]

The Hausa trade to the Middle Volta Basin reached its peak in the nineteenth century. At the beginning of that century Ashanti lost an important source of income by the abolition of the slave trade and it had to pay in gold for transactions with the coast. It became more convenient for the Ashanti to buy clothing and other manufactured goods from the north, where they could pay in kola.[4] As the imports of kola nuts to Hausaland increased, the price of kola fell, and consumption grew even more.[5] The Hausa traders obtained European goods either from North Africa, through the trans-Saharan trade, or from Badagri and other ports on the Nigerian and Dahomean coasts, through Nupe and Borgu.[6] Goods brought by Hausa included also oriental clothing, beads, leatherwork, a limited number of slaves, and natron.[7] The latter was in great demand because of its many usages.[8] Salaga was the southern entrepôt for this flourishing trade in the nineteenth century.

Traders made their way to Salaga and back in caravans. Leading a caravan the long way from Hausaland was a major task. The *madugu*, leader of the caravan, had to choose the route and the halting places, to settle disputes, to negotiate with local chiefs about tolls (*fito*) the

[1] For the chief-list of Kilir, see Bertho, 1949. See below, p. 198, for the calculation of forty years as an average length of generation.

[2] *Proceedings*, 1790, appendix. See below, p. 24.

[3] Dupuis, 1824, p. lxxxv.

[4] Bowdich, 1819, p. 334.

[5] Krieger, 1954, p. 295. Barth (1857, iv. 161–2) describes the great demand for kola among the warriors in Hausaland. This demand is illustrated also by one of the miracles attributed to 'Uthmān dan Fodio, who took a friend to Gonja to pick kola within a few minutes. (*Rawḍ al-jinān fī dhikr manāqib al-shaykh 'Uthmān*, by the *wazīr* Gidadu b. Layma, dated A.H. 1232 [1817], manuscript at the University of Ibadan library, acc. No. 82/28.) Dr. D. M. Last drew my attention to this reference.

[6] Denham and Clapperton, 1826, Clapperton's narrative, p. 87.

[7] Clapperton, 1829, pp. 68, 137–8.

[8] See Barth, 1857, ii. 66–67; Mauny, 1961, p. 334; Boahen, 1964, p. 124.

caravan had to pay, to distribute the burden of toll payment amongst members of the caravan, etc. The *madugu* had indeed far-reaching authority over his caravan. He was assisted by the *jagaba*, the guide, and by the *uban-dawaki* (or *madaki*), who was responsible for collecting the payments for the tolls.[1]

In every caravan there was at least one Mallam. As a literate he kept the records, and as a man of religion he chose the propitious day for setting out, and offered prayers for the success of the adventurous trip.[2] It was mainly through these Mallams that Islam left traces along the trade-routes. Having no direct interest in the trade itself, these Mallams sometimes left the caravan on its way, when they found a local chief to whom they could render religious services. The Mallam would be given a wife, often a daughter of the chief, and a small Muslim community would grow where no Muslims had lived before.[3]

The caravans made their way slowly, travelling each day only five to six hours. A camping place of the caravan was known as *zango*.[4] *Zangos* were never inside a town, but just outside it or near water.[5] Little huts were erected, but since the same routes and camping places were used each year, it was often sufficient just to repair last year's huts.[6] Local people used to come to the *zango* to supply the caravans with provisions.

At present, *zongo* refers to the strangers' section of towns. Although the word itself is derived from the old concept of the caravan's *zango*, present *zongos* are recent. None of the *zongos* in the Middle Volta Basin were founded before the last quarter of the nineteenth century.

Generally speaking, Muslim communities did not develop out of *zangos* in the bush, which were occupied by caravans for one day or two only. Muslim communities developed in different circumstances: around a toll-post put up by a chief to control the trade through his territory (e.g. Djougou and Walwale); around the residence of an

[1] On the caravans, see Krieger, 1954, pp. 296–300; Monteil, 1894, pp. 209–11; Krause manuscripts, No. 26, sec. 41 and 42.

[2] Lander, 1830, pp. 274–5.

[3] This is a current theme in the Muslims' traditions.

[4] Abraham, 1962, p. 967. *Zango* is used both for the camping place and for the distance between two camping places.

[5] At Kulfu in Nupe, Clapperton (1829, pp. 137–8) remarks: 'the Bornu merchants stop in the town in the houses of their friends, while the Hausa merchants stop outside the walls in little straw huts or leathern tents, which they erect themselves'.

[6] Binger (1892, ii. 80, 156) came across a few camping places left behind by the Hausa caravans.

important chief (e.g. Nikki and Yendi); near the crossing of a great river (e.g. Yauri and Gaya); or at the crossing of routes coming from different directions, where goods were exchanged (e.g. Kupela in Mossi and Kulfu in Nupe). These were places where resident Muslims could help passing traders.

In places on the route and in the termini of the caravans, resident Muslims served as hosts to foreign traders. The host was known as *mai-gida* ('house master'). He introduced the trader to the chief, and the latter inquired about events along the routes and in neighbouring countries. Transactions were conducted inside the house of the *mai-gida*, who acted as a broker, drawing commission from the transaction. The *mai-gida* would have information about conditions of the market and fluctuation of prices. In short, resident Muslims acted as means of communication, so essential in this elaborated trade system.

Caravans from Hausa could choose alternative routes, and in following one of the main routes they could take different itineraries. One route went over Kebbi and Dendi, across the Niger at Gaya, past the sparsely populated region of Gurma to Pama and Sansanne-Mango, and thence to Yendi and Salaga.[1] An alternative route crossed the Niger near Say, over Fada-n-Gurma to Kupela (an important trading centre in Mossi), and thence either to Wagadugu,[2] or past Tenkodugu and Bawku to Gambaga and Salaga.[3]

Another route went first to Nupe (where Kulfu was a meeting-point for traders coming from Hausa, Kebbi, Zamfara, Yoruba, Badagri, and Gonja)[4] and thence over Borgu, Djougou, Kotokoli, and Dagomba to Salaga.[5] This was the first route described by Europeans. It appears on the map drawn by Major Rennel according to information furnished by Lucas. It reads: Cashna [Katsina] – Youri – Gangoo Domboo – Nykee – Zeggo [Djougou] – Kottokolee – Kombah [Konkomba] – Dagomba – Gonjah.[6]

Caravans had to pay tolls to the chiefs, who in return tried to ensure security on the routes in their territories. In all routes, however, there were tracts more dangerous than others, notably Gurma on the upper

[1] Dupuis, 1824, pp. cxxviii–cxxix; Barth, 1857, iv. 554–6.

[2] Barth, 1857, iv. 558–9.

[3] Kusasi traditions (in Syme, unpublished manuscript) tell of Mamprusi chiefdoms established in Kusasi land to keep open the route between Tenkodugu and Gambaga.

[4] Clapperton, 1829, pp. 137–8.

[5] Dupuis, 1824, pp. cxxiv–cxxvii; Bowdich, 1819, pp. 491–2.

[6] *Proceedings*, 1790, appendix.

route and Borgu on the southern.[1] Nevertheless, the remunerative kola trade induced traders to take the risks of the long journey. Caravans learned to live with the dangers, and a certain measure of safety prevailed along the routes if the usual precautions were taken.

There were, however, periods when even this precarious balance was violated, and the deterioration of security on one route made the caravans take another. Such disturbances occurred, for example, after the Fulani *jihād*. Reference has already been made to the decline of Katsina as a result of the constant warfare in its vicinity. A comparable situation occurred in the western provinces of the Fulani empire. Kebbi, Dendi, and Yauri carried resistance to Fulani domination throughout the nineteenth century. In 1824 Clapperton found that the route from Sokoto to Yauri was regarded as extremely dangerous, and the trade to Sokoto was inconsiderable 'owing to the disturbed state of the surrounding country'.[2] On his way to Timbuktu, Barth ventured to pass through this disturbed country and reported the constant strife between the emir of Gwandu and the rebellious chiefs of Kebbi, Dendi, and Jerma.[3]

In contrast to the difficulties on this upper trade-route, Clapperton described huge caravans that 'consisted of upwards thousand men and women, and as many beasts of burden' passing through Nupe and Borgu to Salaga.[4] It appears that in the nineteenth century most of the trade passed along the southern route. There the whole country from Kano down to Nupe was well mastered by the Fulani emirates. This was a period when the trade was ever growing, and with it the Muslim communities along the route, in Djougou and Parakou, in Bafilo and Sokode. Above all, this was the period of Salaga's prosperity, when this town became famous throughout West Africa.

[1] In 1888 Binger (1892, ii. 54–55) noted that the routes through Gurma and Busanga were unsafe, and the Hausa preferred to go to Salaga via Nupe, Dendi, and Yendi. (Dendi here refers to Djougou.) The Gurma chief of Kantindi (in northern Togo) used to attack the caravans at the head of his cavalry (Froelich, 1963, p. 184). The people of Borgu were notorious as thieves and murderers (Clapperton, 1829, pp. 274–5). A treacherous attack on a caravan in Borgu is described in the Krause manuscript, No. 26. A. Freeman (1898, p. 366) tells the story of his 'boy', who was captured in an attack on a caravan in Borgu.

[2] Denham and Clapperton, 1826, pp. 91–93, 113. In this context Dendi is the proper Dendi on the Niger.

[3] Barth, 1857, iv. 164–5. See also Boahen, 1964, pp. 242–3; Urvoy, 1936, pp. 96–110; and below, pp. 151–2.

[4] Clapperton, 1829, p. 68; also Lander, 1830, p. 127.

CHAPTER III

The Trading Town of Salaga

TRADITIONS remember the towns of Buipe, Mpaha, and Kafaba as important markets on the northern bank of the Volta, before the emergence of Salaga.[1] This may be inferred also from European documentary evidence. Several maps in the atlas of de l'Isle (1700–46) show the gradual 'discovery' of this area by Europeans. The map of 1707 presents roughly the same picture of the hinterland of the Gold Coast as did the Dutch maps of the previous century, a picture derived from Portuguese sources. 'Goaffi' (Buipe) is first mentioned in a map dated 1714. The map of *c.* 1720 shows 'Gonge' (Gonja), and that of 1722 adds the 'kingdoms of Telowe' (Tuluwe) and 'Caffaba' (Kafaba).[2] These names reached the Europeans through Muslim traders, and the localities known were, in all probability, associated with trade.[3]

As late as the end of the eighteenth century Kafaba was the best-known place in this region. In 1788–9 Lucas heard from the governor of Mesurata (near Tripoli) about 'the extensive kingdom of Caffaba'.[4] Major Rennel, relying on Lucas, placed 'Caffaba' in his map so as to comprise the terminus of the route from Katsina; 'ten days or more through desert to Cashna'.[5] Salaga is not mentioned by name on this map. The Gonja Chronicle, written in the middle of the eighteenth century, mentions the name of Kafaba, but not that of Salaga.

The earliest reference to Salaga by name appears to be in the routes described by Abū-Bakr al-Ṣiḍḍīq. Abū-Bakr's account is related to the period before his captivity by the Ashanti in 1804.[6] This account,

[1] *GNQ*, iii, 1961, pp. 16–17, 26–27.

[2] These maps were first studied by J. Goody, 1964, p. 203 n.

[3] The name 'Goaffi' for Gbuipe is typically Muslim. 'Gb' is rendered in Arabic as 'Gh' (compare Ghuna for Gbuna, i.e. Buna), and 'P' is replaced by 'F'. Dupuis read names of places in the interior from Arabic manuscripts, and called the town 'Ghofan' (e.g., p. 170). Bowdich, who could not read Arabic and wrote names as he heard them, called the town 'Boopee' (e.g., p. 171).

[4] *Proceedings*, 1790, p. 194.

[5] Ibid., appendix. This picture of the interior did not change on subsequent maps by Major Rennel; see his maps in *Proceedings*, 1810; and in the appendix to Mungo Park, 1799.

[6] Renouard, 1836, p. 111. The biography of Abū-Bakr and his information are discussed in a forthcoming paper by I. Wilks.

however, was recorded in 1835 only. By that time Salaga had already been known through the information of Bowdich and Dupuis.

For Bowdich, Salaga was 'the great town of Inta [i.e. Gonja]', situated at the junction of several important routes.[1] Dupuis had more information: 'Salaga is reported to be of twice the size of Coommassy, and its population, of whom nearly one sixth part are Moslems, to be about four hundred thousand souls.'[2] Such figures as given by travellers, a hearsay evidence, are far from being accurate, but the impression remains that Salaga was an important town at the beginning of the nineteenth century.

It is likely that Salaga was a market of some importance even before the end of the sixteenth century, as is suggested by the traditions of Nanumba, who occupied the region before the Gonja invasion.[3] Two miles east of Salaga is Kpembe, one of the divisional capitals of Gonja. By analogy to other divisional capitals—Buipe, Daboya, and Bole—it would seem that the Gonja chose to establish their political centres in the vicinity of old trading centres.[4]

Qiṣṣat Salagha Ta'rīkh Ghunjā, 'the Story of Salaga and the History of Gonja', includes a compilation of the traditions of the town's founding families as recorded in the 1890s.[5] The traditions, corroborated in interviews with representatives of these families, cover the foundation of the important wards of Salaga.

The transfer of the principal market of Gonja to Salaga is associated in these traditions with the settlement of a Muslim, said to have been of Arab origin, who came from Hausaland. He is remembered as *Bature* ('the white' or 'the Arab'), and his descendants at Salaga are known as *Magaji-n-Bature* ('the heirs of *Bature*'). It is said that *Bature* built houses for himself and his children, a small market, as well as a place for his guests.

Bature was followed by Mallam Chediya, a pious and learned Muslim, who left his village near Katsina after a war had broken out there. He built the Friday mosque (*jāmi'*) of Salaga, and his ward became known as *Unguwa Mallam*, 'the ward of the learned man'. Sanūsī, the great-grandson of Mallam Chediya, was the headman of that ward in 1892, at the time of the Civil War.[6]

[1] Bowdich, 1821, pp. 17–18.
[2] Dupuis, 1824, p. xl.
[3] Tamakloe, unpublished manuscript; Tait's manuscripts; see also above, p. 18, about a Muslim at Salaga in the pre-Gonja period.
[4] See below, pp. 61, 64–65.
[5] *GNQ*, iii, 1961, pp. 24–29. On the author and the date of writing, see the introduction by I. Wilks, op. cit., p. 9.
[6] *GNQ*, iv, 1962, pp. 12–13.

Next came a group of *Beriberi*, namely Muslims from Bornu. In another version of the same account the names of the three leaders of the Bornu group are given as Ḥasan, Tsofo, and ʿUmar.[1] The latter, known as Mallam Moru, was the great-grandfather of the present headman of the ward founded by this group, and the grandfather of Imam Abarshi (ʿAbbās) who officiated immediately after the Civil War of 1892.[2]

'Then', says the tradition, 'a notable elder from Djougou Kilinga, called Alfā Sābī, left the land of Dendi. He was a pious man, whose sole interest was to study and worship Allāh.' The great-grandson of Alfā Sābī, alias Mallam Ibrāhīm, is al-ḥājj Mai-Suna, a respectable elder living at Salaga. The latter said in an interview that his ancestor was of the Jaʿara family, the Earth-priests of Djougou. He converted to Islam after the Gurma stranger had taken over the chieftaincy from the Earth-priest.[3] The conversion may have been under the influence of the people of Wangara, the Muslim section of Djougou. Wangara, it is suggested, was founded about the middle of the eighteenth century. If a certain period is allowed for the growth of Islamic influence at Djougou and for Alfā Sābī's studies, his arrival (as a 'notable elder') at Salaga may, tentatively, be dated late eighteenth or early nineteenth century.

A similar date for the arrival of the founders of Salaga's wards is suggested also by their genealogies. They came three or four generations, spanning about a century, before *c.* 1900. Thus traditions and genealogies agree with the documentary evidence that Salaga's development as an important trading centre dates from the turn of the eighteenth century, when it replaced Kafaba as the main terminus of the Hausa caravans.

At that period Gonja was under Ashanti domination. The Ashanti, who pursued a policy of tight control over the trade within their dominions, must have had special interest in controlling the principal market of the interior. Gonja, however, was regarded as a protectorate or a tributary kingdom of Ashanti,[4] and the current control of the market had to be administered by the local chief. Salaga, only two miles from the seat of the divisional chief of Kpembe, was more suitable for the main market than the more remote Kafaba.

[1] The Hausa version by Mallam Alḥassan was translated by J. Withers-Gill, *A Short History of Salaga*, Accra, 1924.

[2] Information at Salaga.

[3] See above, p. 21.

[4] Bowdich, 1819, pp. 235, 320–1; Dupuis, 1824, pp. 244, 249.

The Gonja chief of Kpembe was known to Europeans as the king of Salaga.[1] In 1876 Gouldsbury speaks of the first and the second kings of Salaga, but it is difficult to suggest who the second king was.[2]

I could not find out [says an experienced traveller like Binger], who exercised authority at Salaga. There is however a village chief who lives at the Kopepontou ward, called *Salaga massa*. But every ward is under the authority of the eldest Muslim and the Imam. The ward of Lampour has even a king, who has the pompous title of *Lampour-massa*, or *Lampour-éoura*. I believe, however, that Salaga is subject to the chief of Pambi or Kwambi.[3]

Binger's better acquaintance with the political system at Salaga is a result of his intimate communication with the local people. Because he spoke Mande his informants were the Dyula residents of Salaga, hence the occurrence of the title *massa*, a Mande term for 'chief', in place of the Gbanyito term—*wura*.

The *Salaga-massa* mentioned by Binger is probably the *kasaweli-wura*, 'the Earth-priest'. At Salaga he is of Nanumba origin, because the Nanumba had occupied the place before the Gonja conquest. His duties are purely ritual with no political authority.

Binger rightly asserted that each ward was governed by its own elder (the *mai-unguwa*); there was no official chief of the whole foreign community at Salaga.[4] Lampur-wura, mentioned by Binger, is in charge of the Gonja ward of Salaga only; he has no jurisdiction over the Muslim population. Salaga is under the supervision of Leppo-wura, one of the senior sub-chiefs in the Kpembe division. Because of the importance of his office Leppo-wura is appointed by the Kpembe-wura from his own 'gate'.[5]

A recurring theme in the traditions, as recorded in the Arabic history of Salaga, is that the founder of each ward built up houses for himself, for his children and followers, as well as 'for his guests'. The 'guests' were probably traders who came to Salaga from all parts of the hinterland. It was the custom of traders from one country to stay

[1] Dupuis, 1824, pp. 170, 174.

[2] Gouldsbury's report, 1876, unpublished manuscript.

[3] Binger, 1892, ii. 93–94.

[4] A new office, that of Salaga-wura, 'chief of Salaga', was created by the British (in 1936, according to Tomlinson, unpublished manuscript). They appointed to this office a Muslim of the Kamaghte patronymic group, a son of Kpembe-wura's daughter. (Information from the present Salagāwura, son of the first holder of this office.)

[5] Memorandum from Kpembe-wura to Yabum-wura, dated Kpembe, 2 August 1957. Consulted at the D.C. office, Salaga.

in a particular ward at Salaga: Unguwa Mossawa ('the ward of the Mossi') was founded by a man from Bornu, but it had its name from the Mossi traders who used to lodge there. Traders from Dendi (Djougou), Borgu, and Kotokoli stayed in Unguwa Kapate, the residence of the Ligby. Mande-Dyula traders were guests at Unguwa M'beima. Hausa traders, by far the most numerous, stayed in several other wards.[1]

The first Europeans came to Salaga only after it had entered the period of its decline. Hence there is no contemporary description of Salaga in its prime. Binger visited Salaga in 1888, when its trade dwindled. He describes Salaga as a ruined village, irregularly built of wards separated from each other by land torn by trenches with standing water, and houses of which the walls were ruined or the roofs missing.[2] In the past, it is said, all the open spaces now separating the wards were congested with huts and shades, the lodgings of the guest traders.[3] It is possible that what Binger described were the remains of these lodgings, which had fallen into neglect when traders no longer called in as great numbers as before.

'Salaga', says the first European visitor in 1876, 'contains a fixed population of, I should say, about eight thousand souls, but there is a considerable floating population, which a few years ago was a very large one.'[4] The floating population consisted of traders who came during the high season (November to May), and stayed at Salaga for a short period. There were also foreigners who stayed for longer periods: people attracted by the fabulous name of Salaga, traders who had to make good a debt, or others who married at Salaga. It was this floating population which imparted life to Salaga and gave it its cosmopolitan character. But it was also the least loyal population; it deserted Salaga when decline set in and contributed to the emergence of new trading towns, such as Kintampo and Kete-Krachi.

The supply of provisions to this growing population was an important source of income to the neighbouring Gonja villages. A subsidiary trade in provisions flourished along with the prospering trade in kola and slaves. Salaga, however, had one serious disadvantage, which made it somewhat unpopular, namely a water dearth. Barth heard from traders who had visited it that 'Salaga is a most miserable

[1] Information at Salaga. During his visit to Salaga, in 1888, Binger stayed with the headman of Unguwa M'beima. Binger (1892, ii. 92) calls this ward *Bemadinsou*, a Mande appellation.

[2] Ibid., p. 91.

[3] Information at Salaga.

[4] Gouldsbury's report, op. cit.

town, where even water is very scarce and can only be purchased at an exorbitant price. The merchants always managed to make their stay here as short as possible, awaiting the proper season in Yendi.'[1] The scarcity of water at Salaga is confirmed also by Binger. The busy period at Salaga occurred during the dry season, when the water pits were empty. The Salaga people used to bring water from a distant spring, charging very high prices for it.[2]

Salaga had two markets which served mainly for the supply of provisions and for minor transactions. There were also places for the display of slaves and livestock for sale. The major transactions, however, were carried on inside the houses, where the *mai-gida* ('master of the house') acted as a broker between the transacting parties.[3]

The complexity of the trade between Hausaland and Salaga in the middle of the nineteenth century is summed up by Barth:

> Three points are considered essential to the business of the kola trade; *first*, that the people of Mosi bring their asses; *secondly*, that the Tonawa, or natives of Ashanti, bring the nuts in sufficient quantities; *thirdly*, that the state of the road is such as not to prevent the Hausa people from arriving. If one of these conditions is wanting, the trade is not flourishing.[4]

The last of these conditions, namely the safety of the routes, has already been discussed.[5] Hausa caravans came with a number of beasts of burden not larger than that needed to carry their goods. As kola nuts are bulky, the Hausa traders needed more animals for the way back. The Mossi are famous for their asses, which they brought to Salaga. Binger says that the price of the Mossi asses fluctuated according to the kola harvest; if kola was abundant the price of the asses was higher; if kola was deficient the price of the asses fell.[6]

The trade between the region of the kola plantations in the forest and Salaga was well controlled by the Ashanti authorities, as illustrated by the account of an Ashanti *bata-hene* ('chief trader'):

> I went once to Salaga with forty *apakan* (loads). They were carried by free men. It was no disgrace for a free man to carry a load while trading. Each carrier was allowed to carry as many extra nuts as he was able, attached to the chief's load, and these he could trade on his own account. This was how the carriers were 'paid'.

[1] Barth, 1857, v. 29.
[2] Binger, 1892, ii. 99.
[3] A report by David Ashanti of the Basle mission, who visited Salaga in 1878 (Beck, 1880–1). The same procedure in Bonduku is described by A. Freeman (1898, p. 237).
[4] Barth, loc. cit.
[5] See above, pp. 24–25.
[6] Binger, 1892, ii. 105.

The *amanhene* [chief of a state] sent his heralds with us, carrying an *afona* [state sword] as an insignia of office to show we had been sent by the chief. As soon as we had passed, these heralds closed the path until we had disposed of our kola, i.e. about twenty days. The guards were stationed at Ejura and Attabubu. It was a law in olden times that all kola must first be exchanged for cowries (*sidie*), with which you bought what you had been commissioned to purchase.

After the road was thrown open the heralds remained on duty and exacted a toll of twenty-five nuts on each load (of 1,500–2,000 nuts) from all other traders; twenty for the *amanhene* and five for themselves. There was not any tax on imports from the north.

There was always competition to carry a chief's kola, because thereby the carriers had access to the early market for any surplus which they chose to carry.

Northern Territories men were not permitted to trade south of Salaga.[1]

The last statement of this account is confirmed by the author of the Arabic history of Salaga, saying that the Hausa traders 'could not cross the river Yeji [the Volta] because the Ashanti would not let them do so'.[2]

This policy was part of the efficient control the Ashanti exercised over the trade, and it was sharply criticized by the British as preventing free intercourse between the coast and the hinterland. Subsequent developments proved that once a direct route had been opened to the coast, traders from the north did not fail to use it. But, for the purpose of the traditional kola trade, the location of the terminus on the limits of the savanna, rather than further to the south into the forest, was advantageous for the northern traders. They were people of the savannah accustomed to a dry climate. They used beasts of burden, many of which succumbed in the forest to the tsetse fly and the lack of fodder.[3] The forest people brought their loads on carriers' heads. Hence it was convenient to change goods as well as means of transport on the border between the forest and the savannah.

Muslims, however, were not altogether excluded from the country south of the Volta river. Early in the nineteenth century Bowdich and Dupuis found an established Muslim community in Kumasi. Dupuis mentions Muslim communities in Nkoranza and in eastern Brong, probably in the region of Atebubu and Prang.[4]

[1] Rattray, 1929, pp. 110–11.

[2] *GNQ*, iii, 1961, pp. 30–31.

[3] This became evident when the market moved to Kintampo and the traders complained of losses among the animals on that extended leg of the journey (Lonsdale, 1882).

[4] Dupuis, 1824, pp. 99, 108, 170–1, xxxiv.

Political disturbances in Ashanti were likely to interfere with the supply of kola to Salaga. In 1826 Clapperton met a caravan at Kiama (near Busa, in Nigeria), where the traders, coming back from Salaga, reported that they had been detained in Gonja a long time, twelve months, on account of wars; that the king of Ashanti was dead as also the heir, and that the Ashanti were now without a king.[1] This may refer to the war between the British and Ashanti, and to the death of the Ashanti king, Osei Tutu Kwame, in 1824.

The trade of Salaga flourished under Ashanti protection, yet the Gonja resented Ashanti rule. The Gonja Chronicle recorded the death of the Ashanti king, Opoku Ware, in A.H. 1163 (1750) as follows: 'In this year died Opoku king of the *Tonawa* [Ashanti]; may Allāh curse him and put his soul in hell. He oppressed the people of Gonja and violated their property. He reigned as a tyrant.'

In 1876, after almost a hundred and fifty years of Ashanti domination, Dr. Gouldsbury heard similar grievances from the chief of Kpembe:

> The king spoke most bitterly of the way the Ashantees treated his people when they were subject to them. . . . He told me that the Ashantee often sold into slavery a whole village full of his people. . . . No one's life or property was safe when the Ashantee were in the country. I myself [says Gouldsbury] saw the ruins of several large villages in the country through which I passed, and on inquiring the reply in every case was: the Ashantees sold all the inhabitants.[2]

Captain Lonsdale, visiting Salaga in 1881–2, could add more about the cruelties of the Ashanti: 'No man could say he possessed any thing of his own. His wives, his children, his property, were all at the mercy of passing Ashantis. A small party of Ashantis would come to a village, take a house, turn the men and the old women out, make the other women first cook their food, and then submit to fearful indignities. This was their ordinary conduct.'[3]

The Gonja were waiting for an opportunity to throw off the Ashanti yoke. In September 1839 the brothers John and Richard Lander heard from caravan traders they met in Busa (western Nigeria) of a bid for independence on the part of the Gonja: 'Gonja was till very recently a province of Ashantee. . . . But these *goora* [kola] merchants report that it has lately been separated from that empire, and is now an independent state.' It was, the traders told, before the Ashanti war

[1] Clapperton, 1829, p. 68. [2] Gouldsbury's report.
[3] Lonsdale, 1882.

against the British, that the Gonja refused an Ashanti request for assistance in the coming war. The war ended in the total defeat of the Ashanti (1826). After he had recovered from his defeat the Ashanti king mobilized an army against the disobedient Gonja. Information reached Gonja and its people set out to ambush the advancing force. The sudden attack threw the Ashanti into confusion; they threw away their arms and fled into the wood. The Ashanti king vowed revenge and mobilized a stronger army, commanding it 'to destroy the rebellious city and annihilate its inhabitants entirely'.

The news spread consternation among all classes of people in Gonja, and alarmed the strangers that had located in the country, insomuch that, on the advance of this formidable army, they could not command sufficient resolution to go out against it, but deserted their dwellings and dispersed themselves through all parts of the adjacent countries, till such time as their enemies should think proper to return to Coomassie.

It is almost unnecessary to add, that the city of Gonja was set on fire by the Ashanti soldiers in pursuance of their commands, and every house in it burnt to ashes. The people, however, fancying the king's wrath to be sufficiently appeased, were beginning to return again from the places of their concealment on the departure of the *fatakie* [traders], and were busily engaged in reconstructing their habitations.[1]

'The city of Gonja', referred to in this account, is probably Salaga (or Kpembe). There is no supporting evidence for this revolt. The Lander brothers 'do not place entire confidence in this tale', yet the essence of this account should not necessarily be rejected. It could have been another revolt, like the one led by the Gonja chiefs of Buipe and Daboya in *c.* 1801.[2] The assertion at the beginning of the account that Gonja gained its independence is not supported by what followed; the Gonja were punished, their town destroyed, and the Ashanti maintained their authority.

The Gonja had to wait for another opportunity. This came after the Ashanti's defeat by the British and the fall of Kumasi in February 1874. The Gonja revolted and became independent. Dr. Gouldsbury, visiting Salaga in 1876, reported:

Before the fall of Coomasie, Saharah [Salaga] was in a state of vassalage to Ashantee, sending yearly tribute to Coomasie. . . . As soon however as the intelligence arrived at Saharah that the white man had taken Coomasie and that the Ashantee forces were scattered and broken, the Saharahs seized all the Ashantees in their country (and they were counted by hundreds) and

[1] R. L. and J. Lander, 1832, pp. 191–4.
[2] Dupuis, 1824, p. 248.

killed every one of them, thus taking reprisals for the bitter wrongs which they had for years helplessly groaned under.[1]

This outrage was the deed of the Gonja, rather than that of the people of the trading town. A contemporary Hausa manuscript tells that the chief of Kpembe was incited by his sub-chiefs to attack the Ashanti at Salaga. The people of Salaga (who did not share the hardship of the Gonja villagers) were on good terms with the Ashanti traders to whom they served as hosts. They warned the Ashanti, and during the massacre the latter sought sanctuary in the mosques. The Gonja pressed the people of Salaga to hand over the Ashanti property kept in their houses.[2]

In Dagomba, a state to the north of Gonja, the pressure of Ashanti domination was felt less than in Gonja. Dagomba, too, seized the opportunity to gain complete independence of Ashanti, but there the reaction was not as violent as at Salaga. Captain Lonsdale, who visited Yendi in 1882, found five hundred Ashanti, who happened to be there when the secession from Ashanti took place. 'They are not slaves, and are not, as far as I could find, in any way molested.'[3]

The secession of Gonja and Dagomba was part of a wider movement of revolt against Ashanti. The fall of Kumasi had shaken the Ashanti state to its foundations. Ashanti divisions such as Mampong, Nsuta, Bekwai, Kokofu, and Juaben challenged the authority of the Asantehene, and all the Brong chiefdoms, except Nkoranza, openly declared their independence.[4] The newly independent chiefdoms of Krachi, Atebubu, and Kpembe rallied around the powerful shrine of Dente in Krachi, whose religious influence now gained political significance.[5]

First to report the events north-east of Kumasi was the Frenchman Bonnat, who tried to reach Salaga in 1875. Arriving at Atebubu in August, Bonnat was overtaken by messengers of the Juaben-hene (still in open revolt against Kumasi). Bonnat was escorted back to Juaben and thence to the coast, where he arrived at the end of September 1875. Atebubu, Bonnat reported, wants to be independent of Ashanti. 'All [the Brong] obey the fetish-priest of Crackey [Krachi],

[1] Gouldsbury's report.

[2] Krause manuscripts, No. 24; also reproduced in Olderogge, 1960, pp. 170–4.

[3] Lonsdale, 1882.

[4] On these events, see Claridge, 1915, pp. 170–93.

[5] On the Dente shrine, see Meyerowitz, 1951, p. 139. A tradition on the early contact between the Gonja chief of Kpembe and the Dente shrine appears in a translation of a Hausa manuscript in Goody, 1954, appendix V.

where they took refuge when the British entered Kumasi. . . . These people, as all the tribes of the north, hate the Ashanti, including the Juabens, and *it is more than a year that they blocked the route from Salaga*, and no one of them [of the Ashanti] can penetrate that place.'[1]

Bonnat's information makes it clear that the route to Salaga was blocked by the Brong of Atebubu, and not by the Ashanti. Indeed, the Asantehene showed keen interest in reviving the trade, and allowed Bonnat to proceed northwards with Ashanti guards and porters.[2] The Asantehene wished to restore the Ashanti state to the position it had enjoyed before the 1874 defeat; to this end the road to Salaga had to be opened. The Brong of Atebubu were aware of this, and refused to let Ashanti traders through their territory. Dr. Gouldsbury explained the situation in his report: 'When I was in Coomassie both the king and the chiefs said to me that now that the Juabens were beaten the Ashantees could go back to Saharah. . . . But unless they were introduced under our [British] auspices and kept under our supervision, they would begin as traders and end as masters of it.'

Salaga was immediately affected by this upheaval. 'Since the Ashantee expedition', writes Gouldsbury two years after the event, 'no cola nuts, or next to none, have reached Saharah, and the consequence has been that there has been little or no trade since then in the country, and the caravans have to a great extent ceased to come down to Saharah.'[3]

Dr. Gouldsbury was on an official mission to open trade-routes from Salaga to the coast. Political conditions made it impossible to open the route via Kumasi. Hence, Gouldsbury turned to secure an alternative route, over Krachi and the Volta.

Krachi is situated at the junction of important trade-routes. Early in the nineteenth century Bowdich and Dupuis mentioned a route from Kumasi to Dahomey over Odente, i.e. Krachi.[4] At that time salt was coming up the Volta river, and Krachi was connected with Salaga by an overland route. 'The position of Salaga', says Bowdich,

[1] Bonnat, 1875*a*; my italics.

[2] Bonnat, 1875*b*, pp. 58–59. In 1881 Lonsdale had to dodge an escort sent by the Asantehene, who hoped to use Lonsdale's trip to re-establish Ashanti's authority over the tribes to the north.

[3] Gouldsbury's report.

[4] Dupuis, 1824, p. xxxiv; Bowdich, 1819, p. 483 (routes 10 and 12). The name Odente for Krachi is derived from the shrine of Dente.

'has been pretty well established by the distance and the route overland from Odente, the highest point of the river to which the salt carriers navigate from the coast.'[1]

Salaga and its immediate hinterland were not, however, completely dependent on the sea salt from Ada at the mouth of the Volta. Alluvial salt was mined on the banks of the White Volta river at the Gonja town of Daboya. In 1888 the French traveller Binger noted that the price of Daboya salt was the same as that of the maritime salt from Ada when it reached Salaga.[2] A few decades later, with communications improved under colonial rule, the sea salt became much cheaper in the north than the Daboya salt. As a result of this competition the salt industry of Daboya declined and died. The fact that in earlier periods Daboya salt was in great demand throughout the Volta Basin[3] suggests that the flow of sea salt had at that time been limited.

The limited traffic on the route from Salaga to the coast via Krachi was due to the policy of obstruction pursued by the influential priest of the Dente shrine, as the two companions of Gouldsbury experienced themselves: 'Traders were not permitted to pass either up or down through Brackey [Krachi]. Mr. R. Bannerman and M. Bonnat who went up the Volta to Brackey had the greatest difficulty in getting through the town, and it was not until after three days' delay, and the persuasion of several "dashes" that they were allowed to pass. All the Creepees [Krepis] who accompanied them were stopped.' Gouldsbury met the chief of Krachi and the Dente priest, 'and got them to swear by their fetish Dentio that they would always keep the roads free and open for trade'.[4]

Krachi itself, 'being the Headquarters of the fetish Dente, is avoided as much as possible by all traders and strangers owing to the very stringent fetish laws enforced in the town.'[5] The market was eventually established at Kete, the Muslim twin-town of Krachi, two miles up the river. According to 'the History of the Kratchis as related by the Head Chief Kuji Dente',[6] the Hausa settlement at Kete started with Ceidu Aboakse, who settled there during the reign of Besimuro,

[1] Bowdich, 1821, pp. 17–18.

[2] Binger, 1892, ii. 51–52, 100–1.

[3] The Arabic 'Story of Salaga and the History of Gonja', *GNQ*, iii, 1961, pp. 18–19.

[4] Gouldsbury's report.

[5] Captain Parmeter to the governor, a report written from the right bank of the Volta opposite Krachi, 31 March 1897 (*NAG*, Accra, acc. No. 423/1957).

[6] Recorded by the district political officer at Kete Krachi, April 1920 (*NAG*, Accra, ADM/11/782).

the same chief who had broken the Krachis' allegiance to Ashanti in 1874.

Two members of the Basle mission (David Ashanti in 1877 and M. Buss in 1878) passed Krachi on their way to Salaga. Both say nothing about a market at Krachi.[1] Four years later, in 1882, Captain Lonsdale visited Krachi, and reported of the new town nearby: 'At Kete (a young Salagha), half an hour from Kratshie, and its trading place, there is a large Mohammedan population, the majority being Hausa. It contains about 4,550 houses and 7,000 to 8,000 inhabitants.' Salaga, for comparison, had, according to Lonsdale, 4,000 houses and a population of 10,000.[2] Hence, within a few years a new trading town developed near Krachi, almost as big as Salaga. This instantaneous growth could only have taken place at the expense of Salaga, following the opening up of a direct route to the coast in 1876.

The development of a trading centre in the form of a Muslim twin-town is a common phenomenon in West Africa. Usually such a town would be encouraged and protected by the local ruler. Yet the Muslim population of Kete had an uneasy experience with its Krachi neighbours. In passing through Kete-Krachi, Lonsdale had to settle complaints of the Muslims: 'They complained to me that they receive ill treatment at the hands of the natives of this country, and that they fail to obtain that protection to which they are entitled; that because they are strangers, they are called slaves and otherwise insulted.'[3]

The Krachi's aggression increased in the following years. A German visitor to Kete-Krachi in May 1894 reported: 'Mossomfo the fetishman of Kraki has built a house in the market, as well as on the roads to Lome and Salaga [where fences and huts were erected], and every passing Hausa is plundered. . . . The Hausa are now on the point of leaving Kete.'[4] At that time the Germans displayed a keen interest in the growth of trade to Kete-Krachi and took action to restore order. In November 1894 Bosumfo the shrine-priest and his accomplice Okla (a Grunshi slave) were executed both for plunder and extortion.[5] This, it was reported, brought much relief; the Hausa

[1] Beck, 1880–1, pp. 39–40, 48.

[2] Lonsdale, 1882, pp. 72, 89.

[3] Ibid., p. 82.

[4] An extract from *Deutsches Kolonialblatt*, 15 August 1894; enclosure in No. 41, *Confidential Papers, African* (*West*), PRO, CO. 879/41; see also Lippert, 1907, pp. 202–3.

[5] Ferguson to the governor, 15 December 1894, enclosure 1 in No. 57, op. cit.

sarkin zongo (chief of the strangers' town) was confirmed by the Germans in control of Kete and the trade revived.[1]

The opening up of a route to the coast via Kete-Krachi was only one of the changes in the trade patterns after the upheaval of 1874; another was the emergence of a new entrepôt for the kola trade in Kintampo. Kintampo was mentioned by Bowdich and Dupuis as one of the rest-stops on the route from Kumasi to Buipe and Daboya.[2] Dr. Gouldsbury, who made inquiries about the trade patterns in 1876, had probably no information about an important market at Kintampo. This market first became known through the information of Lonsdale in 1882. 'It is here', he says, 'where the kola trade has its headquarters.' The more important portion of the Hausa caravans went to Kintampo to obtain the kola, which had ceased to reach Salaga.[3] Two years later, in 1884, Assistant-Inspector B. Kirby was the first European to visit Kintampo. 'Qantampoh', he reported, 'is said to be the largest market in this part of Africa.'[4]

The settlement of the first Hausa and the growth of the market occurred during the reign of the Kintampo chief, Nana Kofi Bafo, the predecessor of Nana Mensa, in whose time the British occupied Kintampo.[5] Mahama, the first *sarkin zongo* of Kintampo, was met by both Kirby in 1884 and Binger in 1888.[6] Undoubtedly the market of Kintampo was established only after the closure of the main road to Salaga in 1874.

The rapid growth of Kintampo bears evidence to the vitality of the kola trade, and may give some idea about the importance of Salaga before 1874. Kintampo developed at the expense of Salaga, as a considerable part of the latter's floating population moved there. In 1888 Binger found that many of the inhabitants of the Dandawa ward (that of the Dendi people) at Kintampo had stayed before at Salaga. Other Muslim groups mentioned by Binger at Kintampo were Hausa, Dagomba, Mossi, Mande, and Ligby.[7] The latter came

[1] The British ambassador in Berlin to Lord Kimberely, 21 February 1895, enclosure in No. 62, op. cit.; Lippert, loc. cit.

[2] Bowdich, 1819, p. 483, route No. 9 ('Koonquoontee'); Dupuis, manuscript No. 8 ('Kantano'). On the early history of Kintampo, see Arhin, 1965, p. 138.

[3] Lonsdale, 1882. Part of the report is quoted in Wolfson, 1958, pp. 182–6.

[4] B. Kirby, to Governor Rowe, 'Report of his Mission to Coomassie and the interior provinces of the Ashanti kingdom', 16 April 1884, enclosure in No. 41, *Parliamentary Papers*, 1884–5, lv, C. 4477.

[5] Information from Nana Kobina Danko, chief of Kintampo.

[6] Kirby, op. cit.; Binger, 1892, ii. 135. I recorded the list of the *zongo* chiefs in a meeting with the present *sarkin zongo* and the Muslim elders at Kintampo.

[7] Binger, 1897, ii. 137.

to Kintampo only in 1882, after their villages in Banda had been destroyed by Gyaman.[1]

Kintampo served Ashanti through the Brong chief of Nkoranza. A long tradition of Nkoranza loyalty to Ashanti, which survived even the general uprising of the Brong in 1874, was brought to an end during the reign of the Asantehene Mensa Bonsu (1874–83).[2] The Nkoranza chief complained of heavy fines and taxes imposed by the avaricious Asantehene. The result, Kirby reported, was that 'Koranza had entirely renounced its allegiance to Coomassie. The first step was to block the road at a village called Coffeasi, two days' journey from Koranza.' This happened probably in 1877 or 1878, and the road remained closed till 1884, when Kirby persuaded the Nkoranza chief to reopen it.[3]

Once again, as in the case of Atebubu, a defiance of Ashanti rule led to the closure of a trade-route to the north. Yet this time important kola plantations were included within the area that had been blocked off. 'Koranza region', Kirby noted, 'appears to be rich and prosperous, kola nuts appear to be the chief article of trade; they are sent from Koranza in large quantities to the market of Quantampoh and thence to the interior.' Binger also said that kola nuts were bought from the 'Achanti du Coranza'.[4]

With the closure of the road by Nkoranza and the unsettled conditions in the Ashanti confederation, Kintampo had no direct trade with the coast. Binger noted European goods brought to Kintampo through Bonduku. Salaga deprived of its kola trade, became a centre where:

cattle and sheep, ivory, etc. from the interior and articles of European manufacture from the coast changed hands. [Whereas most of the Hausa traders went to Kintampo for the kola, others took the road to Salaga where they bought] such articles from the coast as they may fancy or which may be of use to them, knives and any implements in the market at the time. A portion of this Salagha party then proceeded to Kantampo to assist in the general business, and return again to Salagha with any surplus money to buy more goods, or to pay for those already obtained there. . . . The leading traders, organizers of the caravans, invariably expressed their hope

[1] See above, p. 11.

[2] W. Tordoff, Ph.D., London, 1961.

[3] Kirby (op. cit.) says that the road was blocked 'five or six years before the outbreak of the revolt' of the Ashanti princes against Mensa Bonsu. That revolt occurred at the beginning of 1883, and the breakaway of Nkoranza probably in 1877 or 1878.

[4] Kirby, op. cit.; Binger, 1892, ii. 142.

that kola may once again be plentiful in the Salagha market as during the time the Ashanti controlled it, primarily because of the increased distance for them to travel to Kantampo, and particularly on account of the loss they suffer on that extended portion of their journey through sickness and death among their horses, mules and donkeys, a large number of which accompany the caravans as beasts of burden, the horses being also for sale. A very small quantity of kola nuts [however] find their way into the Salagha market and are disposed of at once without difficulty. These nuts are imported usually by Kwahe traders from the forest of eastern Akim, but only in a casual way, not as recognized fixed remunerative trade.[1]

When Lonsdale was at Salaga, figures of trade with this town were recorded at Accra. In December 1881, 633 traders went from Accra to Salaga, and 614 came from Salaga to Accra. In January 1882 the figures were 845 and 807 respectively. These traders brought from Salaga shea-butter, cotton clothes, livestock, and leather works. They took to Salaga salt, English cloth, beads, guns, and metal wares.[2]

The abolition of the European slave trade at the beginning of the nineteenth century had not stopped the slave trade among Africans. Undoubtedly the scale of the slave trade decreased, but slaves continued to be in demand in Ashanti, where they were employed in the plantations, as hammock-carriers, or for any other hard labour.[3] Slaves were brought to Ashanti from the north, where they had been taken captive in wars, were paid to the Ashanti as tribute, or bought from slave traders.[4] Salaga was an important centre in this slave trade, which reached a new peak in the last quarter of the nineteenth century as a result of the Zaberma raids among the Grunshi.[5] The continuous raids kept the slave markets in ample supply, and the Basle missioner Buss, visiting Salaga in February–March 1878, remarked that the slave trade at Salaga had not suffered from the 1874 crisis.[6] Ten years later, in 1888, Binger's report suggests that Salaga had to share the prosperous slave trade with Kintampo and Kete-Krachi, with Wa and Bole.[7]

At Salaga, Binger observed a declining spirit of trade and enter-

[1] Lonsdale, 1882.

[2] Governor Rowe to Lord Kimberely, 16 January 1882, enclosure in No. 18, *Parliamentary Papers*, 1882, xlvi, C. 3064.

[3] Rattray, 1929, p. 44.

[4] On the tribute in slaves from Dagomba, see Bowdich, 1819, pp. 320–1. This tribute is a recurring theme in the traditional history of Dagomba: Tamakloe, 1931; Tait's manuscripts. Only a limited number of slaves are said to have been brought from Hausaland for sale to the Ashanti (Clapperton, 1829, p. 68; Lander, 1830, p. 206).

[5] See below, p. 159.

[6] Beck, 1880–1, p. 50.

[7] Binger, 1892, ii. 54, 101, 116, 142.

prise. He heard of people leaving for Kintampo and Kete-Krachi.[1] Because of impoverishment through the diversion of the trade to the southern markets, a spirit of frustration settled on Salaga. This atmosphere may have contributed to the breaking out of a devastating Civil War at Salaga, probably in 1892.[2]

The divisional chieftainship of Kpembe rotates among three families, known as 'gates': Lepo, Sumbung, and Kanyase. For some time before the Civil War (at least during six reigns), succession was confined to two 'gates' only: Lepo and Sumbung. After the death of Kpembe-wura Bambanga of Sumbung the choice fell on Muḥammad Napo of Lepo. But this nomination was contested by the people of Kanyase, who insisted on the right of their turn to succession. Their claim was rejected on the ground that a Kanyase chief's succession was unheard of. The Kanyase people were already resigned to renunciation when one of their senior chiefs, Kabache-wura Yissifa (Yūsuf), refused to withdraw the claim. He retired to his farm and rumours soon became rife that he was preparing for war.

As tension between the two factions mounted, Kabache-wura sent to the Ya-Na, the paramount chief of Dagomba, but a messenger from Yendi failed in appeasing the Kpembe-wura's faction.[3] The Kpembe-wura was under strong pressure from his supporters to take the field. When hostilities broke out Kabache-wura was defeated. He fled to Gjoe, fourteen miles north-east of Salaga, outside the Gonja

[1] Binger, 1892, ii. 107–8.

[2] Our sources for the history of the Civil War are the following: 'The Story of Salaga, etc.', *GNQ*, iv. 1962, pp. 6–25; *Tanbīh al-ikhwān fī dhikr al-akhzān*, a poem by al-ḥājj 'Umar b. Abī-Bakr of Salaga and Kete-Krachi (IAS/AR-27); Nanumba traditions as recorded by Tamakloe (unpublished manuscript), and in Tait's manuscripts. The European records throw light on the aftermath of the Civil War, and not on its origins: 'Report on Yeji country' by Asst.-Inspector Armitage, 9 September 1897, PRO, CO. 96/298/23114; extracts from an article by the German von Zech (written 1898) in 'Notes on the Neutral Zone', enclosure in No. 4, *African* (*West*), No. 564, PRO, CO. 897/54.

On the authority of al-ḥājj 'Umar (in IAS/AR-16/xi) the date of the Civil War is given as A.H. 1309 (August 1891–July 1892). Yet the war began after Ferguson's visit to Salaga on 4 September 1892 (Ferguson's report, enclosure 1 in No. 45 *African* (*West*), No. 448, PRO, CO. 879/38). In his *Tanbīh al-ikhwān*, al-ḥājj 'Umar says that the war started on 13 Rabī' al-Awwal. If the year is updated from A.H. 1309 to 1310, this day falls on 5 October 1892, which is quite probable. In the marginal notes of *Ta'rīkh Daghumbā* by Mallam Khālidu of Yendi (IAS/AR-241), A.H. 1309 is also given as the date of the Civil War, but this date may have been copied from al-ḥājj 'Umar, with whom the author was on close terms.

[3] This is suggested by an Arabic letter from the Ya-Na (*amīr Yandī*) to the chief of Kpembe and the people of Salaga. (Enclosure 1 in: Ag. Governor Hodgson to J. Chamberlain, 6 January 1898, PRO, CO. 96/310.)

territory, where he came under the protection of the chief of Nanumba. Hence, when Kpembe-wura's supporters chased Kabache-wura into Nanumba territory it was regarded as a provocation. Nanumba and Dagomba troops came to the field, and Kpembe-wura's supporters were routed. The people of Salaga ran away in all directions, while the Nanumba and the Dagomba entered the town and plundered it. Kpembe-wura Napo was killed during his flight, and Kabache-wura Yissifa was installed as chief of Kpembe. The Nanumba and the Dagomba withdrew from Salaga after about a year, taking with them much booty, and leaving behind a devastated town.

Such a war, it would seem, could not have broken out under the Ashanti protectorate, a quarter of a century earlier. In 1817 a dispute over the chieftainship of Alfae (whose chief, the Kankulai-wura, is the senior chief of the Lepo 'gate') was settled in the Asantehene court at Kumasi.[1] Indeed, after the independence of Ashanti rule disputes over successions developed into civil wars also at Daboya and over the paramountcy of Gonja.[2]

One may argue further that under Ashanti protectorate an intervention by the Nanumba and the Dagomba was unlikely. The last serious war between Gonja and the states of Dagomba and Nanumba was at the end of Na Zangina's reign in 1713. About twenty years later Gonja was conquered by Ashanti and after another decade Dagomba also became tributary to Ashanti. The Ashanti protectorate eased, or at least held in check, the tension between Dagomba and Gonja. With the overthrow of Ashanti rule, both internal and external tensions again came to the fore.[3]

An early sign of tension between Dagomba and Gonja was reported by Lonsdale in January 1882: 'I find serious misunderstanding exists between this king [of Kpembe] and the king of Yendi [Dagomba], by which the roads from the most important places in the far interior are blocked. They were on the point of going to fight about it.'[4] The reason for the tension, as Lonsdale later discovered, was that a

[1] Hutchison's diary in Bowdich, 1819, pp. 396–7, 401–2.

[2] See below, pp. 59, 70–72.

[3] On the Gonja–Dagomba war, see below, pp. 87–89. Serious disputes over the paramountcy in Dagomba had not been recorded before the second half of the last century, and even then not without a warning from Ashanti (Tait's manuscripts, text B). In Mamprusi, which was not within the pale of Ashanti's effective domination, disputes often developed into civil wars (Rattray, 1932, ii. 548).

[4] Lonsdale to the governor, Salaga, 11 January 1882, enclosure in No. 22, *Parliamentary Papers*, 1882, xlvi, C. 3386.

Dagomba chief had seized a Gonja village, and in revenge, eight men from Dagomba were detained at Salaga. This, however, was part of a more general climate of mutual suspicion, as Lonsdale put it: 'No prince or chief of standing of either country would, without the risk of capture, visit the other.'[1] The slightest provocation was, therefore, enough to bring about the Dagomba intervention.

The dispute between Kpembe-wura Napo and Kabache-wura Yissifa was a chiefly affair. Yet the Muslims of Salaga played an important role in all its phases. In telling the story of the Civil War, two independent Muslim authors accuse the Muslims of Salaga of adding fuel to the fire, thus sharing responsibility for the disaster.[2]

From the beginning of the dispute, the Muslims of Salaga supported Muḥammad Napo. They even challenged Kabache-wura to come out and fight. When Kabache-wura retreated to his farm, it was the Muslims who brought the news that Kabache-wura was preparing for war. In the chiefs' council the Lampur chief, of Salaga, urged the Kpembe-wura to fight. When the latter set out with his troops he saw the Muslims joining him. He ordered them to go back home, claiming that fighting was the business of chiefs, not of Muslims. But, instead of going back to Salaga, the Muslims turned to Dogon-Kade. It was on that front that fighting began. Napo heard the shooting and came to support his Muslims. When the defeated Kabache-wura fled to Nanumba, Napo wanted to stop short at the border, but the Muslims of Salaga urged him to pursue Kabache-wura. They took the initiative themselves and chased Kabache-wura, ahead of their chief, into Nanumba territory. In the fighting which followed the Muslims suffered many casualties, among them 'Uthmān, the imam of Salaga. Once again Kpembe-wura was dragged into battle against his will by the Muslims.

The militant spirit revealed by the Muslims in this crisis was by no means characteristic of Muslims in this area, and certainly not of the

[1] Lonsdale, 1882, p. 74.

[2] 'The History of Salaga, etc.', by Maḥmūd b. 'Abdallāh of Lampur; al-ḥājj 'Umar, the second author, lived at Salaga at the time of the war, and migrated to Kete-Krachi after the disaster. In his poem *Tanbīh al-ikhwān*, al-ḥājj 'Umar strongly criticizes the conduct of the Muslims of Salaga. The poem opens with a scornful description of the debasement of religious values among the Muslims of Salaga, their divinations and prayers for the chiefs, and their arrogance. Al-ḥājj 'Umar represents the puritan view of the Fulani *jihād*'s heritage, which he had adopted during his studies in Hausaland. After the end of the Civil War, when efforts were made to bring people back to Salaga, al-ḥājj 'Umar refused to resettle there.

people of a market town. In the Middle Volta Basin Muslims are regarded as peace-makers rather than bellicose people. Was it not a deep frustration, caused by the continuous decline of their once prosperous town, that lay at the root of the rash and uncalculated conduct of the Muslims?

Indeed, the character trait of the Muslims in this region as peaceful traders may have already been changed by the aggressive nature of the Muslim Zaberma raiders in the north and by the role of Hausa soldiers in the British auxiliary force. In 1888 Binger noted three or four soldiers from the British camp at Kpandu serving the Kpembe chief.[1] When the Asantehene Mensa Bonsu formed a corps of Hausa, mainly deserters from British service, recruits were brought from Salaga.[2] Among the casualties in the Civil War of Salaga was 'Mallam Ibrāhīm *kabīr soja*', or the 'head of the [veteran] soldiers'.[3] This element of Hausa, with soldierly background, may have contributed to the militant spirit of the Muslims of Salaga.

The Salaga Muslims fled to Kete-Krachi, Kintampo, Yeji, and other places. The new Kpembe-wura (Yissifa) appealed to the fugitives to come back; some returned but many did not.

During that period Salaga fell prey to the growing competition between the colonial powers. In 1885 the Germans declared a protectorate over Togoland. In 1888 Britain and Germany agreed on a neutral zone, which included also Salaga and Dagomba. Kete-Krachi fell to the German sphere of influence, while Yeji (the river port of Salaga) came under British authority, following a treaty of protection with Atebubu, signed in 1890.

In 1892 Ferguson was sent by the British to sign treaties with the northern chiefs but was instructed to avoid the 'neutral zone'. Later, in September 1894, Ferguson came again and signed a treaty of trade and friendship with the chief of Kpembe, allowing British and German traders at Salaga. The aim of this treaty was to guard against French encroachment upon the 'neutral zone' which they did not recognize. The Germans, however, became suspicious of these British activities and sent an officer, Dr. Gruner, to Salaga (1895). The Kpembe chief now found himself in the predicament of having to serve two masters. The Germans, suspecting him to be pro-British, decided to take action. They made use of the presence of refugees from Kpembe at Kete-Krachi, among them Sulaymān, son of the

[1] Binger, 1892, ii. 94. [2] Claridge, 1915, ii. 209; Wilks, 1966*b*, p. 218.
[3] 'The History of Salaga, etc.', *GNQ*, iv. 1962, pp. 20–21.

defeated Napo, whom the Germans recognized as the legitimate ruler of Kpembe.[1]

In March 1896 two German officials visited Salaga but failed to induce the chief to accept the German flag. In May another German officer, von Zech, left Kete-Krachi with seventeen soldiers. He took Sulaymān, whom he intended to install as chief after arresting Kpembe-wura Yissifa. The latter had been warned beforehand and met von Zech mounted on a horse and accompanied by armed guards. Von Zech regarded the chief's conduct as offensive and aggressive; he considered himself attacked and ordered his soldiers to fire. 'Three volleys', von Zech reported, 'were enough to drive Kabaki and his people off Salaga and Kpembe. When Kabaki had fled, all the traders then in Salaga came to me and begged to be allowed to migrate to Kete where they would be sure of the protection of the German government, as they were tired of the uncertainty of the conditions in Salaga.'[2]

There were rumours that after driving the chief away this German officer 'burned Salaga, and it is now a total ruin [to the extent that] in fact Salaga no longer exists [and that] he then ordered all the remaining inhabitants to remove to German Kraki, where they are now'.[3] This was denied by von Zech, who claimed that only fifteen huts in Kpembe were destroyed by his orders, whereas all other huts in Kpembe (700 in number) remained untouched. He insisted that not a single house had been destroyed by him at Salaga. It was true, he added, that Salaga lay for the most part in ruins, but asserted that this was as a result of the Civil War 'about four years earlier'.[4]

By that time the Germans were already contemplating eventual partition of the neutral zone (the respective agreement was actually signed only in November 1899), and it was almost certain that Salaga

[1] Ferguson to the governor, Christiansborg, 22 February 1895, enclosure in No. 80, *African* (*West*), No. 479, PRO, CO. 879/41.

[2] A report by von Zech, 3 July 1896, enclosure in a dispatch of the Colonial Office to the Foreign Office, 17 December 1896, consulted at *NAG*, Accra, acc. No. 27/1957.

[3] 'Statements taken from people of British Kraki', enclosure in a dispatch from Governor Hodgson, 17 September 1896, *African* (*West*), No. 562, PRO, CO. 879/54. Also 'Statements of natives' attached to a report by Captain Parmeter to the governor, 31 March 1897, *NAG*, Accra, acc. No. 423/1957.

[4] A report by von Zech, 12 December 1896, communicated to the British Embassy in Berlin, and quoted in 'Memorandum on questions relating to the boundaries between the British and the German possessions on the Gold Coast', *African* (*West*), No. 562, PRO, CO. 879/54, p. 43.

would come under British rule. The Germans' intention, therefore, was to draw all the trade to Kete-Krachi, thus eliminating the Salaga market. To this end they tried to get control over Bimbila and Yendi so as to secure a route to Kete-Krachi within their own dominions. In 1896 the Germans defeated a Dagomba army in the battle of Adigbo (south of Yendi) and established a post at Sansanne-Mango. They started kola plantations in Krachi in order to encourage trade. It was even alleged that they permitted the free sale of slaves at Kete-Krachi as an inducement to traders to come there.[1]

At Yeji, in the British zone, a considerable Muslim community of refugees from Salaga is said to have numbered 15,000 people in 1897. This place was frequented by Mossi caravans, which exchanged livestock for kola nuts. The British hoped to keep the trade in Yeji until such time as the market of Salaga could be restored.[2]

But the Salaga market has never revived. The market of Yeji moved to Atebubu, and thence, in 1927, to Prang which has remained the principal cattle market north of Kumasi to the present day. During the colonial period the trading activities turned southward. Muslim communities spread throughout the Gold Coast, with Kumasi as the important market of the hinterland, accommodating the largest Muslim community in modern Ghana. Salaga remained high and dry on the motor road running north to Tamale and Bolgatanga.

This is the story of Salaga, once the prosperous terminus of some of the busiest trade-routes in West Africa. Salaga had been deserted by its floating population, but was rebuilt by the descendants of the founders of the old wards. These people ran away together with all the Muslims when Salaga was destroyed, but as soon as the storm was over, they came back. To this day they proudly keep up the traditions of their celebrated town.

The Muslim community of Salaga developed around the market, whereas neighbouring Muslim communities in Gonja, Dagomba, Mamprusi, and Wa developed around the chiefs' courts. From this mode of life proceed the different characteristics of the two types of Muslim communities: those in traditional political centres and those in trading towns. Muslims in the local states adopted their hosts' languages; in Salaga the 'official' and everyday language remained

[1] 'Report on the Neutral Zone' by Captain Kenney-Herbert, 24 June 1898, enclosure in No. 442, *African (West)*, No. 549, PRO, CO. 879/52.

[2] Report by Captain Kenney-Herbert, Yegi, 9 February 1898, enclosure in No. 227, op. cit.

Hausa. The former became naturalized, the latter maintained their separate foreign identity.

This in turn conditioned the respective contribution of the two types of communities to the spread of Islam in the Middle Volta Basin. Muslim communities in the traditional states contributed to the diffusion of Islam and Islamic elements among non-Muslims. The contribution of trading communities, on the other hand, was the maintenance of a higher level of Islamic learning. Through their widespread network of trading and family relationship these trading communities maintained uninterrupted communication with Islamic centres in Hausaland and other parts of the western Sudan.

Along the trade-routes, new trends of Islam reached the Middle Volta Basin. These were more readily and fully absorbed in the dynamic trading communities than in the communities living under the chiefs' auspices. The influence of new attitudes generated by the Fulani *jihād* could be detected at Salaga. Al-ḥājj 'Umar b. Abī-Bakr, born and educated in Hausaland, settled at Salaga and established there a school which produced students with sound knowledge of Arabic. Al-ḥājj 'Umar himself composed dozens of poems in Arabic and Hausa, revealing an intimate knowledge of Arabic literature.[1] Indeed, '*ulamā*' of his class introduced into our area some of the intellectual activity of nineteenth-century Islam in Hausaland.

[1] Information from Abū-Bakr, son of al-ḥājj 'Umar, and from Al-ḥājj's former students at Kete-Krachi. Copies of the works by al-ḥājj 'Umar have been collected by IAS from Muslims throughout Ghana.

PART II

ISLAM IN THE MIDDLE VOLTA STATES

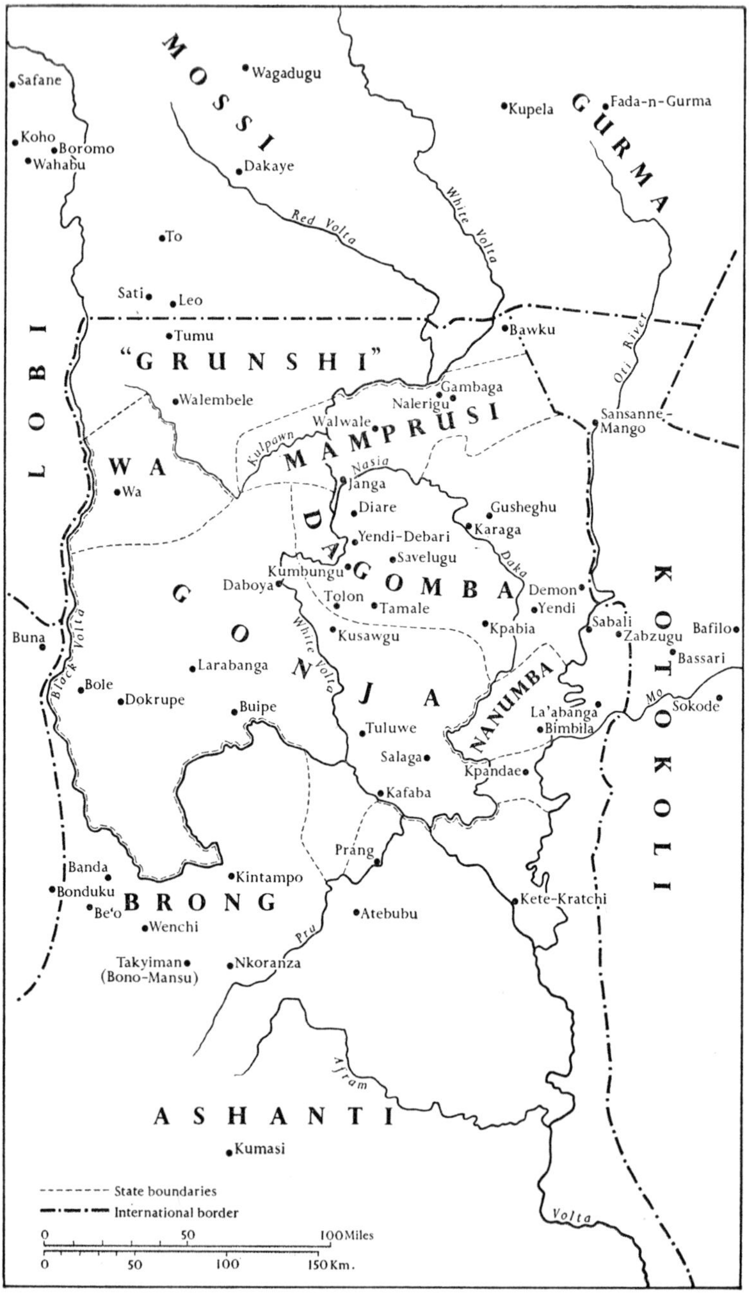

FIG. 2. THE MIDDLE VOLTA BASIN

CHAPTER IV

Islam in Gonja

(a) Chiefs and Muslims

MUSLIMS lived in the territory covered by the Gonja state before the arrival of the Gbanya, founders of this state.[1] Yet Gonja traditions attribute the Islamic influence not to these early Muslims but to other Muslims who are associated with the Gbanya invasion.

There are two traditions about the early contact between the Gbanya warriors and their Muslim followers. Both appear in Arabic manuscripts and might therefore be suspected to represent the Muslim point of view only. However, because of the close relations between chiefs and Muslims in Gonja, and because of the acknowledged contribution of Muslims in preserving Gonja traditions by writing them down, chiefs would subscribe to traditions so recorded.

The first of these two traditions, in its final version, opens the Gonja Chronicle of the mid-eighteenth century. An earlier version, drafted probably in the 1710s, appears in a fragment found at the Royal Library, Copenhagen.[2] This tradition was, therefore, recorded in writing not more than 150 years after the Gbanya invasion and not less than 150 years before the second tradition was written down from memory. The second tradition represents the current oral traditions, known throughout Gonja. It appears as the first part of the Arabic 'Story of Salaga and History of Gonja', written in the 1890s.[3]

The eighteenth-century tradition tells the story of *faqīh* Muḥammad al-Abyaḍ, whose father Ismāʿīl had befriended Nabāʿ the king of Gonja. After the death of his father, Muḥammad al-Abyaḍ left his town Beʿo to greet the Gonja king and to pray for him. He met Maʿūra, Nabāʿ's successor, waging war at Kolo. It was a fierce battle, which the Gonja king could not win. Muḥammad al-Abyaḍ made a miracle, by the name of Allāh, and the enemy was defeated. 'When the king of Gonja saw this it made him wonder. "This faith", he has

[1] See above, pp. 17–18.

[2] See the Introduction to the forthcoming edition of the Gonja Chronicle.

[3] *GNQ*, iii, 1961, pp. 10–25. See Wilks's Introduction, ibid., p. 9. A similar version of the oral tradition is recorded also in Tamakloe, 1931, pp. 21–23.

realized, "is better than our religion." He became devoted to Islam. They converted to Islam; he and his brother Wāmū and Līmu, together with Jāfa and Māfa. . . . When the king of Gonja Maʿūra was converted by the *faqīh*, the latter gave them [Muslim] names. . . .'[1]

The contract between Muslims and chiefs in Gonja is told by the more recent tradition as follows:

> A notable man called Jakpa (he had a name but none is known except this) set out with his people from Mande land to make war. . . . Actually, if you want to wage war and you do not find a Mallam, then it is impossible for you to do so. So he asked Fati-Morukpe to join him in his campaigns. He made an oath: 'by the name of Allāh, I will give you a hundred horses, a hundred slaves (males, females, and boys), a hundred sheep, a hundred gowns, and a hundred trousers with its ropes. If you die, your people and children will take it after your death, and if I die, my people will be kind to you and to your people after my death'. The Mallam accepted and accompanied Jakpa. Jakpa fought and was victorious everywhere. . . . In every town conquered [Jakpa appointed one of his descendants as chief, and] Fati-Morukpe sent out people to live with them, and [one of them] to be their imam.[2]

At first sight the two traditions appear quite different, but a closer examination suggests that both may refer to the same historical events. Fati-Morukpe of the oral tradition is no other than Muḥammad al-Abyaḍ, 'Muḥammad the White', of the Gonja Chronicle. Fati-Morukpe, or as it is otherwise pronounced Fatigi-Morukpe, means in Mande 'the White Learned Muslim'.[3] It is the nick-name which the oral tradition gives to the Muslim called in the chronicle by his proper name, Muḥammad 'the White'.

In the oral tradition Jakpa stands as the conquering founder of the Gonja state, from whom all the chiefs in Gonja claim descent. It is generally accepted in Gonja that Ndewura Jakpa is a title, not a proper name.[4] The Gonja Chronicle does not mention Jakpa by name among the kings of Gonja. The scribe of one manuscript (IAS/AR-12) added after the name of King Lāta: 'the king of Bure, nicknamed Jakpa'. This is undoubtedly a recent intervention, a projection of the

[1] The Gonja Chronicle.

[2] *GNQ*, iii, 1961, pp. 10–11, 18–19. El-Wakkad's translation has been altered in some places according to my own reading of the Arabic text.

[3] In Mande *fotigi* means 'a learned Muslim', *moro* denotes an individual (e.g. *moro-fi* is 'a black man'), *kpe*—'white' (see Delafosse, 1955, vol. ii). The construction *Fatigi-moro-kpe* is, therefore, 'the white learned Muslim'.

[4] See Jones, 1963, p. 4, n. 11: 'I was always told in Gonja that "Ndewura" means "Master of many towns" . . . "Jakpa" is sometimes said to mean "spear holder".'

oral tradition, yet the Chronicle itself suggests a clue to this identification. In the Chronicle Lāta is said to have unified and consolidated the state, which he divided among his sons. All later paramount chiefs of Gonja, and at least some of the divisional chiefs, were, according to the Chronicle, sons or grandsons of Lāta. Lāta, however, was not the first Gonja king nor the conqueror of the land. The oral traditions condensed in the career of its hero Jakpa the history of about a century; from the conquest to the consolidation and the division of the state. All the individual kings, Lāta and his predecessors, have been covered by one title name, 'Ndewura Jakpa'—'the Spear Holder, Master of many towns', a title which the legendary conquering founder well deserved. The span of time between the recording of the two traditions does allow this telescoping.

The Gonja Chronicle begins with the meeting between the Muslim *'ālim* and the Gbanya chief, that is, the point from which Muslims were brought into the orbit of the Gonja state, and could bear evidence on its history. This contributes to the authenticity of the tradition, but also defines its limitation. Nothing can be learned from the Chronicle about the period before the War of Kapuasi, when the Gbanya had already been in the area of their future state. This, it may be inferred from the Chronicle, occurred in the second half of the sixteenth century.[1]

The Gbanya invaders are said to have come from Mande land. The term Mande has a very wide connotation, and may refer to any region of Mande-speaking people. Traditions, however, often refer to Segu.[2] The Gbanya may have come from the Middle Niger, at a period when the empire of Mali was disintegrating. Islamic influence in Mali was restricted to the courts of major chiefs and trading centres. The Mande peasants and warriors were hardly or very superficially touched by Islam. The Gbanya, it is suggested, were of Bambara origin, and the Bambara were among the least islamized of the Mande.[3] But, through their association with the rulers of Mali and with Muslim traders on the Niger, the Bambara could have been acquainted with the religious services rendered to chiefs by Muslims, as the author of 'the Story of Salaga and the History of Gonja' puts it: 'if you want to wage war and you do not find a

[1] On the chronology as inferred from the Chronicle, see below, pp. 195–6.
[2] Goody, 1954, appendixes VI and VII.
[3] On the Bambara origin of the Gbanya, see Wilks, 1961, p. 8; Jones, 1963, pp. 15–16; Goody, 1964, p. 197.

Mallam, it is impossible for you to do so'. This statement projects nineteenth-century attitudes in the Middle Volta Basin, which very likely had been current on the Middle Niger already in the thirteenth and fourteenth centuries. There is no evidence that this role of the Muslims was known in the Middle Volta Basin before the end of the sixteenth century.[1]

The oral tradition does not mention Jakpa's conversion to Islam. On the other hand, the Chronicle explicitly mentions, indeed has as its central theme, the conversion of the Gonja chiefly family. Yet the only actual manifestation of the conversion, as described by the Chronicle, was the adoption of Muslim names by the rulers. Adoption of Muslim names is one of the earliest signs of Islamic influence.[2] Until now every member of the chiefly estate in Gonja has a Muslim name besides his Gonja name. When the Gonja king is said to have been converted by Muḥammad al-Abyaḍ he did not necessarily become a real Muslim. The crucial development was winning over the chief's sympathy towards Islam, by proving how useful to them Muslims could be.

This is also the purpose of the detailed story about the miracle performed by Muḥammad al-Abyaḍ at the Battle of Kolo. This Islamic aspect is represented also in the *alite*, the most powerful religious object in Gonja. It is a pair of clay images, said to have been given to the first Yagbum-wura (the paramount chief of Gonja) by Fati-Morukpe (alias Muḥammad al-Abyaḍ). Believed to be the source from which Yagbum-wura's powers spring, it was carried into war by the Gonja army. One of the clay images is said to have been destroyed in 1895, when the *sofas* of Samori defeated the Gonja at Jantilipe.[3]

The Gonja chiefs have probably never been Muslims. Indeed, there is a clear distinction between being a chief and being a Muslim. But once Muslims became attached to the Gonja chiefs, the latter came under Islamic influence. So a chief is neither a Muslim nor a complete pagan, but what may be defined—in the absence of any better term—as 'half islamized'.[4]

[1] See below, p. 90.

[2] In Dagomba, chiefs have Muslim names since the time of Na Zangina, who is said to have introduced Islam. The same applies to Mamprusi chiefs after the reign of Na Atabia.

[3] Tomlinson, unpublished manuscript.

[4] The term *mukhallit*, or syncretist (cf. Last and Al-Hajj, 1965) is not suitable here. *Mukhallit* is a Muslim who mixes non-Muslim beliefs and customs with Islam. Chiefs in our area do not regard themselves as Muslims at all; they only absorbed Islamic influence.

All male members of the chiefly estate in Gonja are circumcised when seven days old, but the circumcision is performed by a non-Muslim commoner. On the same day they are given a name, chosen by the imam from among the appropriate Muslim day-names, but Muslims are not called to the ceremony, because birth ceremonies are a chiefly affair. In the funeral the imam would pray over the body of the dead chief.

National festivals in Gonja are feasts of the Islamic calendar. Its names and some of the ceremonies are of Dyula origin. The Muslim festivals, however, were transformed to the extent that the original Islamic features can hardly be recognized. *Damba*, on the Prophet's birthday, is the greatest of all the state ceremonies. In the celebrations, commoners and sub-chiefs from the outlying villages come to the divisional capital to pay homage to the chief. Muslims come to pray, and a Muslim slaughters the sacrificial cow.[1]

Gonja society is divided into three estates: the *Gbanya* who are the rulers; the *Nyamase*—the pagan commoners; and the *Karamo*—the local Muslim community.

The commoners are the people of the land, conquered by the Gbanya invaders and incorporated into the Gonja state. They form a number of more or less distinct groups, each with its own linguistic and cultural distinction. They are in fact different tribal groupings associated by 'common submission to the Gbanya, for whom they are simply a residual category of non-Muslims, ineligible for chiefship'.[2]

Communication between commoners and Muslims is limited, and commoners are almost completely untouched by Islam. The chiefs' courts provide the centres for the national culture of Gonja, to which contribution is made by all three social estates. Politically central, chiefs in religion are intermediate between their pagan subjects and Muslim followers. Chiefs refer both to shrine-priests and to their imams; they require the ritual ceremonies of the Earth-priests as well as the prayers of the Muslims.

Among Muslims distinction is made between members of the hereditary Muslim community and stranger Muslims who settled in Gonja after the consolidation of the state. The former alone are completely integrated into the Gonja socio-political system. They are descendants of those Muslims who shared the conquest of the land

[1] Goody, 1967, pp. 190–2. Damba celebrations in the Gonja divisions are described by Tomlinson (op. cit.).

[2] Goody, 1967, pp. 186–7.

with the Gbanya chiefs, praying and making charms for their success. The oath made by Jakpa when he called Fati-Morukpe to help him in his wars, an oath binding also the descendants of both, is the charter for the close association between chiefs and Muslims in Gonja. As all chiefs in Gonja claim descent from Jakpa, so the more important Muslim group claims descent from Fati-Morukpe. This group, which produces the imams, is called *Sakpare*. The *Sakpare* imams pray for the chiefs, and in return the chiefs must support their *Sakpare* Muslims who live around the court.

Besides the imam there is a senior official in the courts of Gonja chiefs called *Nso'owura*. This title may be translated as 'chief of the Dyula' or 'chief of the Muslims'.[1] He is the chief's spokesman, and the head of the *Dogte*s, heralds of the chief. Among five *Nso'owura*s the author met in Gonja, three—in Yagbum (Damongo), Bole, and Daboya—were both *Dogte*s and Muslims; one—in Kusawgu—was a *Dogte* but not a Muslim; and one—in Kpembe—was a *Sakpare* Muslim. There are no *Dogte*s in Kpembe now, and the fact that a *Sakpare* Muslim holds this office, occupied elsewhere by a *Dogte*, suggests some association between the *Dogte*s and the Muslims.

From several explanations given for the origin of the *Dogte* two important points may be singled out: first, that the word *Dogte* means in Mande 'no brotherhood',[2] and second, that formerly the *Dogte*s had the right to the chieftainship, which they exchanged for food. Hence, the *Dogte*s share the chief's food and may take for themselves any food prepared for the chief.[3]

Who are these *Dogte*s? Their middle position between chiefs and Muslims, in a society where the social estates are rigidly marked, suggests that one should look for a certain historical situation which could have created this unique category. This might have occurred in the period between the conquest of the territory and the consolidation of the state. The conquest, extended over a period of about seventy years, was carried by a line of chiefs mentioned by the Gonja Chronicle: Wādih (or Nabāʿ), Maʿūra, Wāmū, and Mūnaʿ. Then Lāta, whom the tradition identifies with Jakpa, succeeded. 'Jakpa on succeeding', says an Arabic manuscript from Bole, 'decided he had

[1] *Nsoko* is the old Akan name for the Mande (Delafosse, 1912, ii. 212).

[2] In Mande *dogo* means 'brother', *te*—'non-existent' (Delafosse, 1955, ii. 136, 731).

[3] In the enrobement ceremony of Bole-wura: 'Finally the *Dogte* reminded him that the *Dogte*s were once chiefs and sold their birth right to their belly' (Bole District Book, *NAG*, Accra, ADM 212/6).

had enough of war, and settled at Buipe. There he said: "I am tired of fighting. All this country belongs to me. I will divide the country between my sons and my brothers' sons.'"[1] The Gonja Chronicle may indicate the way this consolidation was carried out:

As for Lāta [the king of Būra nicknamed Jakpa],[2] it is said that it was he who possessed and subdued all what his predecessors had possessed, [making it] like his own possession, until the possessions of all of them came under his hand. He divided the land of all of them among his sons. He had no rebel or disputant, and the kingdom remained with his descendants until the present time.

Is it not possible that Lāta-Jakpa consolidated the state by eliminating other rulers, or by depriving other rulers' heirs?[3] Could not this be the reason for the general consensus that all the Gonja chiefs are direct descendants of Lāta-Jakpa? The oral tradition, which legitimates the present constitution, consigned to oblivion Jakpa's predecessors of the Gonja Chronicle, as if Jakpa was the first and only founder of the Gonja state.

It is likely, therefore, that during the period of the consolidation one group within the chiefly estate had to give up its right to the chieftainship. In theory, every member of the chiefly estate in Gonja has the right to political office. In order to eliminate one group from rivalry for high offices, it had to be excluded from the chiefly estate. Members of this group could not simply become commoners, because in Gonja there are no individual commoners, as commoners belong to distinct tribal groupings. As chiefs they had already been under Islamic influence, 'half-islamized' as defined above. So, in renouncing their chiefly status they might have chosen to become Muslims. Deprived of the right to political chieftainship, their seniors were given the title of *Nso'owura*, 'chief of the Muslims'. Having been eliminated from the chiefly estate, which is based on kinship (whether real or fictitious), any relationship between them and the chiefs had to be denied. Hence their name—*Dogte*, no brotherhood.

The process described is hypothetical, and taking the same historical

[1] Goody, 1954, appendix VII.

[2] In brackets is an additional note inserted by the scribe of one copy of the Chronicle, IAS/AR-12.

[3] Mr. J. A. Braima, a member of the chiefly estate in Kpembe, has been engaged in the study of the history of Gonja for about thirty years. He postulates a strife between two leaders, Manwura and Jakpa. The latter, the junior among the two, eventually emerged victorious, whereas Manwura's descendants have been eliminated from the chiefly estate.

elements one may suggest another development leading to the creation of the *Dogte* group. Yet, for the purpose of the study of patterns of islamization, it is important to note that they probably moved from the chiefly to the Muslim estate, a process which is by no means common in Gonja.

A member of the *Dogte* group at Daboya said that their ancestor had converted to Islam together with the chiefs. Their Islam, however, had been weak until one of their forefathers went to study at Safane, whence he came back as a real and devoted Muslim. This information suggests that having been islamized in the chiefly way, Islam among the *Dogte*s remained weak even after they had left the chiefly estate. The subsequent development could have been in both directions. Closer association with Muslims, with whom they shared status, could have strengthened Islam among the *Dogte*s. On the other hand, their engagement in chiefly affairs through their office, might have kept Islam among them in its low level. Where they lived in centres without a Muslim community, as in Kusawgu, Islam among the *Dogte*s has completely lapsed.

Though given the status of Muslims, the *Dogte*s still had more in common with chiefs than with Muslims. They remained living near the chiefs, and in return for giving up the chieftainship they received the right to share the chiefs' food. In their new status they became the most intimate officials of the chief, who had nothing to be afraid of their rivalry. A *Dogte* always attends the chief, and it is through the *Dogte*s that sub-chiefs are admitted before the chief. Thus they became quite influential in the political sphere even in their new status.

The functions of the *Dogte*s compare with those of the eunuchs in Dagomba. Eunuchs were the most intimate councillors of the Ya-Na, because being ineligible they did not constitute a threat to the paramount skin. *Mba-dugo*, a eunuch elder in Dagomba, described his duties as follows: 'When anything happens and I am not asleep, I go and tell the Na. . . . I cook for the Na; that is, I superintend the cooking—hence my name *dogo*, a pot. *I share the Na's food.*'[1]

Eunuchs supervised the chief's wives, as did the *Dogte*s. There is a strict taboo on the *Dogte*s not to commit adultery with a wife of the chief. The same taboo applies also to Muslims. (For others it is a criminal offence.) Muslims (and therefore also *Dogte*s) are sometimes referred to as 'wives of the chief'.[2] Like wives, Muslims are close to

[1] Rattray, 1932, ii. 573; my italics.

[2] In the enrobement ceremony of Bole-wura: 'Then a Mallam reminds him that

the chief, his intimates, depending on him for food as well as protection.

A Muslim coming before the chief is not obliged to take off his sandals nor to kneel down while greeting the chief (as members of the chiefly and commoners' estates must do). A Muslim may even sit on the skin of the chief (a grave offence for princes and commoners). These and other privileges are reserved to the local hereditary Muslim community; stranger Muslims do not enjoy them.

(*b*) *Islam in the Divisions*

Power in Gonja rests with the divisional chiefs. There were eight divisions: Buipe, Kpembe, Bole, Tuluwe, Kusawgu, Wasipe (or Daboya), Kun (or Kong), and Kandia. Each divisional chief, except that of Buipe, had the right to succeed in turn to the paramountcy, to the office of Yagbum-wura. The chief of Kandia was eliminated in the eighteenth century, for reasons now not clear.[1] The chiefs of Kun were deprived of the right to Yagbum after one of them 'had invoked the aids of Samori to further his claims to the Yagbum skin'.[2] Wasipe-wura also was ineligible for some time, in circumstances to be discussed later, but his right has been restored since 1931.

Each of the divisional chiefs was given, according to the tradition, a *Sakpare* imam. Each chief may have had also *Dogte*s as his heralds and a *Nso'owura* as his chief spokesman. In Gonja each division is self-supporting in recruiting its office-holders. Chiefs do not move from one division to another (except certainly from the divisions to the paramountcy), neither *Sakpare* nor *Dogte*s do (except when sisters' sons come to live with their maternal uncles). Hence, during almost three centuries since the division of the kingdom, these Muslim offices developed in different ways in the various divisions. In fact, now (and this may have been true at the end of the last century) one finds all the three offices—*Sakpare* imam, *Nso'owura*, and *Dogte*s—in

Mallams were to a chief as his wives' (Bole District Book, *NAG*, Accra, ADM 212/6).

[1] It is possible that the chief of Kandia revolted against the Yagbum-wura. The latter used mercenaries to defeat Kandia. (Inferred from an Arabic manuscript on the history of Sansanne-Mango, IAS/AR-346; see below, p. 79.)

[2] Tomlinson, op. cit. On the origin of this dispute Ferguson reported: 'The king of Gonja died about a year ago, and there is anarchy in the country. The kings of Kosoo [Kusawgu], Gun [Kun], and Boniape [Tuluwe?] were claimants to the stool.' (Ferguson to the governor, 9 December 1892, enclosure 1 in No. 45, *African* (*West*), No. 448, PRO, CO. 879/38.)

Yagbum and Bole only.[1] In all the other divisions at least one of these offices is absent, or has changed from what might have been the original plan.

(I) BUIPE

Among the divisional chiefs in Gonja, the chief of Buipe has a unique status. Buipe-wura is not eligible to the paramountcy, yet he has the right of veto against the candidate chosen for the skin of Yagbum. One of his sub-chiefs, Kagbape-wura, enrobes the new Yagbum-wura, and Buipe-wura himself is the first to be informed upon the death of the Yagbum-wura. There is a taboo against a meeting between Buipe-wura and Yagbum-wura. 'The deep veneration felt by all the Gonjas for the person and office of Buipewura have led many observers to conclude that he is in some ways a greater power than Yagbumwura himself.'[2]

Buipe derives its character of a sacred town from the universally accepted tradition that Jakpa was buried there. Buipe-wura is in charge of Jakpa's tomb, the *Mashiri* or *Mishiri*. The same term is used also for the royal cemetery of the Yagbum-wuras at Mankuma,[3] and of the chiefs at Kpembe.[4] Many terms in Gonja, especially those associated with the early history of the state, are of Mande origin. If it is of Mande origin the term *Mishiri* may have derived from the Mande *misiri*, 'a mosque'.[5] An association between Jakpa's grave and a mosque is suggested by some pieces of tradition.

An additional note in two of the Gonja Chronicle's manuscripts says that Maʿūra (the second king of Gonja and the one 'converted' by Muḥammad al-Abyaḍ) built a mosque at Buipe.[6] This addition appears to be recent, but it does point to a strong tradition that there had been an old mosque at Buipe. This is accepted also by J. A. Braima, saying: 'Jakpa marched to Buipe and rebuilt the mosque that was in ruins. He was buried in the mosque, and the tomb is worshipped annually up to this day.'[7]

'Tradition records', says Tomlinson, 'that the mound [of Jakpa's

[1] My information about the Tuluwe division is incomplete.
[2] Jones, 1963, pp. 22–23.
[3] Rattray, 1932, ii. 577, n. 2.
[4] Information at Kpembe.
[5] Delafosse, 1955, ii. 507.
[6] IAS/AR-11 and 12.
[7] J. A. Braima, *A History of Gonja*, unpublished manuscript.

tomb] was once higher and fenced about with stakes. . . .'[1] This description may well apply to a Sudanese type timber-framed mosque, usually built by Muslims of Mande origin.

Is it not possible that Jakpa (probably Lāta of the Gonja Chronicle) was buried in a mosque—*misiri*; this term eventually was applied to other royal cemeteries? Such an hypothesis, associating the tomb with a Muslim institution, derives support from the fact that the custodian of Jakpa's tomb, the *Mishiri-wura*, belongs to the Jabaghte patronymic group, namely of Muslim-Mande origin.[2]

Buipe was a trading town before the Gonja invasion, with an important Muslim community. In its vicinity, presumably, was the early political centre of Gonja. It is quite possible that Muḥammad al-Abyaḍ made his residence there, and from Buipe the *Sakpare* imams went to establish the divisional imamships. Hence the seniority of the *Sakpare* branch of Buipe. Whereas the paramount chiefship rotates among the divisions, the Yagbum-wura's imam always succeeds from Buipe. That this was the case also in the late eighteenth century may be inferred from a correspondence discovered among the Copenhagen Arabic manuscripts.[3]

An early letter from Bābā, leader of the Muslim community in Kumasi, is addressed to Mālik 'in the imamship of Ghūfe [Buipe]'. This letter can be dated as pre-1810.[4] A later letter (vol. ii, f. 1), written on a paper water-marked '1818', is addressed to Imam Mālik *and* to the imam of *Ghūfe*. Imam Mālik was then no longer imam of Buipe. In another letter (vol. i, f. 73) Mālik calls himself 'imam of Gonja'. It is therefore clear that Mālik was promoted from the imamship of Buipe to that of Gonja, i.e. Yagbum.

The correspondence with the imams of Gonja and Buipe was written by Muḥammad and Ṣūma, two Gonja Muslims resident in Kumasi. As correspondents refer to each other with customary etiquette, it may be possible to explore their relationship.

Muḥammad refers to Mālik, imam of Gonja, as 'our father' (vol. i,

[1] Tomlinson, op. cit.

[2] Information at Buipe. Goody (1967, p. 196) says that a councillor of Yagbum-wura, 'the chief of the now vanished village of Konkrompe was *a Muslim of the Jabagte section, who are said to have lived in the area before the Gbanya invasion*' (my italics). One imam of the Jabaghte patronymic group is mentioned by the Gonja Chronicle (entry for A.H. 1149).

[3] For translations of all the letters mentioned here, see Levtzion, *THSG*, viii.

[4] Copenhagen manuscripts, vol. iii, f. 5. The Queen Konadu, mentioned in this letter, may be identified with the fifth queen mother of Ashanti Konadu Yiadom, who died in 1810 or 1811 (Bowdich, 1819, pp. 240–1).

f. 1), while Mālik calls Muḥammad 'our son Muḥammad *ibn* imam Gonja' in one letter (vol. ii, f. 73), and 'Muḥammad ibn al-Karīm' in another (vol. i, f. 169).[1] The Buipe imam calls him 'Muḥammad ibn al-Muṣṭafā imam Gonja' (vol. i, f. 188). If Muḥammad is referred to as 'son' by Mālik while his father's name was Al-Muṣṭafā, one may assume that Muḥammad was Mālik's nephew.[2] Al-Muṣṭafā, Muḥammad's father, had been imam of Gonja before his brother Mālik. The imam of Buipe, who succeeded Malik upon the latter's promotion to the imamship of Gonja, was of the same generation as Muḥammad, Mālik's nephew. This is why Muḥammad may call the Buipe imam '*ḥabībunā*', 'our beloved friend' (vol. ii, f. 1). ʿUthmān, the Buipe imam's son, being junior to Muḥammad, calls the latter 'our father Muḥammad' (vol. i, f. 126). All these people were, therefore, members of the same kinship group, very probably that of the *Sakpare* branch of Buipe.

About the time this correspondence was written, Dupuis visited Kumasi where he conferred with the leaders of the Muslim community: Baba of Gambaga, Suma, and Kantoma.[3] An Arabic manuscript obtained by Dupuis was written by 'Muḥammad Kamaʿte known as Kantoma'.[4] This is no other than Muḥammad, son of the imam of Gonja.[5] Indeed, Kamaʿte or Kamaghte is now the patronymic of most, if not all, the *Sakpare* imams in Gonja.

Muḥammad al-Abyaḍ came, according to the Gonja Chronicle, from Beʿo. The imams of Namasa, who claim to continue the line of the imams of Beʿo, belong to the Kamaghte patronymic group.[6] Muḥammad al-Abyaḍ may well have been a Kamaghte from Beʿo, who founded the Kamaghte patronymic group of Gonja. That Muḥammad al-Abyaḍ's descendants were imams is confirmed by the Gonja Chronicle. It records the death of Imam Al-ḥājj ibn *al-faqīh* Muṣṭafā ibn Muḥammad al-Abyaḍ in 1691, and the appointment of Sidi 'umar

[1] Mālik refers also to Ṣuma as '*ibn al-karīm*'. In another letter (vol. ii, f. 1) Ṣuma's father is called Muḥammad Bawa. Thus, *al-karīm* is a praising name, 'the noble', not a proper name.

[2] The terms 'brother' and 'son' may be taken also in a wider connotation, indicating relationship in terms of generations in one kinship group.

[3] Dupuis, 1824, p. 170 and *passim*.

[4] Ibid., p. cxxiii.

[5] Among the Copenhagen manuscripts is a magical formula (vol. ii, f. 27) given to 'Muḥammad known as Karamo Toghma'. A letter (vol. iii, f. 6) is addressed to 'Bābā, Ṣuma, and Muḥammad nicknamed Karamo-Toma'. Kantoma must be a contract form of *Karamo Toroma*. (*Toroma*, according to Delafosse, 1955, ii. 373, is a nickname given to a man who has the same name as his father or grandfather.)

[6] See above, p. 10.

ibn Ṣuma ibn Karfa ibn *al-faqīh* Muḥammad al-Abyaḍ as imam in 1747, in succession to Imam Jarawari ibn Sidi Moru ibn Al-Muṣṭafā.[1]

In the oral traditions Fati-Morukpe takes the place of Muḥammad al-Abyaḍ; he is the ancestor of the *Sakpare*, the Kamaghte imams of Gonja. Buipe in central Gonja, an old trading centre and sacred to the chiefly estate, is also the residence of the senior branch of the *Sakpare*.[2]

(2) BOLE

A tradition recorded at Bole says that the *Sakpare* imams came there from Buipe after they had stayed for some time, in between, at Chama.[3] This tradition demonstrates that the *Sakpare* reached the divisional capitals of Gonja from the region of Buipe and the confluence of the White and Black Volta rivers. The version of the Arabic 'Story of Salaga and History of Gonja', that imams were appointed at Bole and other places in the course of the conquest,[4] like other parts of that tradition, is only a simplification of the actual historical process.

Another Muslim group at Bole, the Dabo, also have a central Gonja origin. 'They are', according to one tradition, 'the descendants of a man called Dabo, who at the time of Ndewura Jakpa's invasion lived in a small village in the neighbourhood of Buipe.' He was a Muslim. When Jakpa passed through his village he persuaded him to stay overnight. He provided the army with water, food, and fodder for the horses. Next morning when Jakpa was about to leave, Dabo gave him his son to carry Fati-Morukpe's praying-carpet. To the present time, the Dabo of Bole precedes the imam whenever the latter visits the chief, and acts as the imam's messenger. He winds the turban round a new imam's head at the installation ceremony before the chief's house.[5] Dabo is a Mande patronymic group which is represented in several Muslim communities in the Volta Basin.[6] The tradition shows how an early Muslim group in the area has been integrated, through this office, into the privileged Muslim community.

[1] Al-Muṣṭafā, the last named, may be the same man as *al-faqīh* Muṣṭafā ibn Muḥammad al-Abyaḍ of the former genealogy.

[2] More documentary evidence bearing on the prominent role of Buipe and its region will be discussed in a forthcoming paper.

[3] Information from Imam Abdulai of Bole; see also Tomlinson, op. cit.

[4] *GNQ*, iii, 1961, pp. 10–13, 18–19.

[5] Tomlinson, op. cit.

[6] There are Dabo, or Dao, among the Kantosi (see below, p. 145), and at Sansanne-Mango (see below, p. 82).

Members of the hereditary Muslim community in Gonja usually do not pay tribute. In Bole, however, the *Mbontisuwa* ('the Akan Muslims') who followed Jakpa from the region of Takyiman, pay an annual tribute of a hundred kola nuts. This tribute is collected by their headman, the Taari-wura or Jahori-wura, and is given to the Yagbum-wura at the Damba festival.[1] The annual tribute may represent the reiteration of the allegiance to the Gonja first given to Jakpa by the *Mbontisuwa*'s ancestors in the region of Takyiman. The Jahori-wura, it is said, enrobes a new Bole-wura at the installation ceremony.[2]

Besides the hereditary Muslim community there are in Bole Muslims who came as traders after the foundation of the Gonja state. At Salaga these 'stranger' Muslims live apart from the small local Muslim community of Kpembe. In Bole the two categories of Muslims live together, with the imam, a *Sakpare*, as the leader of the whole community of Believers.

Bole might have been a trading centre of some importance even before the Gbanya invasion. It is remembered by traditions as a thickly populated area, where the Gbanya invaders had fierce battles.[3] An old route seems to have passed from the north over Wa and Bole to Banda and Beʿo.[4] The Ligby who may have been active on this route are said to have settled at Bole before the Gbanya invasion.[5]

In the region of Bole there were several gold-mines, such as those of Wasipe and the mine near the Muslim village of Dokrupe. In 1888 Binger noted that 'these gold fields, although not as rich as those of the Bonduku region, supply gold to the Ligby, who go to Ashanti to buy kola'.[6] Traditions say that the Gonja chief of Wasipe moved to Daboya because of its salt. This was probably in the late

[1] Goody, 1964, pp. 197–8; see above, p. 7.

[2] A letter from Kpembe-wura to Yagbum-wura, of 2 August 1957, consulted at the D.C. Office, Salaga. I could not check this information at Bole, because the document has been consulted after my visits to Bole.

[3] Goody, 1954, appendix VII.

[4] T. G. Reynolds, officer commanding Bole to the officer commanding the Black Volta District, 'Report on my journey to Sikassiko and back', November 1899, sub-enclosure 1 in No. 18, *African (West)*, No. 633, PRO, CO. 879/64; Goody, 1953, p. 45.

[5] Tomlinson, op. cit.; he says that other Muslims—the Kulibali and the Wattara—also came to Bole as early as that, but information at Bole suggests that they did not come before the eighteenth century.

[6] Binger, 1892, ii. 116. A route from Yeji to 'the gold bearing districts of Wasepe and Kui' was described in 1898 (extracts from an article by von Zech, enclosure in No. 4, *African (West)*, No. 564, PRO, CO. 897/54).

seventeenth century. Would he have opted for Daboya if gold had then been known at Wasipe, his former territory? It is possible that gold was exploited at Wasipe only from the eighteenth century. At that time, with the development of Buna and Kong, Bole was on important routes linking these centres with Daboya and Dagomba in one direction, and with Buipe, Kafaba, and Salaga in another.[1] In the last quarter of the nineteenth century Bole became an important market for slaves captured by the Zaberma in Grunshi.[2]

The Zaberma attacked Wa, but did not reach Bole. Bole, however, was devastated by the *sofa*s of Samori in 1896, when this Muslim warrior was called by the Gonja chief of Kun (or Kong) to intervene in a dispute over the paramountcy.[3] In 1902 Delafosse found Bole completely in ruins.[4]

(3) TULUWE

Accession to the divisional chiefship of Tuluwe rotates between two branches of the chiefly family; one living at Tuluwe, the other at Chama. Tuluwe-wura resides in his own village, either Tuluwe or Chama. The *Sakpare* Muslims of Tuluwe-wura live at Chama, whither they moved from Tuluwe along with one branch of the chiefs. There are in Chama also Hausa Muslims, known as *Turewa*, who came there after the *Sakpare*.

Chama is the residence of the *Kagbir-wura*, the priest of the powerful Lansah shrine.[5] The district commissioner commented in the Bole District Book after a visit to Chama: 'No notice is taken of the Gonja chief, and even the imam seems to look at Kibiriwura as his master.' This observation illustrates the complex circumstances to which Muslims in this area must adapt themselves. The influence of the shrine-priest competes with that of the Gonja chiefs, and the Muslims must take account of it, in spite of the apparent dichotomy between shrine-priests and Muslims.

(4) KAFABA

In Gonja, 'medicine shrines', which move about quite freely in contrast to the static Earth shrines, tend to be associated with

[1] Renouard, 1836, pp. 110–11; Binger, loc. cit.
[2] Binger, loc. cit.
[3] Tomlinson, op. cit.; Hébert, 1961, pp. 6–8, 18; Bole District Book, *NAG*, Accra, ADM 212/6; see also above, p. 59.
[4] Delafosse, 1908, p. 131.
[5] Tomlinson, op. cit.

outsiders.[1] In their foreign origin, their mobility, and in recruiting supernatural aid, Muslims have some common traits with shrine-priests. Indeed, one finds cases of Islamic relics becoming shrines, and of Muslims' descendants, who had abandoned Islam, becoming shrine-priests.[2] This is the case of the *Kagbir-wura* (shrine-priest) of Kito, a village four miles south of Kpembe.

The shrine-priest says that he prays twice a day (morning and evening), and fasts three days during the Ramaḍān. He has a rosary, a Koran, and a bundle of Arabic manuscripts. He himself cannot read even one Arabic letter. His ancestors, he said, were formerly Muslims at Kafaba. They left Kafaba for Yeji, and then settled at Kito. It was probably after they had left the Muslim village of Kafaba that his ancestors abandoned Islam to become shrine-priests.

Kafaba, together with other places in the divisions of Buipe and Tuluwe, is associated with pre-Gonja Muslim communities. The integration of the Muslim element of Kafaba into the Gonja political system is peculiar; in Gonja, Kafaba-wura alone has the attributes of both a chief and a Muslim.

Traditions tell that when Jakpa advanced with his army, the Muslims of Kafaba, headed by a chief of Bornu origin, came out to meet Jakpa with water and food.[3] In reward, Jakpa made the village of Kafaba a sanctuary, and its chief a peace-maker and a mediator between a wrongdoer and his chief. In time of war Kafaba-wura goes to Kpembe to pray for victory. He is one of the counsellors (*Beng-bangpo*) of Kpembe-wura. Kafaba-wura does not greet Kpembe-wura in the way a sub-chief greets his senior chief (that is, by kneeling down and taking off both cap and sandals), 'because he is a Mallam'.[4]

At present it is admitted that Kafaba-wura is not a practising Muslim. His acknowledged position as a chief and his involvement in chiefly affairs may have weakened his islamic disposition, as did the decline of Kafaba as a trading centre, and the withdrawal of the trading community from Kafaba to Salaga at the turn of the eighteenth century. Even the imams of Kafaba preferred to live at Salaga, where the Kafaba Muslims have their own ward—Nfabaso. From Salaga the imams of Kafaba, seven in number until *c.* 1900, visit the village for festivals, and on such occasions as chiefly funerals. The

[1] Goody, 1967, p. 201. The Lansah shrine at Chama (mentioned above) is said to have been brought from Takyiman at the time of Jakpa (Tomlinson, op. cit.).
[2] See below, p. 177.
[3] 'The Story of Salaga, etc.', *GNQ*, iii, 1961, pp. 22–23.
[4] Information at Kpembe.

soma, who opens the dance in the *Damba* festival, also lives at Salaga.[1]

(5) KPEMBE

In contrast to the large Muslim community of Salaga, the divisional capital Kpembe has only two compounds of *Sakpare* Muslims, living among non-Muslims. The growth of a trading town, two miles from Kpembe, emphasized the seclusion of the local Muslim community. It is said, however, that until the appointment of a Friday imam to the whole Muslim community of Salaga, probably in the middle of the nineteenth century only, the Muslims of Salaga had been led in the communal prayers of the two festivals by the imam of Kpembe.[2]

It is said that in the past there were more Muslims at Kpembe. The *soma*, who plays a leading part in the *Damba* festival at Kpembe, lives in the Lampur ward of Salaga. He claims that his forefathers had formerly stayed at Kpembe, but moved to Salaga along with Lampur-wura.[3]

With the disappearance of other Muslims from Kpembe, the *Sakpare* Muslims have monopolized all functions. There had been *Dogte*s at Kpembe, but now there are none; a *Sakpare* Muslim holds the office of *Nso'owura*. There were also members of the Sisse patronymic group, whose duty it was to wash the bodies of dead chiefs; this is now done by the *nā'ib*, the imam's deputy, also a *Sakpare*.[4] Besides duties performed by *Sakpare* imams in other divisions, in Kpembe the *Sakpare* imam enrobes the new Kpembe-wura, as well as his senior sub-chiefs.[5]

Sakpare Muslims, it is said, are attached only to the major divisional chiefs. There are, however, *Sakpare* Muslims at the village of

[1] Information at Nfabaso, the ward of the Kafaba Muslims at Salaga.

[2] Information at Kpembe. Salaga had four imams only until the Civil War of 1892. The *first* imam heard of was Imam Kada, of Bornu origin; *second* was Imam Mūsā, probably the one said by the tradition (*GNQ*, iii, 1961, pp. 26–27) to have been appointed by Mallam Chediya; *third*, Imam 'Abdu, who officiated in 1874, when Gonja became independent of Ashanti (Krause manuscripts, No. 24); *fourth*, Imam 'Uthmān, killed in the Civil War of 1892 (*GNQ*, iv, 1962, pp. 16–17, 20–21).

[3] Information from *Soma* Salifu at Salaga.

[4] Information at Kpembe.

[5] A memorandum, Kpembe-wura to Yagbum-wura, 2 August 1957, consulted at the District Office, Salaga. It is concerned with a dispute over the skin of Leppo. The validity of the installation of a new Leppo-wura was challenged on the ground that he had been enrobed by a Muslim from Salaga and not by a *Sakpare* Muslim.

Kulepe (twelve miles south-east of Kpembe), followers of Kulepe-wura (who now lives at Makongo on the main road to Yeji). In the past he had also an imam from among these *Sakpare*, but during the last generation no imam has been appointed. These *Sakpare* Muslims were given by Kpembe-wura, at the request of Kulepe-wura.[1] This privilege may have been granted because of Kulepe-wura's importance among the elders in the Kpembe division. His status is recognized by the fact that he dances the *Damba* in his own village and not in the divisional capital. He is so important, says Tomlinson, 'that he is often given the title *Yeramu* even in the Kpembe-wura's presence'.[2]

(6) KUSAWGU

The clear-cut principle that *Sakpare* Muslims are attached to all senior divisional chiefs, and only to them, is again broken in the case of the divisional chief of Kusawgu, who has the right to the paramountcy. The Kusawgu-wura had no *Sakpare* Muslims at his court. The first Muslim in Kusawgu, it is said, was a Hausa trader called Sanauta. Being the great-grandfather of the present imam, Sanauta may have come to Kusawgu early in the nineteenth century. Only a century later, at the beginning of the colonial period, was the first imam appointed, a Dagomba Muslim from Nantong.[3] Hence, the imamship at Kusawgu is not only recent, but is also held by stranger Muslims, not members of the local hereditary community.

(7) DABOYA

Daboya also has stranger imams, but these replaced *Sakpare* imams who had formerly held this office. It is said that when Wasipe-wura (the Gonja chief of Daboya) moved from Wasipe to Daboya, he had a *Sakpare* imam. The *Sakpare* imams were later dismissed in circumstances which vary according to different versions of the tradition. These versions, however, have one main theme: *Sakpare* Muslims who visited Daboya were not accorded the appropriate treatment. It was reported to the Yagbum-wura, who punished the Wasipe-wura by disqualifying him from succession to the paramountcy. The latter took revenge by dismissing the *Sakpare* imams of Daboya. This tradition, in all its variants, associates the fact that for some genera-

[1] Information at Kulepe and at Kpembe.

[2] Tomlinson (op. cit.) says elsewhere: '*Yeramu* is a courtesy title for important chiefs in a Division, but is more strictly reserved to the Divisional Chiefs themselves.'

[3] Information at Kusawgu.

tions chiefs from Daboya did not succeed to the paramountcy with the fact that the *Sakpare* at Daboya were deprived of the imamship. This association has been echoed by an informant at Daboya who said that since Wasipe-wura can now again succeed to Yagbum (since 1931), the *Sakpare* may now be reappointed imams at Daboya.[1]

Although the *Sakpare* of Daboya do not produce imams, they are still respected for their inherited blessing; they are called to pray at funerals, and at other ceremonies. A *Sakpare* Muslim holds the office of *soma*, who leads the dance at the *Damba* festival. After the dismissal of the *Sakpare* the imamship was given to stranger Muslims. The latter perform the official duties of the imamship, but they do not enjoy some of the privileges of an easy approach to the chief. These are retained by the *Sakpare* (who lost the imamship), because such privileges are reserved for the local hereditary Muslim community, following the contract between Jakpa and Fati-Morukpe.

Eleven stranger imams officiated at Daboya until the end of the nineteenth century. Five other imams officiated during the present century. Collated with the chiefs' list it is likely that the dispute with the *Sakpare* and the appointment of the first stranger imam occurred in the second half of the eighteenth century.[2]

Tradition tells that after the dismissal of the *Sakpare*, a Beriberi (Bornu) Muslim came to Daboya. Wasipe-wura gave him his daughter in marriage, and appointed him imam. He was Imam Banda, the ancestor of the Nkarancha family at Daboya. Later, Imam Banda returned to Bornu, leaving behind his wife and a son. He requested Wasipe-wura to give his wife, the chief's daughter, in second marriage to a Muslim only. So, when ʿUthmān, a Muslim from Larabanga, came to Daboya, he was given the same wife, and was appointed imam. Imam ʿUthmān was the ancestor of the Kamara family at Daboya, the second gate to the imamship. This tradition, repeated by several informants, is the charter for the introduction of a new system of imamship to Daboya.

[1] Versions of this tradition in Tomlinson (op. cit.) and from informants at Daboya and other Gonja towns. The present Wasipe-wura, in an interview, denied that his forefathers had been disqualified from succeeding to the paramountcy. He insisted that they did not want to go to Yagbum because they enjoyed the prosperity of Daboya.

[2] The list of imams has been reconstructed from information collected from representatives of the three families who furnished imams at Daboya. Lists of the Daboya chiefs are given in two Arabic manuscripts, IAS/AR-41 and 42; the former seems to be more reliable. The dispute is said to have occurred in the reign of Wasipe-wura Safo, the tenth ruler back from *c.* 1880.

Two generations later, a third gate to the imamship was created with the arrival of a Muslim from Safane, whose descendants became known in Daboya as Nkombala. This Wangara Muslim, coming along a trade-route which linked Daboya to Safane, carried with him the prestige of Safane, famous as a centre of learning.[1]

The imamship rotated among the three gates—from Bornu, Larabanga, and Safane—for two or three generations, until the Larabanga family withdrew voluntarily. The present imam of Yapei was the candidate for the imamship when the turn of the Larabanga family came, but he preferred to stay at Yapei. Now the imamship rotates between the two remaining families, from Bornu and Safane.

Like other divisional capitals in Gonja, Daboya was also an important commercial centre. It was famous for the alluvial salt of the White Volta in its vicinity. Until late in the nineteenth century Daboya salt was sold as far as Grunshi to the north and Kong to the north-west, where it met the salt bars from the Sahara.[2] The traditional trade patterns of the salt were disturbed with the opening up of the route to the coast, and the improvement of communications under colonial rule. Maritime salt flowed from the coast, and the salt industry of Daboya declined and died under this competition.[3]

Daboya was on the crossing of two important trade-routes. One route from Kumasi to Jenne passed over Nkoranza, Kintampo, and Buipe to Daboya, and thence through Yagaba, Boromo, and Safane to Jenne.[4] This route was crossed by another, which went from Buna over Bole to Daboya,[5] and from Daboya to Yendi, where it joined the great Hausa route.[6] The two routes were neglected during the colonial period, leaving Daboya outside the network of modern roads. Only a cattle-route passes Daboya, which can hardly give any advantage to Daboya itself. Daboya was famous also for its woven clothes. Weaving and dyeing are still practised at Daboya, but this industry has not escaped the fate of other traditional economic activities.

A flourishing town like pre-colonial Daboya attracted traders, and could boast an important Muslim community. But even before the economic decline was felt, Daboya and its Muslim community suffered a set-back through a series of civil wars in the last quarter

[1] In Daboya, Safane is remembered also as the place where an ancestor of the *Dogte*s had spent some time, before he came back a devoted Muslim.

[2] Binger, 1892, i. 315; ii. 51–52, 100–1.

[3] See above, p. 37.

[4] Dupuis, 1824, pp. cxxxi–cxxxii.

[5] Renouard, 1836, pp. 110–11.

[6] Bowdich, 1819, p. 483, route No. 13.

of the nineteenth century. Daboya shared the fate of Salaga and Bole, when internal tensions erupted, following the independence from Ashanti rule.[1]

The first dispute broke between the reigning chief, Takora Abdu, and his younger brother, Achiri Kofi. The latter drove his brother away and seized the skin. The war brought destruction to Daboya; its Muslims fled to towns in Gonja, Dagomba, and Wa. Later, Takora returned to Daboya and expelled the usurper Achiri Kofi. Imam Al-Ḥasan, of the Bornu family, refused to return with those Muslims who came back at the call of Takora. He remained at Salaga, and was succeeded as imam by Al-Ḥasan of the Larabanga family.

The second dispute began over the skin of Yarizori, a gate to the chiefship of Wasipe. Adam Asai aspired to the Yarizori skin, but was prevented by the reigning chief, Darfo Anyami (the successor of Takora), who had been incited by another prince, Zakari. The disappointed Adam retreated to Yabum, north of Daboya, where he was joined by reinforcements from Dagomba. From Yabum Adam sent to Nūḥu, of the Wangara family, who had been at Salaga since the first Civil War, calling him to be his imam. Nūḥu responded. Adam now attacked Daboya, killed Darfo Anyami, and was installed as chief. The imam, Al-Ḥasan, joined the defeated party, and Nūḥu, who came with Adam, was appointed imam. Anyami's supporters, headed by Zakari, went to ask the aid of the Zaberma, who were at that time in the region of Walembele. Three times the Zaberma attacked Daboya without success. In the third attack, Wasipe-wura Adam was fatally wounded.

This account of the Civil War, based on information collected at Daboya,[2] is supported by the evidence of Ferguson who visited Daboya in July 1892, and signed a treaty with its chief, Adam. He noted that 'a Dagomba ally was stationed at Daboya' when he was there.[3] He reported the damage done to Daboya by the Zaberma, and attached a letter from the 'king of Daboya' to the governor, complaining of the disturbances caused by the rebellious princes 'Zakaria

[1] At the beginning of the nineteenth century Daboya was under Owusu Kwantabisa, a son of the Asantehene (Bowdich, 1819, p. 236). In 1872, shortly before the overthrow of Ashanti rule, the chief of Daboya is said to have exploded the hut by putting fire to gunpowder, killing himself together with Ashanti officials who came to collect the tribute (Ramseyer and Kuhne, 1875, p. 231; Northcott, 1899, p. 13).

[2] Tamakloe (1931, p. 53) gives a different account of these events.

[3] Ferguson to the governor, 19 November 1892, enclosure in No. 31, *African (West)*, No. 448, PRO, CO. 879/38.

and Gariba' who were in alliance with the Zaberma.[1] Adam must have been killed during the following two years, because a second treaty with Daboya, in October 1894, was already signed by Daramani Saprapa, Adam's successor.[2] In 1898 it was reported that 'Daboya itself had been almost wholly destroyed'.[3]

(*c*) *The Muslim villages of Larabanga and Dokrupe*

Muslims in Gonja, whether they came before the Gbanya invasion with the founders of the state, or after its consolidation, have all been integrated in different ways into the socio-political system of Gonja. The two unique villages of Larabanga and Dokrupe, which may be described as autonomous Muslim villages, are of particular interest.

The Muslims of these two villages claim descent of Ayyūb al-Anṣārī (better, Abū Ayyūb al-Anṣārī) of Medina in Arabia, who served as host to the Prophet at the time of the *hijra*. They often add the *nisba* 'Lansari' to their names. They keep the history of al-Anṣārī's family, and call the name of Abū Ayyūb and his descendants in their invocations.[4] Their noble descent adds much to their sanctity.

Traditions recorded from Larabanga Muslims say that before embarking upon his conquests, Jakpa had gone to Medina to seek blessing. On leaving Medina he took two descendants of Abū Ayyūb al-Anṣārī with him: Yidana Bureima (Ibrāhīm) and his brother Dokurgu ('the old man'). Yidana Bureima prayed for Jakpa and helped him to victory in his wars until they conquered Gonja, when Yidana settled at Larabanga. Yidana brought with him an old Koran from Medina, which is still kept at Larabanga, and is venerated by the Gonja. The version of the Arabic 'History of Gonja' is somewhat different:

> [In the course of the conquest of the future Gonja state] Jakpa heard that a notable left the land of the Arabs, and was coming to him. So he set out to meet him at a place about three days march away. . . . He lodged him in the house of the first learned Muslim [Fati-Morukpe]. . . . Jakpa said to this Arab elder: 'I will give you land to settle there, because I do not see the end of my march.' Jakpa gave him land to build on. The Arab built this town,

[1] Ferguson to the governor, 9 December 1892, enclosure 1 in No. 45, ibid.

[2] Ferguson to the governor, 1 November 1894, enclosure in No. 68, *African* (*West*), No. 479, PRO, CO. 879/41.

[3] Report on Daboya by Captain D. Mackworth, 6 June 1898, enclosure 2 in No. 382, *African* (*West*), No. 549, PRO, CO. 879/52.

[4] Arabic manuscripts, IAS/AR-342 (from Larabanga), and IAS/AR-345 (from Sansanne-Mango).

which is still there, called Larabanga, meaning 'the Arabs'. Nobody treats them unjustly, rather they are respected by everyone who meets them. If fighting takes place on that land, nobody turns against them or does evil to them.

The Arab copied the Book, the Koran, the Greatest of Books. . . . When he died the Koran remained with his descendants. . . . When any distress falls upon them, or they want anything, they pray to Allāh, seeking his favour, calling: 'Our Lord, for the sake of our forefathers who brought us this Book, we know nothing, it is your Book that knows; for the sake of your Book we turn to you, being omnipotent, praying to give us whatever we ask for.' Then they all say 'Amen', and wipe the palms of their hands on their faces. If there is a cow they slaughter it. Then they fold the Koran and return it to its bag. Others regard this Koran as a shrine. Everybody knows it; the Koran and the town are still there to this day.[1]

The sanctity of the Larabanga Muslims and their claim to be of Arab origin is thus endorsed by Gonja traditions. It is to the headman of Larabanga that the Gonja Chronicle must refer when recording the death of ' 'Abd-al-Raḥman the *shaykh* of the Arabs' in A.H. 1149 (1736/7).

Whereas the myth and the image of the Larabanga Muslims are clear, their historical origin poses difficult problems. Many Muslim groups in West Africa claim an Arab origin, though not all of them can name their Arab ancestor. Yet, even if the Larabanga Muslims in fact had a remote Arab ancestor, it is almost certain that they came to Gonja as Africans.

The Larabanga people are known as Kamara (sometimes pronounced as Kambara or Maara), and their patronymic is Kaute.[2] These names, as well as other phenomena—such as the Sudanese style of their mosques, or the way they recite the Koran—strongly suggest that they are of Mande origin. Yet they speak neither Gbanyito nor Mande, but a Mole-Dagbane dialect. The problem is, therefore, where and when did these Muslims of Mande origin adopt their present language?

[1] 'The Story of Salaga and History of Gonja', *GNQ*, iii, 1961, pp. 12–15. El-Wakkad's translation has been revised in some places.

[2] Kawo or Kao is a Mande patronymic of a clan which gave up the custom of incising tribal marks (Delafosse, 1955, ii. 313). This may well apply to the Larabanga Muslims who have no tribal marks. (Some Muslims at Dokrupe adopted the Gonja tribal marks.) Kamara is also the name of a Mande clan (ibid., p. 379). On the history of the Kamara in the Ivory Coast, see Person, 1964, pp. 325–6. At Wahabu (Upper Volta) I heard of a Muslim at La, known as 'Kamara Lansari', claiming descent from Abū Ayyūb al-Anṣārī. I could not, however, find what relationship exists between this Muslim and the Muslims of Larabanga.

Two members of this group said that their ancestor, Yidana Bureima, had stayed for some time in Mamprusi on his way (with Jakpa) to Gonja.[1] Another tradition says that the Kamara were brought from Mamprusi 'as Mallams' by Cheffigiwura (a chief in central Gonja) to help his father Manwura in the strife against Jakpa. As Manwura was defeated the Kamara were made to pay an annual tribute (in soap, it is said) as a sign of submission. In this, they differ from the *Sakpare* Muslims, followers of the victorious Jakpa, who pay no tribute and enjoy intimacy with the chiefs.[2] A third tradition says that Larabanga was founded by a Muslim who had formerly been imam to the Mamprusi chief of Janga.[3]

These references suggest that before they settled in Gonja, the Kamara had stayed for some time in Mamprusi. They could have been traders who settled along the route passing through Mamprusi in the pre-Gonja period.[4] Like the Yarse in Mossi or the Kantosi in Wa, the Kamara could have adopted their hosts' dialect in Mamprusi.[5]

This proposition presupposes that the Kamara had adopted their language before they had settled at Larabanga. Yet it is also possible that they acquired this language in their present habitation. Before the Gbanya invasion, central Gonja was inhabited by people speaking Dagbane or a related dialect. Some of the *nyamase* (commoners) of Buipe are said to be of Dagomba origin; their headman, the *Kanyampase-wura*, whom Jakpa met when he conquered Buipe, is still the Earth-priest of this place.[6] Only ten miles from Larabanga, at Damongo, the Earth-priest is also of Dagomba origin.[7] One tradition says that the Gbanya attacked a big 'Dagomba' settlement in the direction of Damongo.[8] Even now a Mole-Dagbane dialect, Anga, is spoken by villagers in Murugu and Busunu, twenty-five miles from Larabanga.[9]

[1] Information from al-ḥājj M'beima of Larabanga (regarded as the best authority on the history of that village), and from the imam of Tuna (on the Bole-Wa road), who is of the Kamara group of Buna.

[2] J. A. Braima, personal communication. See also, Jones, 1963, p. 12. On the strife between Manwura and Jakpa, see above, p. 57 note 3.

[3] Mrs. Susan Drucker-Brown, personal communication. She heard it from a government employee who had worked for some time near Larabanga, and knew well this village. On Janga, see below, p. 137.

[4] See above, pp. 5–6. Janga may have been a rest stop on this route.

[5] On the Kantosi, see below, pp. 145–7. Several Kantosi informants alluded to some relationship with the Kamara of Larabanga.

[6] Tomlinson, op. cit.; Jones, 1963, p. 10.

[7] Goody, 1964, p. 202.

[8] Jones, 1963, p. 17.

[9] Tomlinson, op. cit.

A linguist studying the dialect of the Kamara in comparison with other Mole-Dagbane dialects may suggest whether the Kamara adopted their language at their present location, or further to the north. It is, however, significant that, whereas the *Sakpare* Muslims speak the same language as the Gonja chiefs, the Kamara speak a Mole-Dagbane dialect, as do neighbouring commoners. The *Sakpare* became attached to their chiefs, while the Kamara settled in their own autonomous villages.

Traditions say that when Yidana Bureima settled at Larabanga, his brother Dokurgu ('the old man') established Dokrupe ('the old man's town'), fifteen miles south-east of Bole.[1] Dokrupe had twelve imams compared with twenty imams at Larabanga.[2] Although both lists are not necessarily correct, it is likely that Dokrupe is a more recent foundation than Larabanga. It may be suggested that Dokrupe was established on an important route which linked not only the Gonja divisional capitals (Bole, Buipe, Tuluwe, and Kpembe) but also Buna, Kong, and Bonduku with Kafaba and Salaga.[3] Even in this century gold was mined just over a mile from Dokrupe, which had probably been in the past part of the gold-bearing region of Wasipe. It is likely that Dokrupe was founded only when both the trade-route and the gold-fields developed, in the eighteenth century.[4]

Had Dokrupe been founded over three centuries ago, together with Larabanga, one would expect a greater differentiation between the two Kamara communities. In fact, there is a close similarity in the constitution of the two villages. In both, the *tengpiema* (lit. 'the village's old man') is the senior elder, and the imam the spiritual leader. The imam and the *tengpiema* are looked after by the *bendugu*. The latter carries their orders and acts as an arbiter between disputing parties. At the death of either of the two leaders, the *bendugu* keeps the insignia of the office. When a new imam or *tengpiema* is appointed he is enrobed by the *bendugu* at the installation ceremony.

The *tengpiema* is not a chief. Larabanga had no chief in the pre-colonial period. As the British insisted on a chief, one of the village elders was invested with the chiefship. Yet, although the so appointed

[1] Information at Larabanga and Dokrupe.

[2] The list of the Larabanga imams has been recorded at a meeting with the elders of the village. List of the imams of Dokrupe in an Arabic manuscript IAS/AR-341.

[3] Binger, 1892, ii. 116.

[4] See above, pp. 64–65.

chief represents the village before the official authorities, one may notice that in the internal traditional constitution the chief is still overshadowed by the *tengpiema*. One is reminded of the European-made chiefs, imposed over the *tengdana*s among the 'tribes without rulers' of the Upper Region.[1] Indeed, the *tengpiema* may be regarded as a kind of *tengdana*, but Muslims would not use the latter term, which is almost the symbol of paganism in the Volta Basin.

The autonomous character of the Larabanga is marked also by the taboo against any meeting between the *tengpiema* and the Yagbum-wura, the paramount chief of Gonja. The imam of Larabanga, on the other hand, goes to greet the Yagbum-wura and to pray for him. The imam of Dokrupe does the same to Senyon-wura, a senior counsellor of the Yagbum-wura. Tomlinson says that a new Senyon-wura is enrobed by the imam of Dokrupe.

The intimate relations of the *Sakpare* and the chiefs is associated with the contract between Jakpa and Fati-Morukpe, and the latter's participation in the conquest. Gonja traditions make it clear that the ancestor of Larabanga did not take part in the wars. Jakpa said, as quoted above, 'I will give you land to settle there, because I do not see the end of my march'. A certain atmosphere of 'estrangement' dominates relations between the Kamara and the Gonja chiefs. Though in Gonja for over three centuries the Daboya imams of Larabanga origin are classified, together with imams from Bornu and Safane, as strangers.

One finds imams of Larabanga origin only in Gonja chiefdoms with a strong Dagomba cultural influence: in Daboya, where the majority of the *nyamase* in the division speak Mole-Dagbane dialects; at Kakpande, on the border between the Kpembe division of Gonja and Dagomba, where the Gonja people speak Dagbane; and at Yapei, in the division of Kusawgu, which is said to have been conquered by the Gonja from the Dagomba.[2]

An important community of Kamara Muslims lives at Buna. They claim to have come from Larabanga, and relations between the two communities continue to this day. If it is true, as claimed, that the Kamara were among the earliest Muslims at Buna,[3] they may have come there not long after the foundation of the kingdom by a dynasty of Dagomba origin. At that period the affinity of the Buna chiefs to

[1] Rattray, 1932, i, preface p. xvi.
[2] Tamakloe, 1931, p. 24. Information at Kakpande and Yapei.
[3] Information from Kamara Muslims from Buna at Bole and Tuna.

Dagomba might have been more than a remote tradition. The Kamara, one may conclude, inclined to operate within the Dagomba sphere of influence. Indeed, the Larabanga Muslims have played an important role in the diffusion of Islam in Dagomba since the late seventeenth or the early eighteenth century.

In Gonja itself the Larabanga Muslims could have found little scope for propagating Islam. There was not a continuous process of islamization. Islamic elements in Gonja were incorporated into the culture of the chiefly estate; distinct groups of Muslims became attached to the chiefs and integrated into the social and political system; but rigid social stratification and lack of mobility prevented the spread of Islam from the Muslim estate to the other social estates.

CHAPTER V

Islam at Sansanne-Mango

IN the north-western corner of Togo, east of Mamprusi and south of Gurma, lies the Chokossi state, with its centre at Sansanne-Mango. It has chiefs of Mande origin, commoners of Akan origin, and Muslims of Dyula origin. A state of that composition is indeed outside its geographical context.

All the traditions agree that these people came from Anno (Grumania), west of Bonduku. The people call themselves *Anufom*.[1] They were given the name Chokossi by their Mamprusi and Dagomba neighbours.[2] The name of their capital Sansanne-Mango means 'the camp of the Anno people'.[3]

Mamprusi traditions say that the Chokossi were brought to Sansanne-Mango by a Mamprusi chief. In 1888, while at Walwale, Binger heard a tradition that following an internal dispute in Mamprusi about 1730, the Mamprusi chief called in people from Gonja, Bonduku, and Grumania to help him. The Mande from Grumania decided to stay and the Mamprusi chief gave them the country of Sansanne-Mango in reward for their services.[4] According to another tradition the Mamprusi chief, Na Atabia, led an expedition as far as Anno, where he was impressed by the fighting qualities of the warriors. He later called these Anno warriors to help him repel an invasion of the Gurma.[5]

An account of the migration of the Anufom is recorded in an Arabic manuscript, written about the beginning of the nineteenth century.[6] It tells of a band of warriors, led by Beima Bonsafo and

[1] i.e. 'the people of Anno'; sing. *Anufo* (Froelich, 1963, p. 176).

[2] Cf. Rattray, 1932, i. 113.

[3] *Sansanni* is 'a war-camp' in Hausa (Abraham, 1962, p. 779); *Mango* is the Mande name for Anno (Binger, 1892, ii. 38, 219).

[4] Ibid., p. 38. Variants of these traditions can still be heard in Mamprusi.

[5] Mackay, unpublished manuscript; Rattray, 1932, ii. 547.

[6] Arabic manuscript in possession of Ṣiḍḍīq b. 'Umar Jabaghte of Sansanne-Mango (IAS/AR-346). The manuscript, its owner claims, was written by his ancestor who took part in the expedition from Anno. It is read, however, as a memorized tradition rather than as a contemporary record. Kurba, the Mamprusi king mentioned in the manuscript, is probably Na Kulba who reigned at the beginning of the nineteenth century. He may have been the Mamprusi ruler when the manuscript was written and not at the time of the expedition, about half a

Soma Ibrāhīma (the former's nephew ?), who set out from Mango. They raided several towns, advancing north-eastward, until they were invited by the chief of Yabo, the Yagbum-wura, to help him in his war against the chief of Kandia (a rebellious Gonja divisional chief). The names of these warriors became famous and they were called by the Mamprusi chief to fight the pagans of Kantindi (a Gurma chiefdom in northern Togo), who had threatened Mamprusi land. Kantindi was defeated, and the Mango people turned to Kunjogu, conquered it, and settled there. It became known by the Hausa name Sansanne-Mango.

In the expedition against Kantindi, the manuscript relates, the Mango warriors were accompanied by the Yagbum-wura's son. His descendants still live at Sansanne-Mango, in the Gbanyaso ward. Their patronymic is Cherba.[1] In Gbanyito, *Cherba* is the title of chiefs' sons who have no chiefship.[2] This patronymic, therefore, supports their claim to be descendants of a Gonja prince.

The Gonja Chronicle may refer to that expedition of Mango and Gonja forces when it says: 'In that year, in Jumādā al-Ākhira [May 1751] 'Uthmān the king of Kapuasi son of Ṣulū king of Diber[3] died while fighting in the land of Gurma in the direction of Gambaga. . . . He was [there] together with the [people of] Mango. In the same month he had an army destroyed together with the Mango people.'

Earlier references in the Gonja Chronicle to the Mango people (in A.H. 1161 or A.D. 1749) show them still west of Gonja. The expedition of the Mango people against the Gurma, at the invitation of the Mamprusi chief, took place in 1751. The foundation of the Chokossi kingdom could have been a little later. Siki, son of Beima Bonsafo, the fourth ruler, is mentioned in an Arabic manuscript written in 1820.[4] Siki was preceded by two of his brothers, who had reigned successively after their father, the founder of Sansanne-Mango. This may be consistent with a date early in the second half of the eighteenth century, for the foundation of the state, as inferred from the Chronicle, and suggested by earlier writers.[5]

century earlier. The same account appears in two German translations, by R. Asmis (1912) and von Seefried (1913), who say that the translation was made for them from manuscripts written in the Mande language.

[1] Information from the headman of the Gbanyaso ward at Sansanne-Mango.

[2] Information at Buipe, given in a different context.

[3] Both Kapuasi and Diber were in central Gonja.

[4] Dupuis, 1824, p. cxxviii.

[5] Von Seefried, 1912, pp. 424–8; Westermann, 1914, p. 24; Froelich, 1963, p. 177.

Sansanne-Mango was founded at a time when the trade with Hausaland was increasing considerably. It became the last place on the road protected by the local states. After Sansanne-Mango the route to Hausaland entered a territory of petty Gurma chiefdoms, sparsely populated and rather unsafe.[1]

Shortly after the foundation of Sansanne-Mango a group of Hausa Muslims arrived. They became hosts to passing traders, and acted as intermediaries between traders and chiefs. Their ward, Baki-n-Gulbi, is comparable to the Gamaji ward of Yendi as a kind of *zongo*.[2]

The chiefs of Sansanne-Mango are members of the Wattara patronymic group. They claim relationship with the Wattara rulers of Kong. Groups of Muslims at Sansanne-Mango also came from Kong, some together with the chiefs, others after the foundation of the Chokossi state. There are still close relations between Sansanne-Mango and Kong. In a way, Sansanne-Mango may be regarded as an offshoot of the Dyula state of Kong. However, the founders of Sansanne-Mango came not directly from Kong, but via Anno.

A reliable history of Anno (Grumania) is still to be written. It is there that the blending of Mande and Akan elements took place, for in Anno, as in Sansanne-Mango, Wattara chiefs rule over an Akan population.[3] The kingdom of Kong was founded by the Wattara at the end of the seventeenth or the beginning of the eighteenth century,[4] that is just over half a century before the foundation of Sansanne-Mango. It was probably during that period that the Wattara operated in Anno, in the fringes of the forest, a country known for its kola. The Wattara chiefs of Kong recruited their troops from among the pagans, mainly Senufo. These troops, known as *Sonangi*, were hardly touched by Islam.[5] The composition of the expeditionary force which established Sansanne-Mango—Wattara chiefs commanding pagan troops (Akan in this case)—suggests that the Wattara in Anno had recruited their troops in much the same way as their kinsmen of Kong. Internal disputes had driven a party of them to adventurous raids, which subsequently took them as mercenaries to the area of their future state.

Kong was regarded as a Muslim kingdom, because it had a

[1] See above, pp. 24–25.

[2] See below, pp. 105–6. The *zongo* of Sansanne-Mango was established only after the German conquest.

[3] Binger, 1892, ii. 236; Marty, 1922, p. 50.

[4] Bernus, 1960; Person, 1964, pp. 326–7.

[5] Binger, 1892, ii. 209; Bernus, 1960, pp. 253–4.

prosperous Dyula community, which made the town an important centre of Islamic learning.[1] But even there the Islamic character of the Wattara chiefs was dubious. Al-ḥājj Mahmadu Lamine of Tenetou told Binger that Kong had Muslims and pagans; the name of the Muslim tribe was *Sanokho* (i.e. Saghanogho), whereas the pagans were the *Wattara*.[2] Compared with the north, the view from the south was always more liberal. Dupuis heard of the chiefs of Sansanne-Mango as Muslims: 'Magho is a kingdom which contains a mixed population of Moslems and heathens—*the former enjoying the government.*'[3]

At present, the Wattara at Sansanne-Mango are not real Muslims; rather they may be regarded as 'half islamized', sitting on the fence between Islam and paganism. Had they practised the same kind of Islam before they migrated to Sansanne-Mango, as may be inferred from the critical view of al-ḥājj Mahmadu Lamine about the Wattara of Kong? Or had they been more thoroughly islamized? Established at Sansanne-Mango the Wattara became detached from the main body of Mande-Dyula peoples. Thus isolated they abandoned their Mande dialect and adopted the Akan dialect of their recruited warriors as well as some of their customs. They retained, however, Islamic customs, such as circumcision, Muslim names, avoidance of pork, and celebrations of Muslim festivals.[4] In this they do not differ much from the Gonja chiefs, though the process of attaining such a degree of islamization might have been different.

The Wattara warriors were accompanied by Muslims from the outset of their adventurous expedition. At first, it is said, the imam was of the Jabaghte patronymic group. Only later, during the expedition itself, did Ghassama, the ancestor of the Kamaghte imams, join the Mango people, and was given the imamship. The old status of the Jabaghte is still remembered; a Jabaghte takes part in the installation ceremony of a new chief, and after the ceremony a Jabaghte acts as the chief's imam for the first ten days, when the Kamaghte imam takes over.[5] It is significant that the two patronymic groups occur also in Gonja: Jabaghte are the guardians of Jakpa's

[1] Cf. Wilks, 1961, p. 22.

[2] Binger, 1892, i. 56. Tenetou is Tementou on the map, about a hundred miles south of Bamako.

[3] Dupuis, 1824, p. xcviii; my italics.

[4] Von Seefried, 1913, pp. 429–30; Froelich, 1963, pp. 179, 181–2.

[5] Information from Ṣiḍḍīq b. 'Umar Jabaghte in the presence of Muslims from other groups at Sansanne-Mango.

tomb, and at least one imam (recorded by the Gonja Chronicle) was a Jabaghte. The *Sakpare* imams of Gonja are, however, Kamaghte as are the imams of Namasa, and probably the imams of old Beʿo.[1] Is it not possible that it was when the Mango people entered this region, where Kamaghte imams are common, that the Jabaghte were replaced by Kamaghte?

The Kamaghte imams, who succeeded Ghassama, were attached to the paramount chief. Most of the paramounts were of one branch of the ruling family, and the Kamaghte imams became closely associated with that branch, the Jermabu. The Jermabu are the descendants of Beima Bonsafo, the senior leader of the expedition. The second leader, Soma Ibrāhīma, died before Beima Bonsafo. Soma's descendants form the junior branch of the ruling family, the Sangbana. In principle they are eligible to the paramountcy, but in practice (during the pre-colonial period) a member of the Sangbana succeeded only when there was no eligible successor from among the Jermabu. Only two of the twelve chiefs in Sansanne-Mango before 1898 were of the Sangbana branch.[2]

The Sangbana chiefs had their own Muslims, members of the Dao patronymic group. ʿAlī, the ancestor of the Dao, did not take part in the expedition, but came directly from Kong. Upon his arrival at Sansanne-Mango, ʿAlī stayed with the Sangbana chief, to whom ʿAlī's descendants remained attached. In 1897 Chief Beima Sabie of the Jermabu was killed when leading the resistance to the German conquest. The Germans appointed Ajanda of the Sangbana as chief. After his death, two years later, his cousin Tchaba, also of the Sangbana, succeeded him. As the chiefship went from the Jermabu to the Sangbana, so was the imamship transferred from the Kamaghte (associated with the Jermabu) to the Dao (Muslims of the Sangbana): Imam Aḥmad of the Dao family was given the imamship. In 1912 the chiefship returned to Jermabu, and the Kamaghte imams were restored. Only recently did both the chiefship and the imamship change hands again. The previous chief, Jambara, was of the Sangbana; he took the imamship from the Kamaghte and appointed Jibrīl, son of Imam Aḥmad Dao. After Jambara's death, the present chief, Tchaba of Jermabu, dismissed the Dao Imam Jibrīl, and restored the Kamaghte Imam ʿAbdallah.[3]

[1] See above, p. 10.

[2] Von Seefried, 1913, pp. 421–4.

[3] Information from the ex-imam, Jibrīl Dao. For the events in 1897–1912, see Trierenberg, 1914, pp. 152–3; von Seefried, 1913, pp. 423–4.

These events demonstrate the close association of chiefs and Muslims at Sansanne-Mango, when one of two Muslim houses gains prominence with the rise of one of the two branches of the ruling family. Kamaghte and Dao have become two gates to the imamship, while the Jabaghte enjoy privileges as representing the oldest Muslim companions of the chiefs. Other Muslim families of Mande, Hausa, Gonja, Ligby, and Larabanga origin complete the composition of the Muslim community at Sansanne-Mango. All these are associated with the role of that town as a commercial centre.

Since the foundation of Sansanne-Mango, the Chokossi have been in contact with their neighbours the Mamprusi and the Dagomba, in whose internal disputes the Chokossi more than once took part.[1] Yet a closer examination of the history of the Chokossi state and its constitution shows that it has more in common with Gonja than with either Mamprusi or Dagomba.[2] There is a striking similarity in the social structure of the Chokossi and the Gonja states, in the division into three social estates:

1. *Chiefs* of Mande origin who adopted the language and some of the customs of the commoners, but retained elements of their original Mande culture. In religion they keep the balance between the two other estates in embracing both Islamic and pagan beliefs and rituals.
2. *Muslims* of Dyula origin, called *Karamo* in Gonja and *Achirama* at Sansanne-Mango (both are derived from the same word of Mande origin). Even the three patronymic groups are represented in both states: Kamaghte, Jabaghte, and Dao (Dabo in Gonja).
3. *Commoners*, whose language (a Guang dialect in Gonja, and an Akan dialect at Sansanne-Mango) was adopted by the two other estates. Commoners in both states have hardly been touched by Islam.

According to the Arabic history of Sansanne-Mango, the Mango warriors had first been introduced into the Middle Volta Basin by the Gonja, and were later recruited by the Mamprusi. The founders of both states, Gonja and Sansanne-Mango, came into

[1] Mackay, unpublished manuscript; Rattray, 1932, ii. 548; Syme, unpublished manuscript; A. W. Davies, unpublished manuscript.

[2] Only von Zech (1949, p. 33) took note of the resemblance between the Chokossi state and Gonja.

the area as warriors, bringing along the nucleus of their future state with them. There are, therefore, some parallels in the circumstances of the establishment of these two states. The background of the Anufom migration should be further explored, mainly in Anno itself. It occurred almost two hundred years after the Gonja invasion, coming from a region which is precisely known. When the history of the Mango is reconstructed, covering many aspects of the Mande warriors' adventures, new lines of investigation for the early history of Gonja may be suggested.

For the purpose of the present study it may already be noted that the chiefs of both states entered the territories of their future states with Muslim followers, the latter having been no strangers to the chiefs. Following this early contact, the infusion of Islamic elements into the culture of the chiefly estate probably took place before the consolidation of these states. The participation of Muslims in the conquest, in both cases, brought them into intimate relations with the chiefs. On the other hand, the differentiation into distinct social estates was crystallized with the conquest, and this in turn conditioned the limits of Islamic influence and propagation. In a comparative study of the patterns of islamization, Gonja and Sansanne-Mango may represent one model, because all these common features distinguish the two states from others like Mossi, Dagomba, and Mamprusi.

CHAPTER VI

Islam in Dagomba

(*a*) *The Introduction of Islam into Dagomba*

'MOHAMMEDANISM here has never made the slightest progress, the Dagomba confederation having been throughout the centuries a firm bulwark against the influence of Islam.'[1] This bold statement, written in the 1920s, should be compared with late eighteenth-century references to 'the Mahometan kingdom of Degombah'[2] to demonstrate the complexity of the actual situation. Dagomba may serve as the best example to illustrate the interaction of Islam and paganism in the Middle Volta States.

The existence of Islamic elements in the national culture of Dagomba and Mamprusi led early observers to suggest that these elements had been brought to this area by the founders of the Mossi-Dagomba states. These founders were a group of invaders from the north-east or east, arriving probably about the thirteenth century. They imposed their authority over the stateless tribes, which had known no headmen other than the *tengdana*, the Earth-priest.[3]

Rattray says of these invaders that they were 'in some cases conversant with the rudiments of Mohammedanism',[4] and that 'they did not contribute to the local religious beliefs, which, *abandoning Islam*, they eventually came to follow'.[5] Rattray is supported by Mackay, who has been told 'that they originally came from a country east of Sokoto, that they were originally Mohammedans, and that an ancestor "Bungwa", the first Na we know of, had gone to Mecca'.[6] That such traditions were current is attested also by Syme: 'The Mamprusi claim to have been Mohammedans themselves at one time, and perhaps this is partly substantiated by the finding of ruined primitive mosques at Pusiga.'[7]

[1] Cardinall, 1927, p. 108.
[2] Lucas, in *Proceedings*, 1790, p. 176.
[3] See above, p. xiii.
[4] Rattray, 1932, i, preface p. xii.
[5] Ibid., ii. 550; my italics.
[6] Mackay, unpublished manuscript.
[7] Syme, unpublished manuscript. The remains of little mosques seen by people still living in 1932, are unlikely to be of such antiquity.

Is it true that the Islamic elements in the culture of Mamprusi and Dagomba are traces of their former Muslim religion? The Mamprusi claims to have been Muslims in the past are rather vague. Indeed, Mamprusi traditions say virtually nothing of the period before their great ancestor Na Bawa. Dagomba traditions go further back but have nothing to say about Islamic traits of the ancestors. Their ancestor Tohajiye rendered military aid to Malle. But this Malle, 'a country adjacent to Hausaland' and east of Gurma,[1] could not be the islamized empire of Mali. It might refer, if the name Mali in this tradition is not a recent innovation, to a southern Mande group, possibly Busa in Borgu.[2] These Mande people were not Muslims, and if any Mande elements were introduced at that stage they could not have been Islamic.[3] The Mossi, for example, who claim a common origin with Mamprusi and Dagomba, had quite a different experience in adopting Islamic elements. It will be suggested, therefore, that Islamic elements were introduced only after the foundation of these states in the Middle Volta Basin.

Dagomba traditions say explicitly that their ancestors were complete pagans until the time of Na Zangina, to whose reign radical changes in the Dagomba civilization are attributed. Not only Muslims say this, but also the traditions transmitted by the non-Muslim official drummers.

Official Dagomba history does not mention Muslims in the period before Na Zangina (*c.* 1700). This does not necessarily imply that there had been no Muslims in Dagomba land in the pre-Zangina period, but it does suggest that Muslims had made no significant impact then, and that relations between chiefs and Muslims had not been close.

Indeed there is some evidence for the existence of Muslims in Dagomba before the end of the seventeenth century. Trade-routes, it has been suggested, passed through Dagomba as early as the sixteenth century. The excavations at Yendi-Dabari raised the possibility of Muslim traders' quarters in the pre-eighteenth-century Dagomba capital.[4] These Muslim traders were Wangara of Mande origin, and one would expect to find them in western Dagomba, known as *Toma*, where the Mande trade-route passed, and where the kingdom of

[1] Tamakloe, 1931, pp. 3–6.

[2] See above, p. xiii.

[3] Duncan-Johnstone and Blair (1932, p. 13) attribute the introduction of Mande Islamic elements, such as the Damba festival, to that period.

[4] See above, p. 6.

Dagomba was consolidated. It is, however, difficult to confirm that any Muslim now in western Dagomba belongs to a group which had settled there three centuries or more ago.[1] For this purpose one needs a crucial event in relation to which one may date the arrival of a certain group to the area. The Gonja invasion was such an event, which helped in dating the arrival of Muslim groups on the northern bank of the Volta river. The same is true of the Dagomba conquest of Konkomba land, now eastern Dagomba or *Na-Ya*, towards the end of the seventeenth century.

Gbanyaghe is the title-name of 'Umar Jabaghte, who came from *Saryartenga*, 'the land of the Yarse', namely Mande. He settled among the Konkomba at Kuga, two miles east of Yendi. Later the Ya-Na (paramount chief of Dagomba) came from *Toma* and drove away the Konkomba. Gbanyaghe stayed at Kuga with the Dagomba, but his early association with the Konkomba is still remembered in the custom that a member of the Gbanyaghe family performs the ceremonial sacrifice to the Konkomba shrine Pabo.[2]

A Muslim elder at Yendi holds the office of *Tsheli-Yarna*. Tsheli is the old Konkomba name of Yendi,[3] and it is said that the first Muslim who held this office, a member of the Sisse patronymic group, had settled among the Konkomba before the Dagomba conquest. He came there from western Dagomba.[4]

It is likely that these early Muslims moved eastwards before the transfer of the Dagomba capital because of the growing importance of the Hausa trade-route in the second half of the seventeenth century. They preceded the Dagomba who, compelled to abandon their old capital under the pressure of the Gonja, found it advantageous to have their new political centre on the route to Hausaland.

Dagomba had first felt the pressure of the Gbanya invaders in its periphery. During the first half of the seventeenth century the

[1] But see below, p. 116, on the *yarnas* of Savelugu and Karaga.

[2] Information from 'Uthmān Gbanyaghe at Binchiritenga, whither he moved from his ancestral village, Kuga. This informant counted seven generations back to his ancestor, the same number of generations as in the chiefly genealogy since the conquest of eastern Dagomba. The patronymic Jabaghte occurs also in Gonja; could the title Gbanyaghe be associated with Gbanya?

The same informant mentioned another shrine, at Turzon, where only a Muslim (any Muslim) may perform the sacrifice.

[3] The Dagomba name of Yendi is Yaa or Yaa-Na. Yendi is probably the Hausa form of this name. For a Konkomba version of the Dagomba conquest, see Tait, 1961, p. 4.

[4] Information from a descendant of the first *Tsheli-Yarna*, and from other elders at Yendi.

Dagomba lost whatever control they had west of the White Volta and south of Daboya. A direct clash between Dagomba and Gonja was inevitable, and it took place at Daboya, in the second half of the seventeenth century.[1] After expelling the Dagomba from Daboya, the Gonja crossed the White Volta river and defeated the Dagomba not far from their capital. In this battle, it is said, the Dagomba chief, Na Dariziegu, was killed. His successor, Na Luro, had a victory over the Gonja, but his son and successor, Na Tutugri, faced a more vigorous Gonja attack. He abandoned the old capital, Yendi-Dabari, and moved to the east where he conquered part of the Konkomba country.[2]

The Dagomba retreat gave them only a brief respite; the Gonja threat continued, as is inferred from Na Zighli's call for unity against the Gonja.[3] Unity was wanted then, as the Drum History is explicit about disputes over the paramountcy. After the death of Na Zokuli the elders consulted soothsayers, who unanimously selected for the paramountcy the chief of the small village of Yamol-Karaga, the poor and sick Prince Gungobili. This choice had reluctantly been accepted, but the princes and the elders vowed to consult the soothsayers no more.

This episode reveals a breakdown in the customary machinery for selecting the Ya-Na. This became evident at the death of Na Gungobili, when many princes contested for the skin. The selection was referred to the Mamprusi paramount chief. The latter, after testing the candidates, decided in favour of the youngest, Zangina son of Na Tutugri, to the indignation of the other princes. It is sometimes alleged that Zangina and his supporters had bribed the Mamprusi chief.

The split between Na Zangina and the other princes continued throughout his reign. It came into the open again when Dagomba faced another Gonja attack. Na Zangina's appeal to the Dagomba chiefs to join him in defending the country was rejected by some of the important princes, who said 'that the subtle manner by which he got the chieftaincy in Mamprusi, he could employ again to ward off the war'. Andani Zighli, cousin to Na Zangina, agreed to command the army on condition that Na Zangina relinquished the skin to him.

[1] On this date, see below, p. 196.

[2] Tait's manuscripts, text A; according to Tamakloe (1931, pp. 23–24, 27), Yendi-Dabari was abandoned by Na Luro.

[3] This and the following account are based on the Drum History as recorded for D. Tait (Tait's manuscripts, texts A and B). Parts of this tradition have been recorded also by Tamakloe (1931, pp. 27–31).

The Gonja advanced eastward from Daboya, threatening the new centre of the Dagomba kingdom. The decisive battle took place near Sang, only twenty miles west of Yendi. The Gonja were defeated, and Na Andani Zighli killed the Gonja chief 'Kumpatia'. This great victory of Dagomba finally checked the Gonja expansion, probably in 1713.[1]

This was the political background to the introduction of Islam into Dagomba, which all traditions agree took place during the reign of Na Zangina. The traditions, it has been suggested, refer not to the arrival of Muslims, but to the beginning of a strong Islamic influence on the Dagomba chiefs. That one should distinguish between these two stages in the spread of Islam may be inferred from the history of Islam in Mossi. The Yarse, Muslim traders of Mande origin, lived in Mossi since the sixteenth century, but their influence on the Mossi chiefs was negligible. Islamic influence entered the court of the Moro-Naba at Wagadugu only towards the end of the eighteenth century with the appointment of the first imam. This was done, according to one Mossi tradition, following the example of the Mamprusi chief who had already been served by an imam.[2] If this tradition has any significance, it suggests that the change in the attitude of the chiefs towards Islam is not explicable only by increased numbers of Muslims, or by the length of their residence in the country. One has to seek another explanation for the change, its nature and timing.

The growth of trade with Hausaland, and the flow of Hausa Muslims since the late seventeenth century, could explain the introduction of Islam during Na Zangina's reign. Indeed, Hausa Muslims have contributed more than any other group to the propagation of Islam in Dagomba. But the traditions suggest that Na Zangina had first approached the Sabali-Yarna, a Wangara Muslim of a group which had already been in Dagomba for some time.

Further, some features of Islam in Dagomba suggest a Mande-Dyula rather than a Hausa influence. Take, for example, the most important national festival of Islamic origin, the *Damba* festival commemorating the Prophet's birthday. The name *Damba*, as in Gonja, is of Mande-Dyula origin.[3] Names of other festivals have

[1] This may be the war of A.H. 1125 (1713) recorded by the Gonja Chronicle; see below, p. 197.

[2] See below, pp. 166–7.

[3] In Hausaland, in Nupe, and in Borgu this festival is known as Gane (Abraham, 1962, pp. 296, 844; Nadel, 1942, pp. 217–19; Lombard, 1965, pp. 331–65).

been translated into Dagbane, but they provide clear parallels to festivals in Gonja. In general, one may suggest that Islamic elements have been incorporated into the Dagomba culture in much the same way as in Gonja. This similarity may reflect a Gonja influence, which is probably not accidental; the changed attitude of the Dagomba chiefs might have resulted from the confrontation with the Gonja.[1]

The indifference of the Dagomba chiefs to the Muslims in the pre-Zangina period, reflected by the silence of the tradition, contrasts with the enthusiasm of the Gonja chiefs towards their Muslim followers. The Gbanya were acquainted with the institutionalized role of Muslims in the Mande chiefdoms, they brought with them the idea of recruiting the aid of Muslims by integrating them into the social and political system of the state, without destroying their own institutions.

In the course of their history, the Dagomba proved capable of adopting such institutions as contributed to the strength of their adversaries. Responding to the challenge of fire-arms, after their defeat by the Ashanti, the Dagomba soon created units of musketeers on the Ashanti model. 'Before the time of Na Garba', Rattray recorded from elders of the Ya-Na, 'the Dagomba did not have guns; they fought with swords, spears, and bows and arrows.' 'Before Na Luro's time', it was added, 'Nas of Yendi wore skins. We got our first robes in the Gonja war.'[2] These were two important landmarks in the development of the Dagomba civilization. Clothing, it will be shown later, is closely associated in Dagomba traditions with the introduction of Islam. Here, therefore, is an allusion to Islamic influence as a result of the war with Gonja.

In the early phases of the struggle with Gonja, the Dagomba suffered humiliating defeats by the Gonja. The young vigorous power (Gonja) had an initial advantage over the two-centuries-old kingdom (Dagomba). The Dagomba, however, may have been puzzled by the defeat they suffered from an enemy, apparently without any decisive technical superiority.[3] The Gonja themselves ascribed their success to the prayers and charms of their Muslim followers, and the *Alite*,

[1] Fage (1959, p. 20) alluded to the possibility of Gonja influence on the introduction of Islam into Dagomba.

[2] Rattray, 1932, ii. 564.

[3] Eyre-Smith (1933, p. 12) suggests that the Gonja might have had guns. This is unlikely; the Gbanya left the Middle Niger before fire-arms became widely known there following the Moroccan conquest. In the Middle Volta Basin fire-arms are associated with Ashanti.

an Islamic relic, is regarded as the source of their chief's power. The Dagomba may have singled out this factor. Responding to the challenge, they turned to Muslims, already in their country, calling for their aid.

Thus, during the period of hostilities with Gonja, the Dagomba chiefs drew closer to the Muslims. The new trend reached its climax at the time of Na Zangina. This ruler, in an uneasy position of isolation and antagonism with many chiefs and princes, found it expedient to build up even closer relations with Muslims than his predecessors had.

(*b*) *The Muslim Elders of the Ya-Na*

The Drum History tells that soon after his enthronement Na Zangina went to seek the blessing of Yamusa, the *yarna* of Sabali, across the Oti river.[1] *Yarna*, a contraction of *yarse-na*, means 'the chief of the [Mande] Muslims', the same as *Nso'owura* in Gonja. At the time of Na Zangina the Sabali *yarna* was regarded as the senior Muslim in Dagomba; other early Muslims were his followers.

The *yarna* of Sabali belongs to the Boghyo or Baghyogho patronymic group, whose fame as *'ulamā'* goes back to the sixteenth-century scholar Muḥammad Baghyogho of Timbuktu.[2] The imams of the Moro-Naba at Wagadugu belong to the same group.[3]

A tradition recorded from *yarna* Qāsim at Sabali tells that Yamusa's father, Sulaymān, came to Dagomba during the reign of Na Tutughri, father of Na Zangina. Na Tutughri asked Sulaymān to find out who would succeed him among his sons. Sulaymān could not point to anyone, but showed the Na the woman who would give birth to a future Na. This woman was Zangina's mother. As a reward Sulaymān was given the title *yarna*. Later the young Zangina was sent to Sabali to study Koran. An echo of this tradition may be heard in the words of Na Zangina to Yamusa, the Sabali *yarna*, as given by the Drum History: 'My mother's home is in this town Sabali, and from you I have learnt the Koran.'

Sulaymān, first *yarna* of Sabali, built a mosque. Its traces, a few stones scattered about, are shown some fifty yards from the *yarna*'s compound. People of the village come to pray there occasionally.

The title *yarna*, which occurs also in Wa and in Mossi (*yar-naba*) is

[1] Tait's manuscripts, text B.
[2] Al-Sa'dī, 1900, pp. 43–47; trans., pp. 71–77.
[3] See below, p. 167.

typical of Muslim communities of Mande origin. It was created when Wanagara, to whom the term *yarse* applies, were prominent in Dagomba. The Sabali *yarna* represents in Dagomba traditions the early contribution of the Wangara Muslims to the spread of Islam in Dagomba. It is said, for example, that he introduced circumcision to Dagomba, and one of his family was commissioned to perform this rite, with the title of *yidan-kafa*.[1]

This early contribution, however, was later overshadowed by that of the Hausa, who outnumbered the Wangara in Dagomba. As the Hausa influence in Dagomba was both more intense and lasting, it is sometimes given the full credit at the expense of the Wangara. Hence, whereas the Drum History tells of Na Zangina's conversion by the Sabali *yarna*, another tradition ascribes the same to Kamshe-Na, who represents the Hausa contribution.

'In those days', says the tradition, 'the Dagomba wore skins of animals. . . . So when Na Zangina with his lion skin arrived in Kamsheghu, this Hausa Mallam . . . took off the lion's skin from Na Zangina and gave him a big gown as well as pantalons and a hat.' One of the Mallam's *wanzams* ('barbers') circumcised Na Zangina, and the Mallam himself taught him how to pray. The Mallam then sent weavers, *wanzams*, and Mallams to Yendi. 'So this Hausa Mallam brought a complete civilization to Dagbong. Na Zangina became happy and made him chief of that village Kamsheghu. . . . So among the Muslim elders in Dagbong, Kamshe-Na is their paramount.'[2]

In the Drum History Kamshe-Na appears as a follower of the Sabali *yarna*, the latter having been regarded as the chief of the Muslims.[3] As Wangara gave way to Hausa as prominent in Dagomba, the Sabali *yarna* retained his title, but the actual status of the senior Muslim elder in Dagomba was given to Kamshe-Na.

Following the tradition that Kamshe-Na gave Na Zangina his first gown, it is a custom that in the installation ceremony of a new Ya-Na, Kamshe-Na presents him with a new gown, specially woven for the occasion. From the time of Na Zangina Dagomba chiefs have had Muslim names. The introduction of these names is also attributed to Kamshe-Na. Na Zangina, it is told, had a pagan name, Wumbi, and

[1] Tait's manuscripts, text C; but see below (p. 100) on *yidan-gunu* the chief of the barbers at Yendi.

[2] Ibid. The introduction of weaving in this region is often attributed to Islamic influence. The Ashanti, it is said, learnt the art of weaving from Muslims in the north (Rattray, 1927, p. 220; Kyerematen, 1964, pp. 46, 67, 71).

[3] Tait's manuscripts, text B.

the name Zangina was given to him by Kamshe-Na.[1] Kamshe-Na, having converted Na Zangina, became his 'spiritual father'. Hence every Ya-Na refers to Kamshe-Na as *nba*, 'my father'. Besides his status as the senior Muslim elder, Kamshe-Na is also regarded as a village-chief: his wives have their heads shaved, like other chiefs' wives; he sits on a leopard's skin, as chiefs do; and he has his drummers to praise him.[2]

Another Muslim chief in Dagomba is La'aban-Na, chief of the small and remote village of La'abanga (near Nakpali). Like Kamshe-Na, La'aban-Na is mentioned as a follower of Yamusa, the *yarna* of Sabali. 'Chief of La'abansi', as he is called in the Drum History, may be translated as 'chief of the Arabs'. Could these 'Arabs' be of the same Muslim group as that of Larabanga in Gonja? This has been suggested by the present La'aban-Na as well as by other informants of Larabanga origin.[3] The historical circumstances of the settlement of the Larabanga people in Gonja is not yet clear, but it is very likely that they were associated with Mole-Dagbane speaking people before their contact with the Gonja. During the upheaval caused by the Gonja invasion, a group of these Muslims, who claim an Arab origin and are known in the area as *La'abansi*, 'the Arabs', may have moved to eastern Dagomba, where they established the village of La'abanga. La'aban-Na, therefore, may represent a third group of Muslims, besides the Wanagara and the Hausa, which contributed to the propagation of Islam in Dagomba.

These early Muslims of Na Zangina's time—the Sabali *yarna*, Kamshe-Na, and La'aban-Na—all settled in villages east of Yendi. Western Dagomba at that time was exposed to the Gonja invasion, which reached a point only twenty miles west of Yendi. After the evacuation of the old Dagomba capital, and while the war with Gonja continued, Dagomba had no fixed capital. The Ya-Na with his court stayed east of Yendi. Na Zangina was buried at Agbandi (between Nakpali and Sabali), where he probably had his court. The

[1] Zangi, in Abraham's dictionary, is 'a man's name'. The name Zangina, I was told at Yendi, is the nickname of a man called Muḥammad.

[2] Information at Kamsheghu and Yendi.

[3] The chief of La'abanga said that his patronymic was Sisse. The Larabanga Muslims, on the other hand, are referred to as Kamara, Kaute, or Lansari—none of these names was mentioned by the chief of La'abanga. Patronymics, it should be admitted, are flexible and subject to alterations. *Yidam-Kambara* (of Larabanga origin) said that the founder of La'abanga is related to the Larabanga as 'a sister's son'. If of any value, this information may help to explain the different patronymics.

court moved to Yendi only during the reign of Zangina's successor Na Andani Zighli, or in the following reign, that of Na Dzinli Binbigho, son of Na Zangina.[1]

It was during the transitional period, before the establishment of the new capital, that relations between chiefs and Muslims in Dagomba became closer. As the court was then moving about there was no place for a Muslim community centred on the court. Muslims therefore settled in villages east of Yendi, not far from the temporary residence of the Ya-Na, as far as possible from the scene of the Gonja invasion. After the victory over the Gonja, when peace was restored and the new capital established, a Muslim community developed around the court at Yendi. Traditions suggest that Muslims from those early groups in the eastern villages were sent to Yendi to serve the Ya-Na and to live with him.

It is said that at first Kamshe-Na, staying in his village, used to whisper a prayer into a bottle-skin, which was then tied up and sent to the Ya-Na. On receiving it the Ya-Na carefully opened the bottle-skin and the blessing came out to him.[2] Later Kamshe-Na sent his 'son' to Yendi to stay with the Ya-Na and to pray for him. This 'son', and his descendants who succeeded him, became known by the title *walgu-Na*, for he had been ordered '*dewalge-na*',' don't leave the Na'. *Walgu-Na* always lives close to the Na in *Nayiri-fo*, the Ya-Na's ward.[3]

Later, Kamshe-Na was visited in his village by one Muḥammad, a learned Muslim from Hausaland. Kamshe-Na introduced him before the Ya-Na, and suggested that this learned Hausa should be appointed imam. Muḥammad was given the office of *Nayiri-limam*, 'the imam of the Na's household'. Together with the imam, Kamshe-Na sent one of his followers, who became known as *yidan-asakiya*. He is described as Kamshe-Na's representative with the imam. It is a custom that the imam sends a piece of his own share in the sacrificial meat with *yidan-asakiya* to Kamshe-Na.[4]

[1] The Arabic history of Dagomba (IAS/AR-241) and Duncan-Johnstone and Blair (1932, p. 50) mention Na Zangina's grave at Adigbo. The two sources (which are not independent, because Mallam Khālidu who wrote the Arabic history had been an informant of Blair) say that Na Binbigho was the first to establish the court at Yendi. In Tait's manuscripts, text A, is another version: 'Then Andani [Zighli] brought Yendi to this town.'

[2] The same way of communicating a blessing was described at Gambaga about Imam Adam and the Asantehene (see below, p. 126).

[3] Information at Kamsheghu and Yendi. Tamakloe (1931, p. 11) attributes the creation of the office of *walgu-na* and other offices to Na Zirli, son of Na Gbewa.

[4] Information at Kamsheghu and Yendi (both from Muslims and members of the chiefly estate).

There is, however, another tradition which attributes the introduction of the imamship to another Muslim elder at Yendi, to *yidan Kambara*. *Yidan-Kambara*, as also his title suggests, is of Larabanga origin.[1] One tradition, recorded for the late Dr. Tait, says that Mūsā, the first *yidan-Kambara*, came in the time of Na Tutugri, Na Zangina's father. The present *yidan-Kambara*, on the other hand, claims that his ancestor came during the reign of Na Binbigho, Na Zangina's son, that is, two generations later. The two traditions may be reconciled if distinction is made between the arrival in Dagomba of a group of so-called La'abansi during the reign of Na Tutugri, who had settled at La'abanga, and the settlement of one of them at Yendi, in the time of Na Binbigho, after the establishment of the new capital.[2]

Yidan-Kambara's duty is to wash the bodies of the dead chiefs at Yendi. It is said that because of this duty he is much respected by the chiefs; he lives in a former residence of the Ya-Nas (with an ostrich's egg on the top of his principal hut, the sign of a senior chief).[3] In other communities, mainly in western Dagomba, the same duty of washing dead chiefs is performed by the *yarna*s. The title *yarna*, 'chief of the Muslims', has lost the original meaning it had in the time of the early Sabali *yarna*s. Yet their old title, and the respect shown to *yidan-Kambara*, do suggest that the rite of washing the dead is one of the most important for the chiefs, and probably one of the first customs associated with Islamic influence.[4] Now, however, the status of the *yarna*s, often of Wangara origin, is below that of the imams, in most cases of Hausa origin. Like the Sabali *yarna* who was replaced by the Hausa Kamshe-Na as the senior Muslim elder in Dagomba, like the *yarna*s who had to give precedence to Hausa imams, was *yidan-Kambara* superseded by a Hausa imam.

[1] Kambara is another form of the tribal name Kamara. In the tradition recorded for Tait (text C) *yidan-Kambara* is said to have come from Hausaland. This could have been a confusion with the name Kambari or Gambari for a group of Hausa traders (Palmer, 1936, p. 109). Hausa traders are known as Kambari in northern Dahomey (Marty, 1926, p. 471).

[2] *Yidan-Kambara* counted five generations back to his ancestor Mūsā, the first holder of this office. Another Muslim elder (the *yarna* of Zohe) is removed five or six generations from the Mūsā, the first *yidan-Kambara*. The same number of generations is given by *madaha-Na*, whose ancestor is said to have been contemporary with Mūsā. Five generations may just take us back to the first half of the eighteenth century, to Na Binbigho's reign.

[3] *Yidan-Kambara*'s compound comprises three huts named as those of the Ya-Na: *yili-bila*, *yili-kpane*, and *zee* (cf. Rattray, 1932, ii. 578–81).

[4] See below, pp. 114–15, on the introduction of Islam to Gusheghu. On the custom of washing the dead, see Trimingham, 1959, pp. 178–9.

A tradition recorded from the present *yidan-Kambara* says that Muṣṭafā, a learned Muslim from Hausaland, stayed at Yendi with *yidan-Kambara*. The latter introduced his guest before the Ya-Na, suggesting that in funerals, after he himself had washed the corpse, the Hausa Mallam should lead the prayer. In this way, through the introduction of *yidan-Kambara*, Muṣṭafā was appointed as the *Nayiri-limam*. The Hausa Mallam was more learned than *yidan-Kambara*, and he soon became the senior of the two.

An Arabic manuscript has sixteen names of *Nayiri-limams* up to the present imam.[1] The first imam on this list is Imam Muḥammad, the name of the imam introduced by Kamshe-Na. Imam Muṣṭafā, introduced by *yidan-Kambara*, appears as the sixth imam on the list. Muṣṭafā is mentioned as the first imam also in Tait's tradition, where it is said that he was appointed by Na Ziblim Andani.[2] Na Ziblim Kulunku, son of Na Andani, was the Dagomba king in 1853.[3] Imam Muṣṭafā officiated, therefore, in the mid-nineteenth century, a date which is consistent with information about the imams who succeeded him.[4]

Whereas information is available about Imam Muṣṭafā and his successors, nothing is known about the first five imams on the list. Only the first, Imam Muḥammad, may be associated with Kamshe-Na's tradition. Is it not possible that the line of imams, including Imam Muḥammad and his four successors, was interrupted for some reason for any length of time, until the imamship was renewed with the appointment of Imam Muṣṭafā, through the introduction of *yidan-Kambara*, in the mid-nineteenth century?

This is a sheer hypothesis, but it does reconcile the two traditions. That the two traditions may claim validity is attested also by the present situation. *Yidan-asakiya*, it has been explained, is regarded as the link between the imam and Kamshe-Na. On the other hand, the imam is always accompanied by *yidan-Kambara* and *madaha-Na*, with whom he is closely associated. *Madaha-Na* is a follower of *yidan-Kambara*; it is said that his ancestor Labaran, a Hausa Muslim who used to recite poems in praise of the Prophet (*madaḥa*), was invited by the first *yidan-Kambara* to stay with him at Yendi.

[1] In possession of al-ḥājj 'Abdulai, the Friday imam of Yendi.

[2] Tait's manuscripts, text C.

[3] Barth, 1857, iv. 556.

[4] The seventh imam, succeeding Muṣṭafā, Ashafa, is said to have come during the reign of Na Sumani (*c.* 1860). Muḥammad Zangbegho, Imam Ashafa's son, officiated as the tenth imam *c.* 1900. The eleventh imam, 'Abdallāh, died in A.H. 1337 (1918/19), according to a note in the Arabic manuscript IAS/AR-241.

About the situation in the nineteenth century one may learn from a letter, written in the 1810s, from Kamshe-Na to Bābā, the leader of the Muslim community in Kumasi. In this letter Kamshe-Na sends instructions for charms to be made for the Asantehene, adding greetings to the Ashanti ruler from 'the Sultan of Yendi'.[1] This letter may be interpreted as the extension of religious services of Dagomba's Muslim elders to the Asantehene, to whom the Ya-Na was then a tributary. Now these religious services are rendered to the Ya-Na by the imam and his followers, Kamshe-Na coming to the court only rarely. This, however, is probably a later development since the mid-nineteenth century. Before that, one may infer from the letter, Kamshe-Na himself (and his followers) was responsible for these services to the Ya-Na. In other words, the appointment of Imam Muṣṭafā, regarded by some authorities as the first imam, marks a further step in the withdrawal of Kamshe-Na from direct responsibility for religious services in the Ya-Na's court, and the growing importance of the resident Muslims in Yendi, led by the imam.

Another group of Muslims at Yendi claims to have come from Mossi. Their senior is *yidan-more* or *yidan-mole*; *more* means 'a Muslim' in the language of the Mossi.[2] Their ancestor Buba (Abū-Bakr?) is said to have come to Dagomba from Mossi during the reign of Na Zangina. Būba stayed at Sabali, and his son Nafaʿu lived at Demon, where he died. Babi, son of Nafaʿu, moved to a place two miles from Yendi, where he established the village of Mole-yiri. Their history concurs with the pattern described above. This group, like the other early Muslim groups of Na Zangina's time, first settled east of Yendi, before they moved nearer to the capital. Their village, Mole-yiri, is now abandoned. A stone plate, said to have been brought from that village, has the following Arabic inscription:

> In the name of Allāh, the merciful, the compassionate.
> This is the name of the owner,
> Bab[i] son of Nafaʿ[u],
> Mole Sirmān,
> The Arab.[3]

The age of the inscription and its authenticity call for a closer study. Yet the agreement between the inscription and the tradition is

[1] Copenhagen manuscripts, vol. i, f. 107; on the date of these manuscripts, see above, pp. xxi–xxii.

[2] Cf. Alexandre, 1953, ii. 257, 465.

[3] The inscription is in the possession of Ḥasan b. Maḥmūd of the Mole family at Yendi, to whom I am indebted also for much of the information about *yidan-mole*. He said that their origin was from 'Sirman in the land of the Arabs'.

by no means accidental. If the inscription is authentic it could have refreshed the tradition, or, alternatively, the tradition could have left its impression on the stone.

Traditions ascribe to *yidan-mole* the introduction of the *Damba* festival to Dagomba.[1] The *Damba*, commemorating the Prophet's birthday, is known as *Gane* in Mossi and is not celebrated there in the way it is done in Dagomba.[2] *Yidan-mole*, therefore, did not introduce the *Damba*, but he is closely associated with this festival. *Yidan-mole* opens the first dance of the *Damba*, followed by the Ya-Na and the other chiefs. He is also responsible for the preparation of the rice cooked in the *Damba*. In this he is assisted by his two followers, *kor-mole* who grows the *Damba* rice in a village near Savelugu, and *taha-mole* who carries the rice to Yendi, to *yidan-mole*.[3] *Yidan-mole* and *taha-mole* were appointed from the same house. Tradition says that originally *kor-mole* was of the same family, but inquiries around Savelugu could lead back only to *c*. 1876. From that date to the present the office of *kor-mole* has been held by members of two families unrelated to *yidan-mole*.[4]

The *Damba* as celebrated by the chiefs in Dagomba has very little of the Islamic character of the *mawlūd* (the Prophet's birthday). The chiefs, the Muslims say, are given plenty of food (rice and meat) so that they may be happy and may dance throughout the night in honour of the Prophet. As in Gonja, the *Damba* festival is an occasion for sub-chiefs to pay homage to their senior chief. The *Damba*, more than any of the other Muslim feasts celebrated in Dagomba, is a chiefly affair. *Yidan-mole* is involved in another chiefly event when he acts as master of ceremonies in the final funeral of a Ya-Na.[5]

More than once the informant of the *yidan-mole* family stressed that their relations with the chiefs were not restricted merely to religious services as rendered by other Muslim elders. *Yidan-mole* and his followers are said to have taken part as horsemen in the wars of

[1] Tait's manuscripts, text C.

[2] In Mossi the *Gane* festival is celebrated by the Yarse and the Fulani, and not as a national festival as in Dagomba (Tauxier, 1917, p. 568; Alexandre, 1953, ii. 129). A comparative study of the way the Prophet's birthday is celebrated in different parts of West Africa might yield interesting results.

[3] *Kor-mole*—'the [Mossi] Muslim who farms'; *taha-mole*—'the [Mossi] Muslim who carries [the rice]'.

[4] Information at Yendi, Libga, Kamshegaw, and Zaji; the last three villages are near Savelugu.

[5] Information at Yendi. Rattray (1932, ii. 581) describes this ceremony, but does not mention the role of *yidan-mole*.

Dagomba. They fought with Na Andani Zighli against the Gonja (1713?), and took part in Na Abdulai I's raid on the Bassari (early 1870s) and in the Battle of Adigbo against the Germans (1896). In 1899 the Germans sent *yidan-mole* Muḥammad to summon Prince Alḥasan from Tampiong to assume the paramountcy.[1]

The *yidan-mole* people have 'joking relations' with Dagomba princes. One *yidan-mole* married a daughter of the Ya-Na (which is common among Muslim elders), but the children of that princess went to live with their maternal kin, the chiefs, and joined their ranks. It is also said that one chieftainess of Gundogo (the eldest daughter of the Ya-Na) 'was a friend in the way of love with *yidan-mole*'.[2] The *yidan-mole* family claims, therefore, exceptional intimate relations with the chiefly estate.

Traditions tell that *yidan-mole* came to Dagomba with his younger brother. This brother was sent to stay with the Ya-Na, and was temporarily accommodated in the *zee* hut of the Ya-Na's compound. He became known as *zee-mole*, 'the [Mossi] Muslim of the *zee* hut'.[3] This may be another case of a Muslim elder, living outside the capital, sending one of his followers to attend the Ya-Na; *zee-mole* may have represented *yidan-mole* in the Ya-Na's court in the same way as *walgu-Na* did for Kamshe-Na. Indeed, *zee-mole* had formerly stayed in *Nayiri-fo*, close to the Ya-Na's residence, where *walgu-Na* still lives. Later, and it is difficult to say when, *zee-mole* moved to another section of Yendi to live among the Muslims. He is now regarded as a *nā'ib*, or the *Nayiri-limam*'s deputy; three of the last five imams held the office of *zee-mole* before they were promoted to the imamship. Originally the office might have been in one house, but now, and probably since his status has changed, *zee-mole*, like the imam, is appointed by the Ya-Na from among the distinguished Muslims in Dagomba.

After *zee-mole* left the *Nayiri-fo*, only one Muslim elder continued to live in the Ya-Na's section together with *walgu-Na*. He is *yidan-tkim* (or, *yidan-tchim*), whose duty is to roast the sacrificial meat of *'id al-aḍḥā* ('*chimsi*' in Dagbane) for the Ya-Na. *Yidan-tkim* accompanies *walgu-Na* when the latter comes to pray for the Ya-Na.

Barbers in Dagomba shave all babies on the eighth day after birth,

[1] The last episode is confirmed by the Arabic history of Dagomba (IAS/AR-241).

[2] Information at Yendi, recorded independently from members of the chiefly estate and at the house of *yidan-mole*.

[3] Tait's manuscripts, text C.

and circumcise all boys, Muslims and non-Muslims, between the age of five and seven years.[1] Every Friday the barbers shave the heads of the Ya-Na's wives, a custom observed by the wives of all senior Chiefs. The headman of the barbers (*wanzami*) at Yendi is *yidan-gunu*.[2] The first *yidan-gunu* is said to have come from Daboya (in Gonja) during the reign of Na Binbigho, in the first half of the eighteenth century. This, it has been noted above, was the period when the office of *yidan-Kambara* was created, and probably also other Muslim titles at Yendi, because this was also the period of the establishment of the new capital at Yendi.[3]

The introduction of circumcision to Dagomba is ascribed by the traditions to Islamic influence. The first Muslim appointed to perform the circumcision was *yidan-kafa*, a follower of the *yarna* of Sabali. Like the latter, *yidan-kafa* remained at Sabali, aloof from the Ya-Na's court. He became only a symbol of the introduction of circumcision, whereas the actual performance of the rite is carried out by *yidan-gunu* and his men.

At Yendi, as in other communities, the chief-butcher is one of the richest and most influential Muslims. His title at Yendi is *yidan-Baba*. The history of this office is of much interest as all informants said that it originated in the chiefly estate. The versions, however, differ in details, and the following is an attempt to present the main theme of the various traditions.[4] The first butcher, who traded in meat, was Na Dimani (seven generations before *c.* 1900). Upon his order a bush cow was brought and slaughtered. Na Dimani divided pieces of meat among his wives and children for sale. He left his remunerative knife to one of his sons, who succeeded him as a butcher. But the son was not as powerful as his father; he could not rely on game brought to him, but had to buy sheep for slaughtering. Later (one tradition suggests that it was in the time of Na Dzinli Binbigho),[5] a Hausa Muslim, nicknamed Baba, came to Yendi. He helped the 'royal' butchers in their trade and married into the chiefly family. Subsequently, the office of chief-butcher was given to his descendants, who have since held the title *yidan-Baba*.

[1] Anderson, 1954, p. 259; see also Trimingham, 1959, pp. 161–3.
[2] *Guni*—one who circumcises the boys (Alexandre, 1953, ii. 146).
[3] *Yidan-gunu*'s genealogy, like that of *yidan-Kambara*, extends over five generations back to his ancestor who came at the time of Na Binbigho (see above, p. 95, n. 2).
[4] Information from the chief-butchers at Yendi, Tamale, Savelugu, and Zoghaw, as well as from a drummer at Demon.
[5] Tait's manuscripts, text C.

The genealogical list of the *yidan-Baba*s is reliable only three generations back, then it continues in a rather obscure way to Na Dimani. But even where the genealogy seems reliable the chiefly element is clear. *Yidan-Baba* is the chief-butcher's title at Yendi only; elsewhere in Dagomba *Baba* is the title of the chief-butcher's deputy. (The chief-butcher himself is called *nakoha-Na*.) It is likely that at Yendi also *yidan-Baba* had formerly been the chief-butcher's deputy, as suggested by the traditions.

The meat trade is closely associated with Muslims; not only because Muslims carry the cattle trade from north to south, but also because of the Muslim ritual slaughtering which chiefs in Dagomba (as in other 'islamized' states) are supposed to observe. This is clearly demonstrated in occasional ceremonies, when a Muslim slaughters for the chief. The tradition, as presented above, may therefore describe the 'islamization' of the chief-butcher's office, which already existed, associated with the chiefs. Both *tengdana*s and chiefs have the right to a share in their people's game.[1] Powerful chiefs may have had a surplus of meat which they could sell. Hence the traditions about the chiefly origin of the butchers, and the Dagbane term for a butcher—*nakoha*, 'the chief's trader'.[2] Later, the office was taken over by Muslims, both because of the ritual slaughtering, and because of the growing importance of the meat trade.

In concluding the historical survey of the Muslim elders of the Ya-Na, one should note the *diversity* in origin of the Muslims in Dagomba, and their *integration* into the political system through the creation of many offices attached to the Ya-Na's court.

It is peculiar to Dagomba that Muslim groups of different provenance took part in the propagation of Islam. The contribution of these groups is recognized by the titles and offices held by their representatives. The early contribution of the Wangara, Muslims of Mande origin, is represented by *Gbanyaghe*, *Tsheli-yarna*, Sabali-*yarna*, *yidan-kafa*, and according to one tradition also by *Mallam Albarka*.[3] Elders of Larabanga origin are La'aban-Na and *yidan-Kambara*.

[1] Cf. Rattray, 1932, i. 262; ii. 368, 489, 493.

[2] In More (the Mossi language), the term for a 'butcher'—*nem-koasa*—is translated as 'a trader in meat' (Alexandre, 1953, ii. 271).

[3] According to Tait's tradition (texts B and C), *Mallam Albarka* was the son of *Sabali yarna*, sent to Yendi to serve the Ya-Na. At Yendi I was told that the first *Mallam Albarka* was a Hausa Muslim. *Mallam Albarka* is officially imam of the village of Gbungbalga (near Yendi), but he often resides at Yendi, where he is counted among the Muslim elders who accompany the imam to the Ya-Na.

Hausa Muslims held the following titles: Kamshe-Na, *walgu-Na*, *yidan-asakiya*, *madaḥa-Na*, *yidan-Baba*, and according to some traditions also *Mallam Albarka*. Most of the *Nayiri-limams* were of Hausa origin, but at least two (the present imam, Muḥammad, and his father, Imam Zakāriyā) are of Larabanga origin. Gonja is represented by *yidan-gunu* who came from Daboya. Yarse from Mossi created the 'Mole' group of elders: *yidan-mole*, appointed always from the same house, and *zee-mole* which ceased to be a hereditary office.

Some of the Muslim elders perform such functions as circumcision and shaving (*yidan-gunu*), washing the dead chiefs (*yidan-Kambara*), or officiating in festivals (*yidan-mole* and *yidan-tkim*). Traditions ascribing the introduction of customs to the elders who perform them seem to interpret the past from the actual functions. There is not necessarily any association between the origin of the elders and their functions. A significant division is that between the Wangara Muslims on one hand, and the Larabanga and Hausa Muslims on the other. Whereas the Wangara represent the past contribution, the Larabanga and Hausa Muslims, closely associated with each other in Dagomba, carry on the propagation of Islam and render religious services to the Ya-Na at Yendi as well as to other chiefs in the countryside.

The Muslim elders may be classified also according to their place of residence and the frequency of their contacts with the Ya-Na. The earliest Muslims—Sabali *yarna*, La'aban-Na, and Kamshe-Na—live in villages east of Yendi. Among them Kamshe-Na alone still calls at the Ya-Na's court on rare ceremonial occasions, such as the installation of a new Ya-Na. Current religious services are rendered by two categories of elders who reside at Yendi: (*a*) those who live at *Nayiri-fo* and have daily contact with the Ya-Na—*walgu-Na*, *yidan-tkim*, and formerly also *zee-mole*; (*b*) those who live in the Muslim sections of Yendi, and come to pray for the Ya-Na occasionally, on Fridays, festivals, and other state ceremonies. They are in order of seniority: the *Nayiri-limam*, *yidan-Kambara*, *madaḥa-na*, *Mallam Albarka*, *yidan-asakiya*, and *yidan-kama*.[1] *Zee-mole* has moved from the former to the latter group, and is now second to the imam.

All these elders are appointed to serve the court, except the Friday

[1] *Yidan-kama* is an attendant of the imam; to him presents for the imam are handed over. The distinction between the two groups of Muslims and the order of seniority in the second group were observed at a Friday morning ceremony at the Ya-Na's court which I attended.

imam (*imām jum'a*), who is the spiritual leader of the Muslims at Yendi. Although he is appointed by the Ya-Na he has nothing to do with chiefly affairs. His duties, as described by the Friday imam Khālid, are to be the custodian of the Muslim law (*shari'a*), to settle marital problems among Muslims, and to lead the prayers on Fridays and at the two Muslim festivals.[1]

The office of Friday imam at Yendi is recent, having been created at the turn of the last century only. During the present century it has been held by four imams of two families distinguished for their Islamic erudition: a Hausa family from Katsina, and a Fulani family from Massina.[2] The need for the creation of a new imamship rose with the increased number of Muslims in the late nineteenth century, and the growth of the *zongo* at Yendi. The newcomers, mainly Hausa, represented a more puritan brand of Islam, influenced by the Fulani *jihād*, and a higher standard of learning than that of the older Muslims in Dagomba. The *Nayiri-limam*, involved in magical and ritual services to the court, had to be superseded by a second imam of scholarly reputation, acceptable as leader to all Muslims at Yendi.

(*c*) *Yendi as a trading centre*

The two layers of Islam in Dagomba, the Wangara and the Hausa, are associated with the two trade systems, the north-western and the north-eastern respectively. It so happened that the Dagomba capital was always on a flourishing trade-route. The old capital, Yendi-Dabari, was on the Mande route to Jenne, and had traders' quarters. The Dagomba retreat east, under the pressure of the Gonja, coincided with the increase of traffic on the route to Hausa. The Drum History associates trade development on the new route with Na Zangina's conversion: 'There were no traders on the main roads to Dagbong. Na Zangina prayed to God, and the roads opened, and many travelled by them. That is why the drummers say that Na Zangina made the world wise.'[3]

[1] A note on the front page of the Arabic manuscript IAS/AR-241, describing his appointment by Na Abdulai II, in September 1926. On the application of Muslim law at Yendi, see Anderson, 1954, pp. 258–63.

[2] Imam Ya'qūb, a Hausa from Katsina (*c.* 1900–15), and his son Mallam Khālid (1926–35). Imam Ḥasan, whose ancestor came from Massina (1915–26), and his son al-ḥājj 'Abdallāh (since 1935). The latter is the *muqaddam* of the Tijāniya in northern Ghana, whose reputation is widespread, as far as Djougou in northern Dahomey.

[3] Tait's manuscripts, text B.

By this route Dagomba became known in the wider world. In 1788/9 Lucas heard from *Sharīf* Imhammed, in Fezzan, that traders went to 'the Mahometan kingdom of Degombah' where gold was abundant.[1] The Hausa trade system linked Dagomba also with the Bight of Benin, where Sir William Young heard that 'the Slatees of Old Calabar are said to carry on their trade to Degombah northward'.[2] Bowdich, who had already been acquainted with these reports of the fame of Dagomba, collected further information about Yendi in Kumasi: 'Yahndi is described to be beyond comparison larger than Coomassie, the houses much better built and ornamented. The Ashantees who had visited it told me they frequently lost themselves in the streets. . . . The markets of Yahndi are described as animated scenes of commerce constantly crowded with merchants from almost all the countries of the interior.'[3]

Dupuis, who does not always agree with Bowdich, similarly describes the Dagomba capital:

> Yandy, the chief city, is said to be at least four times as extensive as the capital of Ashantee. . . . Yandy enjoys great celebrity all over the African continent for its riches and manufactures. The natives are, moreover, highly enterprising and commercial, and they maintain a constant communication with the neighbouring kingdoms; but particularly with Haoussa and Sarem, for the conveniency of whose traffick their city becomes a depôt, and a periodical mart, as well for their own manufactures, as for those of Fezzan, Egypt, Smyrna, etc., as also for slaves, gold and ivory collected in and upon the confines of Wangara.[4]

Both Bowdich and Dupuis may have exaggerated, as Barth remarked some thirty years later: Yendi is 'an important place, but not near so large as was believed by the travellers to Ashanti'. But even Barth confirmed that Yendi was far larger than Salaga.[5]

What could have been the basis of that flourishing trade of Yendi, as described in the late eighteenth and early nineteenth century? Dupuis says that most of the gold of Gyaman was carried to Hausa through Salaga, Yendi, Djougou, and Nikki.[6] Abū-Bakr al-Ṣiḍḍīq, referring to the late eighteenth century, says that his father sent gold

[1] *Proceedings*, 1790, pp. 176–7.
[2] Quoted by Bowdich, 1819, p. 177.
[3] Bowdich, 1819, p. 178.
[4] Dupuis, 1824, p. xc.
[5] Barth, 1857, iv. 556. Five thousand inhabitants at Yendi compared with a thousand at Salaga. Estimates of population are often erratic even if the traveller himself visited a town, let alone through information collected hundreds of miles away.
[6] Dupuis, 1824, pp. lvii–lviii.

from Buna to the 'countries of Bernu and Kashina'. The route from Buna to Hausa passed over Daboya.[1] Daboya was linked to the main route to Hausa by a road to Yendi.[2] It is likely that while the Gonja markets, on the Volta river, were primarily for the kola trade, Yendi specialized in the gold trade. When drummers in Dagomba praise Muslims they often say that the Dagomba had not known gold until it was brought by the Muslims.[3] Is it not possible that this refers to a flourishing trade in gold, carried by Muslims?

In comparison with the information of Lucas, Bowdich, and Dupuis, very little is said later in the nineteenth century about trade in Yendi or about the gold trade on this route. During the last century the gold trade dwindled and became negligible beside the growing importance of the kola trade. For the kola trade Salaga was the main entrepôt, and to this town the Hausa caravans went. In Yendi, according to Barth, the merchants awaited the proper season before going to Salaga, where they preferred to stay as little as possible because of the water dearth.[4]

Turning from documentary to traditional evidence it is surprising that informants in Yendi had hardly anything to say about Yendi as a trading centre. Whenever this question was raised they pointed to Gamaji, a hill about two miles west of Yendi, where, it is said, traders used to stay, and where the people of Yendi went to buy salt and kola.

The history of Gamaji has been recorded from descendants of its founder. A Hausa Muslim came to Yendi in the time of Na Andani I (early in the nineteenth century). He built a house (now in the Zohe ward of Yendi), which became known as *Madugu-fo* ('the caravan headman's ward') or *Zangbere-yiri* ('the Hausaman's house'). At that time, it is said, Hausa was not spoken at Yendi. A son of this Muslim, born at Yendi, could speak both languages Dagbane and Hausa. He was sent to live on a hill outside Yendi where he served as host to Hausa traders, and introduced them to the chief. Hausa traders were directed to this place, having been told: '*ga ma ji*', i.e. 'there is one who hears' ('who can speak your language'). Hence the name of that place, Gamaji.

Hausa must have been spoken elsewhere at Yendi, and the traders were sent to this place presumably to keep them out of the capital.

[1] Renouard, 1836, pp. 103–4, 110–11.
[2] Bowdich, 1819, p. 483, Route No. 13.
[3] Information from both drummers and Muslims throughout Dagomba.
[4] Barth, 1857, v. 29.

The Muslim in charge of Gamaji was indeed a kind of dragoman, for he acted as intermediary between strangers and the chief. Hence Gamaji served both as a *zongo* and as a quarantine.[1]

The separation of the traders' quarters from the town at Yendi underlines the difference between the two great Muslim communities of Salaga and Yendi. Salaga was a commercial and cosmopolitan town, where everyone could come and stay. Yendi, on the other hand, was a political centre, where precautions had to be taken against strangers. The Muslim community of Salaga developed around the market, whereas at Yendi, though individual Muslims could have been engaged in trade, the community as such centred on the court.

(*d*) *Chiefs and Muslims*

Dagomba's fame as a commercial centre also carried the idea of Dagomba as a Muslim kingdom. Lucas called it 'the Mahometan kingdom of Degombah', but added that 'there is reason to believe from the Shereef's account that the Musselman and the Pagan are indiscriminately mixed'.[2]

Looking northward from the pagan south, Dagomba and other states in the hinterland seemed more islamized than was really the case. Bowdich, for example, had good reason to regard Dagomba as a Muslim kingdom, for he found that the Dagomba king was sending Muslim amulets to the Asantehene.[3] This is now confirmed by the finding of an Arabic letter comprising instructions for charms, sent to the Asantehene in the name of Na Andani of Dagomba.[4] This letter, written by Kamshe-Na, was addressed to Bābā, the leader of the Muslim community in Kumasi. Bābā, a native of Gambaga in Mamprusi, acted as the representative of Dagomba in the Ashanti capital. He was 'a member of the king's council in affairs relating to the believers of Sarem and Dagomba'.[5] On one occasion, witnessed

[1] Lonsdale (1882, notes on the route) mentions a place of thirty houses, forty-five minutes from the Daka river and twenty-seven minutes from Yendi, which he calls 'Sangu'. The location of this place suggests that it was Gamaji, 'Sangu' may be *zongo*. In August 1892 Ferguson was told by the Ya-Na: 'The Frenchmen had been here too. They were not allowed to stay in the capital, and they stopped about two miles away at Gamalzi' (Ferguson to the governor, 9 December 1892, enclosure 1 in No. 45, *African* (*West*), No. 448, PRO, CO. 879/38).

[2] *Proceedings*, 1790, p. 176; quoted also in Hallett, 1964, pp. 97–98.

[3] Bowdich, 1819, pp. 235, 271.

[4] Copenhagen manuscripts, vol. i, f. 107.

[5] Dupuis, 1824, p. 97.

by Dupuis, the Muslims officially represented the Dagomba king: 'The Muslims of Dagomba and Ghunja, headed by the Bashaw [namely, Bābā], Abou Becr, Cantoma, and Shoumo, came in a body to return thanks, in the name of their sovereign, the king of Yandy, for a present he had already despatched to that monarch.'[1]

Not surprisingly Bowdich regarded these Muslims he met in Kumasi as representing also the characteristics of the Dagomba people. He therefore contrasted the 'commercial disposition' of the Dagomba with the 'military genius' of the Ashanti.[2] Bowdich was informed that the Dagomba king 'Inana Tanquaree has been converted by the Moors, who have settled there in great numbers'.[3]

The Muslims in Kumasi were interested in building up the image of the hinterland as overwhelmingly Muslim, thus increasing their own prestige in the eyes of the British who were seeking contact with the north. In this way the majority of the non-Muslim population of the northern states were not heard of, whereas the 'half-islamized' chiefs of these states were presented as real Muslims.

Barth obtained his information about Dagomba in the Muslim north, presumably in Hausaland, where the Muslims (then under the influence of the Fulani *jihād*) held a more critical view about the people of Yendi: 'they are idolators, and drink busa or peto in great quantity'.[4]

The verdict of the *jihād* leader, ʿUthmān dan Fodio, on the Islamic character of Dagomba was uncompromising. For him Dagomba, with Mossi, Gurma, Busa, Borgu, Kotokoli, and Gonja, are countries where 'infidelity is overwhelming and Islam is rare. . . . All these countries are, doubtless, lands of infidelity because authority is with the majority, and the rulers of these countries are also all unbelievers; the law of the country is the law of its ruler.' All Muslims, he concludes, must emigrate from these lands of the unbelievers.[5]

[1] Dupuis, 1824, p. 170; Kantoma and Suma represented the Gonja Muslims (see above, pp. 61–62).

[2] Bowdich, 1819, p. 235.

[3] Ibid., pp. 177–8. 'Inana' is the title Ya-Na; the name 'Tanquaree' does not appear on any chief list of Dagomba. From the letter of Kamshe-Na, mentioned above, it is clear that the reigning Ya-Na was Andani. On the position of Islam in Na Andani's reign, see below, p. 121.

[4] Barth, 1857, iv. 556.

[5] ʿUthmān b. Fūdī, *Bayān wujūb al-hijra ʿalā ʾl-ʿibād* ('An exposition on the obligation of the Believers to emigrate'), manuscript at the University of Ibadan, 82/53, written A.H. 1221 (1806).

As an authority for this classification of African peoples Dan Fodio refers to the treatise on slavery by Aḥmad Bābā of Timbuktu, *Kitāb al-kashf wa-ʾl-bayān*

Had all Muslims held these puritan views Islam would never have made any progress in the Volta Basin. Islam spread there only because of the compromising attitude of the Muslims. They created favourable conditions for the growth of Muslim communities, secured the position of Muslims in the chiefs' courts, and infused Islamic elements into the ceremonies and customs of their chiefs. They were satisfied with the inclination of the chiefs towards Islam. The position of Islam at the Ya-Na's court is well illustrated in the following remarks by Professor Anderson:

> For years Muslims have occupied an honoured place in the Ya tribal system, with various *limams* and other functionaries appointed by the Ya-Na each to some special duty; yet the whole has been strangely blended with that paganism which is still frankly professed by the Ya-Na and the majority of his people, while such subject races as the Konkomba are solidly pagan. An interesting illustration of the position is provided by members of the Ya-Na court. All eight with whom I talked denied that they were Muslims, yet all performed Muslim prayers (learnt by heart in Arabic). When asked why, therefore, they did not claim to be Muslims they first said that they could not read the Qur'ān; later, however, they admitted that they still believed in paganism, which they regarded as more powerful than Islam, but they added Muslim prayers as a sort of insurance policy, because Muslims assured them that he who prayed five times a day was sure of Paradise. Those who had really turned Muslim, they added, abandoned the fetish—except, perhaps, in times of special distress.[1]

The situation becomes somewhat clearer if descending grades of devotion to Islam are distinguished. Muslims literate in Arabic, or with some training in Arabic, are known as *alfanema* (singular: *alfa*).[2] They are distinguished from those who profess to be Muslims but cannot read or write even a single word in Arabic. For the latter praying is the main manifestation of their Muslim faith, and they are referred to as *puhera dzanli*, 'those who pray'.[3] This term may refer to a wide range of people, from illiterate Muslims to professed pagans who pray occasionally. It is often used in reference to members of the

li-aṣnāf majlūb al-Sūdān, written in A.H. 1024 (1615/16). With the help of Dr. A. D. H. Bivar, who is preparing an edition of this text, it was found that Aḥmad Bābā had not mentioned Dagomba and Gonja in his list of tribes, and these two names had been added by Dan Fodio himself.

[1] Anderson, 1954, pp. 258–9.

[2] The term *alfa* is common among the Songhay, and it is equivalent to *mallam* among the Hausa, *modibo* among the Fulani, and *karamoro* among the Mande. In the Gonja Chronicle the term *al-faqīh* occurs where the colloquial *alfa* (and its equivalents) are used.

[3] Tait, 1963, p. 141.

chiefly estate (*nabihe*), because they all pray occasionally. To the question whether a certain chief was a Muslim, the answer is 'he was praying'. One would not say of a chief that he was a pagan; although chiefs are not Muslims, neither are they completely pagan.

The majority of the Dagomba commoners do not pray at all; these are often denoted *Dagbandu*. The Dagbane word for 'a pagan' is *chefera* (from the Arabic *kāfir*). This term applies mainly to non-Dagomba tribes, such as the Konkomba and the Tchamba (Bassari), who are completely untouched by Islam. It implies that the Dagomba are regarded as less pagan than the Konkomba. This distinction is valid, because all the Dagomba people have been drawn into the orbit of an islamized civilization, as they take part in ceremonies and festivals strongly influenced by Islam, in which Muslim prayers are said. Islamic influence reaches the commoners in a diluted form through their chiefs' courts. In the pre-colonial period communication between Muslims and commoners seems to have been casual only, while that between Muslims and chiefs became institutionalized.

Na Zangina, credited by traditions with the introduction of Islam, may have been more than a nominal convert. His personal inclination towards Islam contrasts, in the Drum History, with the attitude of his successor, Na Andani Zighli: 'Then Na Zighli returned to Na Zangina, and told him: "you took the Koran and improved the country, I shall also take this spear of mine and put order in the country, but I shall take these Konkomba and Tchamba to buy medicine." '[1]

Na Andani Zighli restored the balance, which might have been shaken by the excessive attachment of Na Zangina to Islam. Dagomba chiefs referred both to Muslim *alfas* and to local soothsayers; they gave presents to Muslims, and sent animals for sacrifice to shrines and to Earth-priests. Some of a chief's duties, required by his obligations to the non-Muslim majority of his subjects, are inconsistent with the proper conduct of a Muslim. In Dagomba, as in other Voltaic states, there is a clear distinction between a chief and a Muslim; that is, being a chief implies not being a real Muslim. Yet, constitutionally, a Muslim has not been barred from chieftaincy if he had the right to it. Although the office is here generally regarded as incompatible with Islam, individual chiefs were able to find a compromise to keep both.[2]

[1] Tait's manuscripts, text B.

[2] The present paramount chief of Kotokoli, al-ḥājj Yūsuf Ayeva, is a devoted Muslim. He has delegated all the ritual duties of the chief, that are incompatible

As early as the beginning of the eighteenth century a divisional chief is remembered by traditions as a Muslim. He was Puusamli, chief of Savelugu, mentioned in the Drum History as one of the Sabali *yarna*'s followers. His Islamic character is stressed again in his own words to Na Andani Zighli: 'I shall take the Koran more than the spear.'[1]

There are two traditions about Puusamli. According to one of them, he was a Muslim, who had cured and fed a sick prince, detested by the other princes. Later this prince was appointed Ya-Na, and when the skin of Savelugu became vacant, the Ya-Na made this Muslim chief of Savelugu.[2] The other version, recorded from a drummer at Demon, says Puusamli was son of Na Zighli. His father sent him to study Koran with a Mallam, and he became a Muslim. He was appointed chief of Savelugu by his brother, the Ya-Na Andani Zighli.[3]

The second tradition seems more acceptable. It is unlikely that Savelugu, one of the three senior chieftaincies in Dagomba, and a 'gate' to the paramountcy, strictly reserved for sons of a Ya-Na, was given to an outsider, even by a ruler who had been abused by his brothers and cousins. The respectable status of Puusamli among the chiefs, as reflected by the Drum History, would have been incompatible with such a breach of the constitution. The second tradition, on the other hand, is explicable within the historical context; chiefs used to send a son (or a grandson) to study Koran, and these princes sometimes turned Muslim. A prince did not lose his right to a chieftaincy just because he had become a Muslim.

Chiefs often gave their daughters in marriage to Muslims. It was regarded as a generous gift, and brought the Muslims closer to the chiefs. Giving a chief's daughter in marriage has often been described as a device to bind a Muslim to the chief's court. Descendants of such

with Islam, to his uncle. (Froelich, 1963, p. 55; P. Alexandre, 1964, p. 247; information at Sokode.)

[1] Tait's manuscripts, text B. Puusamli was appointed chief of Savelugu after Na Zangina's reign, and his association with Sabali *yarna* in the Drum History, can only mean that he is remembered as one of the earliest Muslim chiefs in Dagomba.

[2] Tradition recorded from several informants, Muslims and non-Muslims, at Yendi. Tamakloe (1931, p. 32) tells of Na Binbigho that he was cured from yaws by a Mallam. The meaning of the name Puusamli is said to be 'the debt of the stomach' and this may be associated with one of Puusamli's drum-names (Tait's manuscripts, text B): 'the debt of the stomach is paid yearly, but it can never be paid in entirety.'

[3] About the former version that drummer said: 'it is also true, but this is the story of old men, not of the drummers.'

marriages, between a princess and a Muslim, were usually brought up as Muslims. The more ambitious among them could, however, aspire to certain chieftaincies open to sons of the Ya-Na's daughters.[1]

Dahmani, chief of Diare (*c.* 1900), was the son of Na Andani I's daughter. His grandfather Zakāriyā', of Larabanga origin, was the imam of Nantong. Dahmani's own son, al-ḥājj Abū-Bakr, is the present (1964) *zee-mole*, a leading Muslim personality at Yendi. Here is a chief of a family boasting a continuous line of learned and devoted Muslims, who was very probably a practising Muslim himself.

Another son of a Muslim (who held the office of *yidan-tkim*) and a princess (also a daughter of Na Andani I) had a thrilling political career, which deserves a more detailed treatment. This young man, Laghfu, first helped his maternal uncle, Na Ziblim Kulunku, son of Na Andani (*c.* 1853), to overcome a disputant Sumani, son of Na Mahama. After Na Kulunku's death Sumani succeeded in obtaining the paramountcy. Laghfu, then the chief of Gbungbaliga, plotted against Na Sumani; at the head of a coalition of princes he defeated Na Sumani and killed him. Laghfu thus helped Na Yaʿqūba, another brother of his mother, to the paramountcy.

Having been instrumental in bringing Na Yaʿqūba to the skin, Laghfu became very influential. In his lust for power he began to accumulate chieftaincies, a most unusual precedence, adding to that of Gbungbaliga, one by one, the skins of Korle (Nakpali), Dzenkungu, and Yelzoli (Zabzugu). On top of these he also had the Muslim office of *yidan-tkim*, to which he succeeded through his father. Laghfu was helped in this by Na Yaʿqūba's weakness of mind. At last Na Yaʿqūba became insane. He used to walk about in the market, killing people for sport. No one dared to act, for the person of the Na is sacred. Laghfu came to Yendi to tend his uncle, and ran the country in his name. The princes, already suspicious, became furious when Laghfu suggested that the Na should be chained with silver fetters to prevent him from killing people. When the skin of Savelugu became vacant, Laghfu had his eye on it. Not being the son of a Ya-Na he had no right to Savelugu. The princes, alarmed by this ambitious son of a princess, united and killed Laghfu in a battle.[2]

Did Yelzoli-lana Laghfu remain a practising Muslim in spite of his involvement in chiefly affairs? Was he thought of as a Muslim by his

[1] For the classification of these chieftaincies, see Rattray, 1932, ii. 576.

[2] Tait's manuscripts, text B; A. W. Davies, unpublished manuscript; Tamakloe, 1931, pp. 35–36.

supporters and opponents among the chiefs? These questions remain unanswered, but it is significant that Laghfu combined territorial chieftaincies with the Muslim office of *yidan-tkim*.

These are only two among several examples of Muslims who became chiefs as sons of Ya-Na's daughters.[1] Yet, compared with Muslims' sons becoming chiefs, the opposite cases of chiefs' sons becoming Muslims are more numerous; many Muslim genealogies can be traced back to a Ya-Na.

Imam Idrīs of Tolon is the great-great-grandson of Na Yaʿqūba: Imam Idrīs b. Ibrāhīm b. Imam Muḥammad b. ʿAbdallāh b. Ya-Na Yaʿqūba. Na Yaʿqūba gave his grandson Muḥammad (grandfather of the informant) to a Muslim to be taught Koran. This, it is said, was a custom, whereby a Muslim called upon to pray for a chief sometimes received in return a chief's daughter in marriage or a chief's son to be taught Koran. In both cases the ultimate result is an increase in the number of Muslims through the chiefs' issue. Muḥammad, grandson of Na Yaʿqūba, became a devoted Muslim, and even converted his brothers. One of them, Ibrāhīm, became the first imam of Tolon. He was called there, it is said, because the chief of Tolon was his maternal uncle. Upon his death Ibrāhīm was succeeded as imam by his brother Muḥammad.

Al-ḥājj Sulaymān, an old Muslim from Tamale, had the personal experience of crossing from the chiefly to the Muslim estate. He is a descendant of Ya-Na Ziblim Bandamada (late eighteenth century): al-ḥājj Sulaymān b. Aḥmad chief of Sankuni b. Imoru chief of Demon b. Ya-Na Ziblim.[2] His father and grandfather were chiefs; 'they prayed but were not Muslims'. Sulaymān's mother came from a Muslim family at Yendi.[3] After his father's death, Sulaymān went

[1] Other examples: Mahama, chief of Kpugi, who was also a son of Na Andani I's daughter, and Khālid, chief of Zagbeli, who was a son of Na Abdulai I's daughter. An interesting case is that of a Muslim who inherited, through his mother, the office of Kpati-Na. The chief of Kpatia (about seven miles north of Yendi) is the custodian of a sacred stool (*bolong*), which confers supernatural power to a newly installed Ya-Na (see Duncan-Johnstone and Blair, 1932, p. 31; Tamakloe, 1931, p. 68). The present Kpati-Na told me that he was a Muslim and prayed regularly. This is an extreme case of compromise, because *Kpati-Na*'s duties are exclusively ritual in the sphere of the traditional religion. Kpati-Na Salifu's claim to be a Muslim may not be accepted by the Muslims themselves.

[2] The genealogy is corroborated by the Drum History (Tait's manuscripts), where Imoru, son of Na Ziblim Bandamada, is mentioned as chief of Demon.

[3] The *sharīʿa* forbids marriage between a Muslim woman and a pagan man, but this seems to have been unavoidable in this area (see Anderson, 1954, p. 259). Were chiefs 'who pray' accepted as non-pagans?

to live with his maternal uncles, where he studied Koran and became a Muslim.

The genealogy of the Friday imam of Ziong goes back to Na Andani Zighli. He is: al-ḥājj Abū-Bakr b. al-ḥājj ʿAbd al-Raḥman b. Muḥammad Thānī b. Hārūna b. Dasana chief of Sekpe b. Ya-Na Andani Zighli. When Na Andani Zighli's son, Dasana, was chief of Sekpe (mid-eighteenth century?) traders passed through his village. They used to stay with the chief, and Hārūna—the chief's son—became accustomed to them. Hārūna was then sent to Hausaland with a trader. After studying in Hausaland, Hārūna came back a devoted Muslim, and settled at Yendi.

The genealogy of the imam of Kosuriyiri (nine miles north-west of Tolon) converges with the former genealogy: Imam Hārūna b. Imam Shuʿayb b. Sulaymān b. Abū-Bakr chief of Lungbanga b. ʿAlī chief of Zoghu b. Dasana chief of Zoghu b. Ya-Na Andani Zighli. According to the Drum History Dasana son of Na Andani Zighli was chief of Sekpe as well as of Zoghu, not simultaneously.[1] In this genealogy the turning-point is the conversion of Imam Shuʿayb, the informant's father. He went to study Koran and became a Muslim because, I was told, he realized that he had no chance of obtaining any chieftaincy.

What is the significance of Shuʿayb's conversion? The number of chieftaincies in Dagomba is always far below the number of potential candidates. A son of the Ya-Na has a good chance of getting a chieftaincy; he may become a divisional or a village chief. A son of a village chief may still hope for a junior chieftaincy or any other political office. But a grandson of a chief, whose father was not a chief, may be eliminated. Within one or two generations his descendants may be absorbed into the mass of the commoners, preserving the memory of their chiefly origin only. Against this background of continuous elimination from the chiefly estate, Shuaʿyb's conversion may be understandable. He may have preferred the privileged status of a Muslim to the alternative of becoming a commoner.

These examples of chiefs' sons becoming Muslims indicate a pattern of islamization in Dagomba. It was by no means a general trend, and only a limited number of princes were converted. Yet the proportion of converts, as distinct from Muslim immigrants, in the composition of Muslim communities in Dagomba is higher than in any other state

[1] Tait's manuscripts, texts A and B. Chiefs were promoted from one village to the other.

in this area. Most of the converts came from the chiefly estate, because of the close relations between chiefs and Muslims, and because of the intermediate position of Dagomba chiefs between Islam and paganism.

(*e*) *Islam in the Dagomba villages*

Dagomba, the largest state in northern Ghana, is also the most cohesive and homogeneous. The Ya-Na's court at Yendi is central in the Dagomba political system. Dagomba is divided into territorial chiefdoms, graded as divisional and village chieftaincies. Certain chieftaincies are reserved for sons of Ya-Nas (*bihi-nam*), others for grandsons (*yanse-nam*). All these are for princes of royal blood, while some chieftaincies are held by elders of the Ya-Na (*kpamba-nam*). Elders who hold senior territorial chieftaincies also have functions in the central government, e.g. commander of the cavalry, of the archers, etc.[1] Hence all territorial chiefs, whether royal princes or elders, are closely linked to the paramountcy. This unified political system contributed to the spread of Islam in Dagomba. By the end of the last century Muslims lived in almost every village with a chief of some importance (including all the twelve villages of the divisional chiefs).[2] Chiefs, it will be shown, were instrumental in the creation of new Muslim communities.

Gushiegu, an important chieftaincy about forty miles north of Yendi, may be taken as first example of that process. It is told that a chief of Gushiegu sent his son to establish a toll-post on the trade-route to Salaga, which passed near Gushiegu. Living in the post, the chief's son communicated with Muslim traders, from whom he learnt to pray in the Muslim way. Learning also that a man should be buried in a shroud, he began to prepare shrouds for the burials of the chiefs. He became known as *Kakarse*. Though praying, he was not regarded as a real Muslim. Later, Muḥammad Boba, a Muslim from Kukawa in Bornu, came to stay with *Kakarse*. Through the introduction of *Kakarse* this learned Muslim was appointed by the chief as the first imam. This is commemorated in the custom that *Kakarse* accompanies

[1] Rattray, 1932, ii. 575–7.

[2] Three 'gates' to the paramountcy: Karaga, Miong (Sambu), and Savelugu. Four divisions reserved to sons or grandsons of Ya-Nas: Korle (Nakpali), Yelzoli (Zabzugu), Demon, and Nantong. Five divisions of the Ya-Na's elders: Gushiegu, Kumbungu, Tolon, Sunson, and Gulkpiegu (Gulkpe-Na is the chief of Tamale). See Manoukian, pp. 55–56.

the imam when the latter goes to pray for the chief. The office of *Ka-karse*, created by a chief's son, was later given to Muḥammad Boba's son, and has been held since by Muslims.[1]

It is interesting to note some parallels between *Kakarse* and *yidan-Kambara* of Yendi. Both are associated with burial customs (shroud, and washing the corpse, respectively), both are said to have introduced an imam to the chief, and both accompany the imam to the chief. Another parallel to Yendi is the tradition that the imam appointed one of his followers to live with the chief, to slaughter animals, and to pray for him. His title is *yidan-fati*, and his office compares with that of *walgu-Na* of Yendi. The imam of Gushiegu has a messenger, *yidan-sannu*. He also washes dead chiefs and Muslims, a duty performed at Yendi by *yidan-Kambara*, and in other Dagomba Muslim communities by the *yarna*.[2]

The tradition suggests two stages in the introduction of Islam to Gushiegu: an early period of elementary Islamic influence, preparing the ground for the next phase, when the position of Islam is established with the appointment of an imam. While no date may be suggested for the earlier phase, the appointment of Muḥammad Boba as the first imam took place, probably, early in the nineteenth century.[3]

The two phases are noticeable also at Karaga (fifteen miles west of Gushiegu), where the early phase is represented by the *yarna*. It is said that the first Muslim at Karaga was Ṭāhir Sisse, of Mande (Wangara or Yarse) origin. His son Mushe (Mūsā) was appointed the first *yarna*. Only later, in the second quarter of the nineteenth century, did the chief of Karaga, Ziblim, son of Na Andani, appoint the first imam, a Hausa Muslim called Shuʿayb Ture.[4] At Savelugu also the first imam, a Hausa, was preceded by a *yarna*, of Mande origin. It is said that when Mahama Ture, the first imam, came to Savelugu he found there a *yarna*, who used to go occasionally to the

[1] Information at a meeting with the Muslim elders at Gushiegu.

[2] See above, p. 90.

[3] An Arabic manuscript in possession of the imam of Gushiegu records the names of nineteen imams at Gushiegu. Ten of the imams held the office after *c.* 1900. The genealogy of the oldest man present goes back to Imam Muḥammad Boba in four generations. The third imam, Saʿīd, son of the first imam, was the teacher of the eighth imam, Muḥammad, whose successor, the ninth imam, Qāsim, saw the arrival of the Europeans (information from the Muslim elders).

[4] Information from the Muslim elders at Karaga. Ziblim, mentioned here as chief of Karaga, was later installed Ya-Na. He reigned in 1853 (see below, p. 197). The second imam, 'Uthmān, held the office in the early 1860s, during the Civil War between Na Abdulai and his uncles.

chief to recite the *Fātiḥa* (the opening *sūra* of the Koran) as an invocation (*duʿā'*). The arrival of the first imam may be dated at the beginning of the nineteenth century.[1]

Dates for the creation of the imamship at Karaga and Savelugu are suggested by the genealogical lists of the imams. On the other hand, the lists of *yarna*s in both villages are unreliable, and it can only be said that they were there before the nineteenth century. Karaga and Savelugu, however, are the two senior chieftaincies in western Dagomba, where one might expect traces of pre-eighteenth-century Wangara Muslims. Is it not possible that the *yarna*s of both villages are descendants of such early Muslims? Indeed their histories reflect a more general process, in which the early Wangara Muslims were superseded by Hausa Muslims.[2] In other Muslim communities in western Dagomba (Tolon, Zorro, Kosuriyiri, etc.) it is clear that the office of the *yarna* is recent (two or three generations old), having been preceded by an imam.

The appointment of the first imam at Karaga is another example of the role of chiefs in diffusing Islam. Shuʿayb lived in Yendi where he became a friend of Prince Ziblim, son of Na Andani. When the latter became chief of Karaga he invited his friend Shuʿayb, and appointed him first imam.

At Yendi, it has been shown, the presence of Islam was well felt, and the court was frequented by Muslim elders. Princes at Yendi could regard these elders and their functions as an integral part of the social and political life; they may also have had personal friends among Muslims. As princes proceeded from Yendi to assume chieftaincies, some found it appropriate to have an imam for praying and producing amulets, as they had experienced at Yendi.[3]

Princes coming from Yendi are promoted from one chieftaincy to another, looking ahead towards the most senior chieftaincies, which may lead them to the paramountcy. Yūsuf, son of Na Yaʿqūba, had first been chief of Pisigu (on the road to Karaga), and was later

[1] The third imam of Savelugu, son of the first imam, Mahama Ture, officiated during the Civil War of the early 1860s. The British occupied Savelugu (1897) when a grandson of the first imam held the imamship (the fifth imam, Idrīs). Information from the present imam of Savelugu.

[2] See above, p. 95.

[3] At Zoghaw (eight miles north-east of Savelugu) the first imam is said to have been invited by the Chief ʿIsā, son of Na Yaʿqūba, who wanted to have an imam (information at Zoghaw).

On personal relations between princes and Muslims in Borgu, see Lombard, 1965, p. 229.

promoted to the chieftaincy of Zorro (near Kumbungu). He brought a Muslim called Danganafi with him to Zorro, whom he appointed imam. Danganafi is remembered as the fourth imam of Zorro, interrupting a continuous line of imams from two related families. He is regarded as an outsider, and left no descendants at Zorro. The few Muslims now at Pisigu have come there in this century. They knew nothing about Muslims in that village in the pre-colonial period. A drummer, however, mentioned the name of Danganafi, a Muslim who had stayed at Pisigu for some time as an imam. Nothing more was known to him about Danganafi; not whence he had come nor whither he went.[1] Imam Danganafi is remembered in two villages, linked only by the promotion of a chief from one to the other. He was attached to his patron chief and moved with him. This case may represent a more common phenomenon.[2]

Muslims may have lived in villages before the appointment of an imam by the chief. These Muslims were strangers, living on the margins of the village society. The creation of the imamship brought the whole community closer to the centre, for the imam served the chief, and was called to pray at festivals and at other ceremonies. An official recognition is thus accorded to the presence of Muslims, and as a result the Islamic influence increases.

When going to the chief the imam is accompanied by a Muslim retinue. The attendance of Muslims at the court of the chief of Karaga may have caused Binger, who visited that village in September 1888, to say that 'the majority of the people are Muslims'. 'But', he added, 'there is no mosque. I have been told that in all that region there are mosques at Yendi and Kompoungou [Kumbungu] only.'[3]

The mosque at Kumbungu, referred to by Binger, is a Friday mosque (*jāmiʿ*). It was built in the third quarter of the last century by a Wangara Muslim, al-ḥājj Iṣḥāq, who visited Kumbungu and found there a large Muslim community without a mosque. After the building of the mosque a Friday imam was appointed to lead the

[1] Information about Danganafi has been recorded independently at Zorro and at Pisigu. During the fieldwork I was not aware of the connexion between these two villages through Danganafi (the imam) and Yūsuf (the chief).

[2] ʿIsā, chief of Diare, was the son of the chief of Karaga. He brought with him a Muslim from Karaga to be imam at Diare. This was Imam Alḥaṣan who was not, however, the first imam of Diare (information at Diare). Imam Albarka of Sang followed his chief, Yinifa, son of Na Yaʿqūba, to Karaga (information at Sang).

[3] Binger, 1892, ii. 65. Karaga was the only large village in Dagomba visited by Binger.

prayer.[1] Whereas a Friday imam is appointed to lead the Muslim community, the other imam, appointed earlier, may be regarded primarily as the agent of Islam with the chief.

The imamship at Kumbungu dates probably from the first half of the nineteenth century. Traditions suggest an Islamic influence at Kumbungu from Daboya. It is said that Muḥammad Nā'ib, a junior chief's son, the ancestor of all but the first two imams, was sent to study Koran 'in the direction of Daboya'. His son, Imam ʿUmar, fled to Daboya when Na Andani II fought Kumbungu in 1888.[2] Influence from Daboya came along an important route to Yendi, which passed over Kumbungu.[3]

After Kumbungu, the same route from Daboya, as described by Bowdich, reached Nantong and Tampiong. Both villages have imams of Larabanga origin, who settled there at the beginning of the nineteenth century.[4]

Dagomba is intersected by trade-routes, and every village of some importance claims a route passing near it. The traders' caravans stayed in *zongos* near the villages, but communicated with the chiefs. Sometimes passing traders stopped at a Dagomba village to live with the chief, as did, for example, the ancestors of two families, one from Hausa, the other from Bornu, who settled at Zabzugu at the beginning of the nineteenth century. The imamship rotates between the two families.[5]

Zabzugu was on one of the two routes from Salaga to Hausa, the route which led to Bafilo and Djougou.[6] On the other route, via Sansanne-Mango, the village of Kpabia was a halting-place for caravans before they crossed the border between Dagomba and

[1] Information from al-ḥājj ʿAbbās of Kumbungu, who retired on account of his age from the imamship of that mosque. His own father was the second Friday imam at Kumbungu.

[2] Information at Kumbungu and Tamale. On the date of this war, see Binger, 1892, ii. 52. ʿUmar is said to have been the third imam; if the list is complete, the first imam may have been appointed towards the end of the first half of the nineteenth century.

[3] Bowdich, 1819, p. 483, route No. 13.

[4] Imam Zakāriyā', the first imam of Larabanga origin at Nantong, was the grandfather of Dahmani, chief of Diare *c.* 1900 (see above, p. 111). He was appointed imam by the chief of Nantong Bleima, grandson of Na Zangina. Hence, both the imam (Zakāriyā') and his chief (Bleima) were three generations back from *c.* 1900, and may, tentatively, be dated *c.* 1800.

[5] Information at Zabzugu. The first imam was appointed during the reign of Na Andani I.

[6] Zabzugu is mentioned on this route by both Bowdich (1819, p. 491) and Dupuis (1824, p. cxxiv).

Gonja. As early as 1820 Dupuis noted 'Wabia, a capital city, as large as Coomassy, and a territory purely Moslem'.[1] The development of Kpabia was very probably linked with the emergence of Salaga as the principal market, in the late eighteenth century.

Before Muslims settled at Kpabia it was a small Dagomba village. At Kpabia Muslims did not come to stay with the chief, as in other Dagomba villages, but to live on the route for commercial purposes. Hence the development of the Muslim community left the Dagomba chief in the shadow, giving the place an Islamic character, as noted by Dupuis, and asserted by Binger: 'Pabia, with no more than 200–300 inhabitants,[2] has a square mud construction which serves as a mosque, and [accommodates] two Muslim schools. Almost all the women pray. Except for the slaves, who appear to be quite numerous, I believe that all [the people] are Muslims.'[3]

In Dagomba villages a chief could appoint an imam to pray for him before the latter had a congregation to lead in prayer. In trading communities an imam was appointed only after a congregation existed. Both at Djougou and at Salaga the imamship was created some decades after the establishment of the community.[4] The same is true of Kpabia, where the first imam, a Fulani called Mahama, was appointed in the first half of the nineteenth century. He was succeeded by two sons, and then, late in the nineteenth century, the imamship was transferred to a family from Gurma.[5]

North of Kpabia, about a mile off the road, a small village, completely Muslim, is called Alfayiri, i.e. 'the *alfa*'s residence'. The following tradition tells the history of that village: Mahpi, a village a mile or two north-east of Alfayiri, was on the trade-route. Traders had befriended the chief of Mahpi, who later sent one of his sons, Muḥammad, with a *madugu* (a caravan leader) to Hausaland. When Muḥammad came back, a learned Muslim, he refused to stay at Mahpi with the non-Muslims, and settled at Botrung (over a mile

[1] Dupuis, 1824, p. xcvii.

[2] Lonsdale (1882, p. 90) counted at Kpabia 600 houses and 1,800 inhabitants.

[3] Binger, 1892, ii. 72–73.

[4] On Salaga, see above, p. 67, note 2. In Djougou the community had been established in the mid-eighteenth century, but the first imam was appointed only about half a century later. The French conquest occurred in the time of the tenth imam of Djougou, while the first imam, a Fulani, came after the beginning of the Fulani *jihād* (information at Djougou).

[5] The first imam was the great-grandfather of the present *nā'ib* of Kpabia. The first Gurma imam was appointed shortly before the German conquest (information at Kpabia).

south-west of Alfayiri. The Ya-Na Ziblim Kulunku (who reigned in mid-nineteenth century) gave his daughter in marriage to Muḥammad. When in Hausaland Muḥammad had been given the nickname Kondo, which remained the patronymic of his descendants. Abū-Bakr, son of Muḥammad Kondo, left Botrung and founded Alfayiri.[1]

Going from Salaga to Yendi at the end of 1881, Captain Lonsdale noted two villages: Mallam Kondo (four hours from Yendi) and Bukari Kondo (three hours and forty-five minutes from Yendi).[2] The first village, Mallam Kondo, is Botrung where Muḥammad Kondo settled. The second village, Bukari Kondo, is Alfayiri itself whither Abū-Bakr (Bukari) moved from Botrung. In 1881 the Kondo family was divided between the two villages, but ultimately all moved to Botrung. Lonsdale's notes thus confirm at least part of the tradition recorded.

Tamale is now the largest town in northern Ghana with the largest Muslim community. It reached this position only in this century after it became the capital of the Northern Territories. In the pre-colonial period Tamale was a small village. Its headman was the *Dakpiema* ('the old man of the market'), whose status is that of *tengdana* rather than that of a *Na* (territorial chief). Tamale was distinguished as a market for its surroundings. Muslims might have frequented the market but they settled there only in the third quarter of the nineteenth century.[3]

The information analysed in this chapter suggests that imams were not appointed in Dagomba villages before the beginning of the nineteenth century. Even at Yendi, it has been noted, the history of the imamship before the middle of the last century is obscure.[4] At Yendi, and in some villages like Karaga and Savelugu, chiefs had first been served by Muslim elders other than imams. The imamship

[1] Information at Alfayiri. Compare the story of the Friday imam of Ziong (above, p. 113).

[2] Lonsdale, 1882, p. 90.

[3] Information at Tamale from Dakpiema and his elders and from Muslim elders. The first Muslims settled in the time of the third Dakpiema, back from *c.* 1900. At the turn of the last century the imam, *yarna*, and the chief-butcher, were all sons of the first holders of these offices.

[4] See above, pp. 94–96. It should be noted, however, that our dates for the appointment of imams were based on lists of imams and on private genealogies, both liable to distortion, mainly through omitting names from lists or telescoping genealogies. Hence the general tendency is to shorten the past, and our conclusions that imams were appointed since the beginning of the nineteenth century might have been reached following inconclusive evidence. See below (pp. 126–9), where documentary evidence helped in overcoming the deficiency of the list of imams of Gambaga.

represents an institutionalized form of relations and communication between chiefs and Muslims. It is therefore a later stage in the introduction of Islam to Dagomba.

In the earlier phase, during the eighteenth century, Islamic elements were incorporated into the culture of the chiefly estate, and relations between chiefs and Muslims were moulded. The process took place mainly at Yendi. Several independent sources throw light on Na Andani I, who reigned at the beginning of the nineteenth century. He gave daughters in marriage to Muslims, whose sons became chiefs. In his name instructions for charms were sent to the Asantehene. Bowdich even heard that the reigning Dagomba king (very probably Na Andani) had been converted.[1] This evidence suggests that by that time the patterns of islamization at Yendi had already been established. It was probably thereafter that Islamic influence was more effectively diffused from the centre to the divisions and the villages.

By the end of the last century Islam was making considerable progress in Dagomba. Muslim communities spread throughout the country; through conversion many Dagomba families had Muslim members; even alien Muslims were integrated and became regarded as Dagombas. The term 'Dagomba Muslims' has come to stay.

(*f*) *Islam in Nanumba*

Nanumba claims to be an independent state, yet throughout its history this state was closely associated with Dagomba, its more powerful sister-state.[2] Islam in Nanumba may be regarded as an extension of Dagomba Islam.

The first Muslim remembered in Nanumba was a *yarna*, Neina by name, who stayed in the village of Kwalga, four miles west of Bimbila. He is said to have come from Dagomba during the reign of Bimbila-Na Toli Dahmani, in the second half of the last century. His successor moved from Kwalga to Bimbila.[3]

[1] See above, pp. 97, 107, 111–12.

[2] A case for the independence of Nanumba as presented by its paramount chief is recorded in A. J. Furley, 'Senior Political Officer's Diary 18 January to 18 March 1915', NAG, Accra, ADM/11. The Nanumba took part in the wars of Dagomba against Gonja in 1713 and 1892 (Tait's manuscripts; Tamakloe, unpublished manuscript). It is said that the approval of the Ya-Na was needed for the appointment of the Bimbila-Na, the paramount chief of Nanumba (Gilbert, unpublished manuscript).

[3] Information at Kwalga and Bimbila. Bimbila-Na Toli was the third chief

The *yarna* was followed by an imam. The first imam of Bimbila, Imam Kafa, came from Nantong. But at that time, it is said, Islam was weak and there was no *'ilm* ('erudition'). Islam was firmly established at Bimbila only towards the end of the nineteenth century with the coming of the second imam, a Hausa Muslim, Muḥammad, grandfather of the present (1964) imam.[1]

In 1911 the German Fisch found a fairly large Muslim community at Bimbila, living in its own quarter with a mosque. In Wulesi, south of Bimbila, Fisch came across another Muslim community with an imam and a mosque.[2] It is said in Wulesi that the first imam came there from Yendi after the German occupation. The growth of these Muslim communities, which took place with the advent of the Germans, may be connected with the increased traffic on the route between Yendi and Krachi, over Bimbila.[3]

As residents of a state capital the Muslims of Bimbila imitated the Muslim community of Yendi in creating titles for Muslim elders: *walgu-Na* is the title of the Friday imam of Bimbila, *zee-mole* that of the imam's deputy (*nā'ib*), while *yidan-kama* is, as in Yendi, the imam's attendant.[4]

In conclusion, Islam is recent in Nanumba country, and it has made little progress among the Nanumba themselves; there are hardly any Nanumba converts. Festivals of the Muslim calendar are celebrated in Nanumba, as in Dagomba, but, unlike the Dagomba, the Nanumba do not circumcise.[5] Muslims remained strangers in Nanumba, and are often referred to as Dagombas.

Why has this small state, an offshoot of Dagomba, reacted in such a different way to Islam? No definite answer may be suggested at the present stage of our knowledge of Nanumba history and its social and political system; only a few preliminary thoughts may be put forward. Although closely linked with Dagomba, the Nanumba chieftaincies were not part of the Dagomba system, where the movement of chiefs from the capital to the villages, and from one village to the other, acted as a blood-stream carrying with it Islamic influence. On the

back from *c.* 1900. There had probably been Muslims in Nanumba before that period but only as temporary residents.

[1] Information from the Muslim elders at Bimbila. The fifth imam, Abū-Bakr, son of the second imam, Muḥammad, officiated in 1931 (NAG, Tamale, C. 12).

[2] Fisch, 1911, pp. 46–49.

[3] See above, pp. 46–47.

[4] Information from the Muslim elders of Bimbila.

[5] Gilbert, unpublished manuscript; Nanumba festivals are described in Tait's manuscripts, text D.

other hand, in their southern position the Nanumba were in constant contact with such pagan peoples as the Konkomba, the Krachis, and the Gonja *nyamase* (commoners). Lastly, although one early route (from Salaga over Zabzugu to Djougou) passed Bimbila, Nanumba country was off the main network of trade-routes which brought life to Gonja and Dagomba.

CHAPTER VII

Islam in Mamprusi

(*a*) *Chiefs and Muslims—Gambaga and Nalerigu*

NA BAWA, the traditional ancestor of Mamprusi (and the other Mole-Dagbane states), resided at Pusiga, in the north-eastern corner of Ghana, where his grave is still venerated. After his death the split occurred between Dagomba and Mamprusi; Na Sitobu of Dagomba moved south-westward, while Na Tusogo of the Mamprusi settled at Mamprugu, where he died and was buried.[1] Tusogo's successor moved to Gambaga, which remained the capital of Mamprusi until Na Atabia removed the capital to Nalerigu.[2]

This résumé of early Mamprusi history lacks a solid chronology, because the list of the Mamprusi chiefs and their genealogy before Na Atabia appears to be defective.[3] Na Atabia's reign may be dated A.H. *c.* 1100 (1688) to A.H. 1154 (1741/2), as recorded by the Gonja Chronicle: 'in that year [A.H. 1154] Atabia king of Ghabagha died. He is said to have reigned for fifty-odd years.'

Na Atabia's reign, in the first half of the eighteenth century, coincided with the growing importance of the trade between Hausaland and the Volta Basin. One route, from Hausaland, over Fada-n-Gurma and Kupela, passed Gambaga. In order to secure that part of the route between Tenkodugu and Gambaga, Na Atabia is said to have established three Mamprusi chiefdoms among the Kusasi: Sinibaga, Binduri, and Bawku.[4]

Na Atabia's interest in safeguarding the trade-route appears also in the tradition, recorded independently from several informants at Gambaga, about the settlement of the first Muslim. Traders passing through Mamprusi were attacked and robbed by the princes. Na Atabia appointed a Muslim as toll-collector over the traders, and in return promised to stop the princes' brigandage. This Muslim acted

[1] According to Hilton (1963, p. 80), Mamprugu is now in Togo.

[2] Rattray (1932, ii. 546–7) and Mackay (unpublished manuscript) recorded the traditions of Mamprusi at about the same time, and probably had the same informants. Their versions vary only in minor details. The history of Mamprusi, incorporated in *The Moshi Tribe* by Mallam Alhasan (translated by J. Withers-Gill, 1924) is unreliable.

[3] See below, p. 199.

[4] Syme, unpublished manuscript; see also Hilton, 1963, p. 83.

also as host to the traders and served them food. He used to carry the food in a wooden bowl, called *akushi* in Hausa. His name has been forgotten, but he and his descendants became known as *Magaji Akushi* or Mangoshi.[1]

Drummers praise Mangoshi's house as '*zuu yiri dima*', 'the house of the chief's first-born son'. The Nayiri (the Mamprusi paramount), it is said, appointed one of his sons as protector of Mangoshi, in order to prevent other princes from robbing Mangoshi. Close relations developed between Mangoshi and the chiefs. One tradition tells that a son of the Nayiri frequented Mangoshi's house, and studied Koran together with the Muslim's children. With the Nayiri's approval this son was renamed Ibrāhīm and became a Muslim. He refused to return to live with the chiefs, and built a house for himself opposite Mangoshi's residence. This house, still shown at Gambaga, is known as *yidana-yiri*, and its people trace their genealogy back to *yidana* Ibrāhīm, son of the Nayiri. The first conversion of a chief's son in Mamprusi is thus recorded.

The patronymic of Mangoshi's family was Taraore. Taraore is also one of the praise-names of members of the Mamprusi chiefly estate.[2] Binger, who first noted the name Taraore applied to the chiefs, assumed that the Mamprusi chiefs were of Mande origin.[3] By analogy with the chiefs of Buna, who adopted the patronymic Wattara of their resident Muslims, it is possible that the Mamprusi chiefs acquired the patronymic Taraore as a praise-name, from Mangoshi.

Mangoshi, one informant said, came from Syria (Shām), but others remarked that nobody could say whence he came. The patronymic Taraore suggests he was a Wangara. Since the seventeenth century Wangara Taraore formed the nucleus of the Muslim community in the region of Wa. Mangoshi could have been of that group. Not a newcomer to the region at the time of Na Atabia, he may have emerged from obscurity on entering the service of the Nayiri as intermediary between the latter and the Muslim traders from Hausaland. The traditions suggest that Mangoshi was regarded not only as the first Muslim in Mamprusi, but also as distinct from those who followed him. He may represent an early group of Muslims, already in Mamprusi before Na Atabia's reign.

[1] One may suggest that the first Muslim was called *Mai-Akushi*, 'the owner of the wooden bowl', and his descendants *Magaji-Akushi*, 'the heirs of [the owner of] the wooden-bowl'.

[2] Information from the Dulana, chief of Walwale.

[3] Binger, 1892, ii. 38.

The appointment of the first imam in Gambaga follows a pattern already observed in Dagomba; the first Muslim—Mangoshi—introduced a learned Hausa Muslim before the Nayiri, to be appointed imam. Mangoshi's role in the creation of the imamship is commemorated in the custom that a new imam, after the installation ceremony, is taken to sit under the tree where Mangoshi is believed to be buried.

It is said that the first imam, Maḥmūd, accepted his appointment reluctantly, and only after he had made a contract with the Nayiri, that the latter would comply with the imam's advice as to what was forbidden by Islam. The agreement proved unworkable and Maḥmūd swore that his descendants would not be imams. Maḥmūd was succeeded by a relative, Ibrāhīm. Imam Ibrāhīm was succeeded by his brother, Timani (ʿUthmān), and Timani by his son, Imam Al-Ḥājj. When the latter died the imamship was given to another family, of Gurma origin, that of the present imam of Gambaga.[1]

The first imam remembered from the Gurma family was Imam Adam, whose son and successor, Imam Baba, officiated at the time of the European occupation. Since both Adam and Baba had long tenure of office, the former may have succeeded to the imamship about the middle of the nineteenth century. Imam Adam is famous for his communication with the Asantehene, who used to send annual presents to Adam in return for blessing. The following tradition, related by Imam Saʿīd Nasamu of Gambaga, describes the origin of this contact: an Ashanti army came north to capture slaves. Among those captured was a woman of the family of Baba, grandfather of Imam Adam. Baba went to Kumasi and persuaded the Asantehene to set the woman free. The Asantehene, impressed by Baba's piety, allowed Baba to send the woman to Salaga, but made Baba himself stay with him. Baba's son, Dawūda, had two sons: Adam and Ramaḍān. Baba sent for his grandson Adam, who came to Kumasi. He stayed for some time with the Asantehene, who admired Adam's religious power. The close relations with the Asantehene continued after Adam became imam of Gambaga.

Ramaḍān, Imam Adam's brother, was the founder of one of the 'gates' to the imamship of Walwale. Ramaḍān's grandson, ʿAbdulai, the Friday imam of Walwale, said that his grandfather was appointed imam after he had returned from Kumasi, where he had visited his own grandfather Yao. Yao, a famous Mallam from Gambaga, was called by Ashanti troops, who raided slaves in the north, to help them

[1] Information from descendants of the first imam, Maḥmūd, at Gambaga.

in crossing a river. He did so, and followed them to Kumasi, where the Asantehene asked him to pray for victory in a war. As the king won this war he asked Yao to stay with him. Yao's family left Kumasi only a few years before the arrival of the British, when they moved to Salaga, Masaka, and Yeji.[1]

Fortunately, this is one of those rare occasions when such traditions are corroborated by contemporary documentary evidence. Among the Copenhagen manuscripts, there is a short work 'On the Advantages of the Month of Ramaḍān', ending with the following colophon:

> The scribe is Ramaḍān son of Dāwūda the imam of Ghambāgha; the owner is Karamo Ṭāma; the town Kumāsi; Saturday the 22nd.[2]

The scribe is none other than Ramaḍān son of Dāwūda, the future imam of Walwale and brother of Imam Adam of Gambaga, who copied this work when visiting his grandfather before 1820.[3] Yao (an Ashanti name) of the Walwale tradition is to be identified with Baba of the Gambaga tradition, and both with Baba, the leader of the Muslim community in Kumasi, whom Bowdich and Dupuis met in 1817 and 1820 respectively. Both visitors noted that Baba was from Gambaga.[4] They give, however, different accounts of the circumstances of Baba's arrival in Kumasi.[5] The fact that even these contemporary authorities do not agree only suggests that the traditions of Walwale and Gambaga should not be discarded because of disagreement in details.

More light is thrown on Baba by the Arabic correspondence in the Copenhagen manuscripts. In two letters, one to Baba, the other written by him, Baba is referred to as son of the imam of Gambaga.[6] Two other letters, probably written earlier, are worth quoting:

From ʿAlī, known as Bābā, to Alfā ʿUmar,

I thank you for what you have done. You have fulfilled your promise to the imam. . . .[7] May Allāh give you long life. I heard all you had done for me. I send you some oil for the lantern. I am tired of this world affairs. I

[1] The imam of Masaka, near Salaga, is related to the house of the Gambaga imams (information at Masaka).

[2] Copenhagen manuscripts, vol. ii, ff. 117–18.

[3] On the date of the Copenhagen manuscripts, see above, pp. xxi–xxii.

[4] Bowdich, 1918, p. 240; Dupuis, 1824, p. cxxix.

[5] Bowdich, loc. cit.; Dupuis, 1824, p. 97.

[6] Copenhagen manuscripts, vol. i, f. 107 (a letter from Kamshe-Na of Dagomba to the Asantehene, addressed to Baba); vol. iii, f. 5 (a letter from Baba to the imams of Gonja, Buipe, and Daboya).

[7] Here comes an obscure phrase: 'I was afraid the imam had died.'

have with me all our brothers, our father's wives, our wives, and our paternal uncle. Not one of them left.

Concerning what we have talked about, explain it to me in a letter and send it with my sister. Put her with my sons Marzūq and Yamūsā until I finish my work. Then I will certainly come. May Allāh bring us together in a blessed hour. Let me know her price in a letter.

Greetings to you from the imam of Ghambāgha, from Mallam Shaʿbān, Alfā Maḥmūd, and all the Muslims.

The reply to this letter is on the back of the same folio:[1]

From ʿUmar Kunāte to Alfā ʿAlī Samisiku, known as Bābā Samisiku, son of the late imam Kusu.

You sent us a letter about your old woman (*kabīratuka*), asking us to tell you her price. It is impossible for us to sell her, because of her father, nicknamed Ghunu (may Allāh have mercy upon him), and because of you, my brother. I have taken her from the unbelievers in exchange for one slave. . . .

Our greetings to you, to all your neighbours, to our imam, and to all the Muslims, men and women. Please send me a white gown for praying.

ʿAlī Bābā sends greetings from the imam of Gambaga, which suggests that he wrote from that town. His patronymic Samisiku resembles that of the imam of Gambaga's family—Samso, or, as it is pronounced by the branch of that family at Masaka—Samshegu. The affair of the captive woman recalls the Gambaga tradition about the departure of Baba to Kumasi. Indeed ʿAlī Bābā promises to come down, which he probably did. In Kumasi ʿAlī Bābā Samisiku (or Samso), son of the imam of Gambaga, became the leader of the Muslim community. Indeed W. Hutton, a member of Dupuis's mission, who met this Muslim elder, called him Ali Baba.[2] According to Bowdich, Baba came to Kumasi about 1807.[3]

The documentary evidence clearly shows that Imam Adam of the second half of the nineteenth century was not the first imam of his family. Among imams who preceded him one can mention: Imam Dāwūda, father of Ramaḍān and Adam, Imam Ghunu, father of the captive woman, and Imam Kusu, father of ʿAlī Bābā Samisiku.[4]

[1] Copenhagen manuscripts, vol. i, f. 75.

[2] Hutton, 1821, p. 215. I was told at Gambaga that Imam Baba of the late nineteenth century was named after Baba of Kumasi. In one list (communicated by al-ḥājj ʿUthmān Isḥāq Boyo of IAS) Imam Baba (the younger) is called ʿAlī Bābā, which may suggest that this was also the name of his great-grandfather, Baba of Kumasi.

[3] Bowdich, 1819, p. 240.

[4] The imam of Gambaga mentioned Imam Sulaymān Gunu as the first imam

Imams of that family had, therefore, held office already in the late eighteenth century. Hence the five imams of Hausa origin who preceded them officiated earlier in the eighteenth century.

It is remembered that at the time of the first imam, Maḥmūd, a Muslim from Dakaye in Mossi came to study Koran at Gambaga. This information from Gambaga is corroborated by a tradition recorded at Dakaye that a Muslim from that place went to study at Gambaga during the reign of Naba Kom I, who reigned in the first half of the eighteenth century.[1] It is thus permissible to accept the tradition, recorded also by Rattray, that the first imam was appointed by Na Atabia.[2]

Na Atabia (late seventeenth century to 1741/2), in whose reign Muslims settled at Gambaga, moved the seat of the court from Gambaga to Nalerigu, five miles to the east. One tradition says that the court was transferred after Na Atabia had repelled a Gurma invasion, which reached as far as Nalerigu.[3] This may explain why it was possible to establish the court at Nalerigu, freed from the Gurma threat, but not why it was necessary to remove the court from Gambaga.

With the development of the trade-route and the growth of the Muslim community at Gambaga this town, which became open to strangers, may have been regarded as unsuitable for the residence of the chief. He therefore moved to the secluded and walled village of Nalerigu, which was far enough from the cosmopolitan atmosphere of Gambaga, and yet close enough to secure some control over this important centre. The chiefs preferred to live apart from the Muslims, or, as put by the imam of Gambaga, the Nayiri left Gambaga because he could not stand the supervision of the Muslims over the chiefs, following the contract between the Nayiri and the first imam that the chiefs would avoid practices incompatible with Islam.

When Na Atabia moved to Nalerigu, 'he put a Liman (a Mohammedan priest) and a Gambarana in charge of the town of Gambaga'.[4] Gambarana is the *tengdana* (Earth-priest) of Gambaga. He told

he knew of. The genealogy of a Muslim from Paga (near Navrongo) now seems authentic: Mu'minu b. Yamūsā b. Imam Adam b. Imam Dāwūda b. Imam Sulaymān.

[1] Bichon, 1962, pp. 82–83. The information at Gambaga was given without any leading question.

[2] Rattray, 1932, ii. 547.

[3] Mackay, unpublished manuscript. A Gurma invasion is mentioned also in connexion with the arrival of the Mango people, see above, pp. 78–79.

[4] Rattray, loc. cit.

Rattray: 'Dead game found on the land belongs to me, save a foreleg, which goes to the finder. Bangles and beads and any other valuables belong to me, *save when found by the Mohammedans who refuse to hand them over*. Such things belong to me because I own the land.'[1]

The Muslims challenge the *tengdana*'s claim because they regard him as the symbol of paganism, and refuse any association with him. The tension between Muslims and pagans has been extended to a competition between the imam and the *tengdana* over the authority at Gambaga. Rattray noted in 1930: 'At Gambaga the Limam had posed and passed as being the head of the town, whereas the rightful holder of the office was the old Tendana, who, I am glad to record, has now been reinstated.'[2]

At the head of the big and wealthy Muslim community of Gambaga, the imam appeared also to have enjoyed some political independence of the Nayiri, as observed by Binger in 1888: 'Gambakha s'est affranchi et obéit aux ordres de l'Imam Baraga.[3] Oual-Oualé est entre les mains de l'imam Seydou Touré, et le reste du pays est commandé par quantité de *naba* et de *nabiga* plus ou moins puissants, tels que ceux de Zango [Janga] et de Ouango [Wungu] aux environs de Oual-Oualé.'[4]

The Mamprusi state was divided into four large territorial divisions: Nalerigu, Wungu, Janga, and Pasinkpe. The chiefs of the last three can be traced back over many generations to sons of Nayiris, but since then succession has been from the chiefly estate of each division, and not from the paramount chief's court, as in Dagomba. This allowed the divisional chiefs to build up a certain independence, as noted above by Binger.[5]

The Nayiri's suzerainty was acknowledged in certain periods over several neighbouring tribes, from Navrongo in the north-west to Sanga (in Busanga) in the north-east.[6] Mamprusi's authority over these peoples was seldom effective, but these were drawn into the

[1] Rattray, 1932, ii. 459–60; my italics.

[2] 'Annual Report by Captain R. S. Rattray, April 1929–April 1930', NAG, Tamale, file C. 1.

[3] Binger confused here the names of the reigning Nayiri, Na Berega, and of the imam of Gambaga, then Imam Baba.

[4] Binger, 1892, ii. 38.

[5] On the political divisions in Mamprusi, see Rattray, 1932, ii. 555; Manoukian, 1951, p. 62.

[6] Statements of local chiefs forwarded by Lieut.-Col. Northcott, May 1898, NAG, Accra, 1046/57. See also Prost, 1953, p. 1337; Fortes, 1940, p. 257; Syme, unpublished manuscript.

orbit of the Mamprusi political system, adding to its complexity. Subject and neighbouring tribes—the Kussasi, Konkomba, and Chokossi—took part in internal disputes among princes over the paramountcy.[1]

Mamprusi is therefore less unified and more heterogeneous than Dagomba. In such a polity with various pressure groups, the imam as leader of the Muslim community had more influence in the political sphere than could have been expected in Dagomba.

The transfer of the court to Nalerigu left Gambaga still the most important town in Mamprusi. Outsiders regarded it as the capital.[2] The earlier European visitors to Mamprusi called at Gambaga, where they were received by the imam.[3] The proud Nayiri Na Berega (d. 1902) refused, it is said, to deal with the white men, and it was, therefore, Imam Baba of Gambaga who communicated with the Europeans. This caused some confusion in the minds of the Europeans as to the realities of political authority in Mamprusi, as reflected in an early British report of 1898:

> The king of Gambaga is a fetish king and must remain in his town which is called Nalerigu. The inhabitants are partly fetish and partly Mahommedans. As is always the case, the Mahommedans are the leading party. Their headman is the imam of Gambaga, Baba. He is virtually the ruling power though he always makes a great point of referring matters to the king.[4]

The same impression is conveyed by Watherston, the commissioner of the Northern Territories. His headquarters was at Gambaga, and he must have spoken with personal experience when he said: '[Mamprusi is] ruled nominally by a King who lives at a small town near Gambaga, but in reality by the Liman of Gambaga, a patriarchal looking Mahommedan.'[5] This may have been the apparent situation at the beginning of the colonial era, but it is likely that in his dealings with the Europeans, in the name of the Nayiri, the imam built up not only political influence, but also his own image as the virtual ruler.

[1] Of the last six chiefs of Mamprusi before the colonial occupation, four had to defeat other claimants to the paramountcy before they secured the skin (Rattray, 1932, ii. 457–8; Mackay and Syme, unpublished manuscripts).

[2] In Mossi, for example, the chief of Mamprusi is known as 'the king of Gambaga' (Delbosom, 1932, pp. 204–5).

[3] *Bulletin du Comité de l'Afrique Française*, 1895, p. 349.

[4] 'Report on Mamprusi', by Captain D. Mackworth, 30 May 1898; enclosure in No. 366, *African (West)*, No. 549, PRO, CO. 879/52.

[5] Watherston, 1907–8, p. 349.

Two episodes throw light on the imam's influence in the nineteenth century. Early in that century, during the reign of Na Kuligaba, the latter's subordinate, Bawku-Naba Seteem, had raided cattle in Busanga country. The imam of Gambaga advised the return of the cattle lest the Busanga retaliate. No attention was paid to his warning, which proved justified some years later when the Busanga attacked Bawku, killed its Chief Seteem, and devastated the Kusasi land. In 1895 the Kusasi of Kugri sent a present of two sheep and two thousand cowries to Imam Baba of Gambaga, asking him to prevent the Nayiri from punishing them for a certain wrong they had done. The Nayiri rejected the imam's solicitation.[1]

The two episodes indicate that the imam's influence on the Nayiri was limited. Indeed, in both cases the imam acted well within the traditional concept of his office: advocating prudence, making peace, and pleading for wrongdoers.

An element of tension between the imam and the chief in Mamprusi cannot, however, be denied. This tension finds expression mainly in the sayings of Muslims, who do not pose as humble subjects of their chief as would Muslims in Gonja and Dagomba. In presenting the history of Gambaga the imam claimed that the Muslims had preceded the chief in that town, and that the Nayiri had abandoned Gambaga under the Muslims' pressure. Binger's information, quoted above, on the autonomous status of Gambaga and Walwale under its respective imams, was received from Muslims. Going back to the beginning of the last century, the account of Baba's migration to Kumasi as recorded by Bowdich reflects tension between the Nayiri and the imam's son: 'Whilst the invasion [of the Fanti kingdom in 1807] was meditating, Baba, now the Chief of the Moors, presented himself to solicit an asylum in Coomassie, having been driven from Gamba by the rapacity of the king, his near relative. . . .'[2]

Notwithstanding this moment of tension, relations between chiefs and Muslims in Mamprusi follow a pattern known from neighbouring states. A Muslim, for example, addresses the Nayiri as *nsira*, 'husband', whereas a Muslim is sometimes called *na-pwaaba*, 'the Na's wife'.[3] This fictional relationship excludes the idea of political rivalry, and indicates the dependence of Muslims on the chief. The

[1] Syme, unpublished manuscript.

[2] Bowdich, 1819, p. 240. Chiefs give their daughters in marriage to prominent Muslims. This may explain why the king is regarded as a 'near relative' of Baba, the imam's son.

[3] Mrs. Susan Drucker-Brown, personal communication.

fictional relationship between the Nayiri and his sub-chiefs is that of 'a father' and 'a son', where elements of mutual suspicion and possible replacement exist.

The Mamprusi, like the Dagomba, celebrate festivals of the Muslim calendar as national feasts. The Mamprusi are circumcised, and are given Muslim names besides proper Mamprusi ones. Blessings of Muslims and their amulets are demanded. Rattray recorded that 'at least at Gambaga and its environs' Muslims come to pray in the funeral 'even when the deceased was a "pagan."'[1] Muslims, of course, take part in a chief's funeral.

Muslims are involved also in the installation ceremony of a new Nayiri. The *yarna* enrobes the Nayiri with the ceremonial gown.[2] The *yarna*, whose patronymic is Taraore, claims to be of chiefly descent. The first *yarna* was a converted prince said to have helped his brother Na Salifu (first half of the nineteenth century) to the paramountcy. In reward, Na Salifu wanted to give his brother a chieftaincy, but the latter refused, asking to be appointed *yarna*, 'chief of the Muslims'.

Before the installation ceremony, the Na-designate is hidden in a certain house at Nalerigu, known as Kondiyiri.[3] It has been related at Nalerigu that the founder of this house was *Alfa* Bukari, a Muslim from Gurma, who came to stay with Na Atabia after the latter had moved from Gambaga to Nalerigu. The Nayiri wanted a Muslim to be close to him. *Alfa* Bukari, praying for the chiefs, also had the right to intercede for people condemned to death; the Nayiri was expected to accept that intercession. *Alfa* Bukari's descendants, having lived for many years with the chiefs, abandoned Islam. Although Kondiyiri is not a Muslim house any more, its role in the ceremony is probably associated with its Muslim origin.

In war, the *yarna* is said to have been on the Na's left, praying for victory.[4] Muslims, however, took part in wars not only as clerics, but also as warriors. In the war against the Kusasi of Kugri in 1895, the Na's army was commanded by Wakoso, the chief-butcher of Gambaga.[5]

In Dagomba the office of the chief-butcher had a chiefly origin. In Mamprusi its history is less complicated. The first chief-butcher is

[1] Rattray, 1932, ii. 462.

[2] Information from the *yarna*. Rattray does not mention it in his description of the ceremony (ii. 557–9), but it was confirmed by Mrs. Drucker-Brown, who studied the political structure of the Mamprusi.

[3] Information as above.

[4] Mackay, unpublished manuscript.

[5] Syme, unpublished manuscript. Wakoso was the eighth chief-butcher of Gambaga.

said to have been al-ḥājj Ibrāhīm, a Hausa from Gobir. He came to Gambaga along the trade-route together with Maḥmūd, the first imam. As both were made to stay with Mangoshi, al-ḥājj Ibrāhīm used to buy cattle for meat which he prepared for the passing traders. Later he was officially appointed chief-butcher. From this house at Gambaga, a chief-butcher was sent to Walwale. By custom, when the chief-butcher of Gambaga died, that of Walwale succeeded him, and a new chief-butcher was sent from Gambaga to Walwale.[1]

(*b*) *Muslims in the divisions*

Walwale, it is said, started as a toll-post on the route from Mossi. As the route passed some miles away from Wungu, the residence of the divisional chief, Wu-Naba, the latter sent his son to establish the post, and to collect tolls from passing traders. This chief's son was given the title Dulana. To this day Dulana is in charge of Walwale, as a representative of Wu-Naba.[2]

Soon after the establishment of the post a market developed around it. The new market attracted a group of Muslims who had previously lived in a village, said to have been about five miles to the south. When these Muslims settled at this new place, Walwale, Wu-Naba appointed their headman as imam. The first imam, remembered as *Limam kuru* ('the old imam'), was appointed in the time of the first Dulana, that is not long after the foundation of the toll-post.

In 1888, when visiting Walwale, Binger met the imam, 'Seydou Touré'.[3] This Sa'īd Ture was the grandfather of the present imam, Sulaymān, and the grandson of the first imam, *Limam kuru*. He was the sixth imam, the present one being the thirteenth.[4] This suggests a date in the second half of the eighteenth century for the appointment of the first imam, and for the foundation of Walwale. The settlement of Yarse communities south of Wagadugu—at Kombissiri, Dakaye,

[1] Four out of eight chief-butchers of Walwale succeeded from Gambaga; all eight were of the Gambaga house.

[2] Information from the Dulana. Imam Sulaymān of Walwale referred to the Dulana as an 'Earth-priest', probably in analogy to the Gamba-rana. The title Dulana which may raise some doubts about his chiefly origin is explained as 'owner of the room', because the chief's son, bringing the toll revenue, had free access to the chief's room. The chiefly origin of the office is confirmed by the fact that princes compete to attain it, as well as by the Dulana's tribal marks and his patronymic Taraore.

[3] Binger, 1892, ii. 38.

[4] The list of imams and their genealogies have been reconstructed from information collected from representatives of the three 'gates' to the imamship, and from the Dulana. The latter's genealogy, like that of the imams, goes back to the foundation of Walwale in five generations.

and Sarabatenga—during the eighteenth century, presupposes an increase in the trade of Mossi southward at that period.[1]

The name of the village, whence the first group of Muslims had come, is given as Kamshe. Imam Sulaymān, a descendant of that group, added that their family was related to the family of *yidan-asakiya* of Yendi. *Yidan-asakiya*, as previously stated, was a follower of Kamshe-Na, sent to Yendi from Kamshegu.[2] Kamshe and Kamshegu are two villages with similar names, the inhabitants of both are said to be relatives. Is it not possible that one of the earliest groups of Hausa Muslims, which came at the very beginning of the eighteenth century, had branches in both Mamprusi and Dagomba?

Limam kuru was succeeded by his son Ramaḍān as imam. Then a new 'gate' to the imamship was created with the appointment of Imam Bawa Mandé, a Muslim from Bornu. It is said that he was on a visit to Walwale when Imam Ramaḍān died. As no suitable candidate was found, Wu-Naba appointed the guest Bawa as imam.

Imam Bawa was followed by Imam Ramadān, already mentioned as the brother of Imam Adam of Gambaga. A third 'gate' had thus been opened, very probably through recommendation from Gambaga and Nalerigu. Ramaḍān was succeeded by his son, Imam Dāwūda, and after him the imamship returned to the house of *Limam kuru*, to Imam Sa'īd, whom Binger met in 1888. Next came Imam Adam, son of Imam Ramaḍān, who held the office in 1898.[3] Hence, at the end of the last century the imams of the two principal towns in Mamprusi—Imam Baba of Gambaga and Imam Adam of Walwale—were cousins.

At Walwale Binger distinguished three elements:

1. The autochthons, or those who could be regarded as such. . . . Their tribal marks offer analogy to those of the Mossi.
2. Another group, also very old in the country, but certainly of Mande origin, including Taraore, Diabakhate, and Kamara. They still have the authority. They are marked like the Mande-Bambara of the Upper Niger.
3. Hausa immigrants, known as Dagomba, who came to the region after 'Uthman dan Fodio's wars, at the beginning of the century.[4]

[1] See below, p. 166. On the routes from Mossi, one over Gambaga and the other over Walwale, see 'Report on Mamprusi' by D. Mackworth, op. cit.

[2] See above, p. 94. Information not in reply to a direct question.

[3] In his report (op. cit.) Mackworth says: 'perhaps the best friend to the English is "Adam" Imam of Walwale.'

[4] Binger, 1892, ii. 39–40.

The last group is that of the Muslim section of Walwale, where the three groups which provide imams live.[1] The autochthons of the first group are the Mamprusi commoners. In his second group, Binger confused two distinct elements; the Taraore are members of the Mamprusi chiefly estate, represented in Walwale by the Dulana. They indeed have the authority, but they are not of Mande origin. Muslims of Mande origin—the Jabaghte and Kamaghte (the 'Diabakhate' and 'Kamara' of Binger)—came only at the beginning of the nineteenth century, the Jabaghte from Sansanne-Mango and the Kamaghte from Bonduku.[2] They seem, however, to have closer relations with the Dulana than the other Muslims; the Mande Muslims live in the Dulana's ward, and it is said that they came there as his guests.

A visitor to Walwale is impressed by the Friday mosque in the timber-framed Sudanese style, which elsewhere in this area (Larabanga, Dokrupe, or the Yarse villages in Mossi) indicates a community of Mande origin. Binger did not mention this mosque for it was built after his visit, at the beginning of the present century. The mosque, standing in the ward of Hausa, Bornu, and Gurma Muslims, is typical not of the community, but of its builders; for it was built by men brought from Wa.[3]

The imam of Walwale, like that of Gambaga, is both the head of the great Muslim community and the imam of the chief. He is appointed by the Wu-Naba, and officiates (himself or through a representative) at festivals and ceremonies. The other two divisional chiefs in Mamprusi—Wulgu-Naba and So-Naba—have also their own imams.

Formerly Wulgu-Naba resided in the village of Wulugu (eight miles north of Walwale), but he now lives at Pasinkpe (near the White Volta river). The Muslims of Wulgu-Naba live in the small village of Nabari, on the track between Wulugu and Pasinkpe. The history of Nabari is not very clear; a tradition recorded from his descendant says that the founder of Nabari, Muḥammad, was a friend of Na Atabia. The latter gave him the land of Nabari to

[1] Earlier, Binger (ii. 19, 25) referred also to Mamprusi Muslims as 'Dagomba'. He may have been influenced by the Mande word *Maraba* used for both Hausa and Dagomba (ibid. i. 31). Binger's suggestion that they came after the *jihād* is probably based on information he got from two Hausa Muslims from Dagomba whom he met at Tengrela, in the Ivory Coast (ibid. i. 188).

[2] Information from representatives of the Jabaghte and the Kamaghte at Walwale. The latter counted four generations since their arrival in Walwale.

[3] Information from al-ḥājj Isḥāq Wala, whose father built the mosque.

settle in. Living not far from Wulgu-Naba's residence, Muḥammad and his descendants became like Mallams of the divisional chief. They had the title of *somo*, and their main duty was to lead the *Damba* festival dance at the court of Wulgu-Naba. Wulgu-Naba had no official imam until quite recently when a Kantosi Muslim, Yaʿqūb, approached the chief and was created the first imam (the present one being the second).

Janga, the residence of the divisional chief, So-Naba, is near the confluence of the White Volta river and the river Nasia. A trade-route formerly going from Yagaba to Savelugu is said to have passed near Janga. On this route a Muslim, not known by name, came to Janga and died there, leaving behind a son. This son married a daughter of So-Naba, who gave birth to Moru (ʿUmar), the first imam of Janga. All the Muslims at Janga claim descent from that first Muslim. Their patronymic Sisse may suggest a Wangara origin.[1]

The Janga Muslim community appears to be quite old. Its antiquity may have added to the obscurity of the tradition. The shallow genealogies recorded (four generations from the present only) is typical of Muslims who are removed far in time from the crucial historical event, that of the migration to the present habitation. This is a single-cell Muslim community, somewhat isolated from the outside, but closely associated with the local chiefs, to whom they are linked through their ancestress, daughter of the chief, and with whom they inter-married in subsequent generations. Not only did Muslims marry the chiefs' daughters, but they also admitted giving their own daughters to the local non-Muslim people. Giving a Muslim wife to a non-Muslim is not allowed by Islamic law, but it is unavoidable in small Muslim communities living intimately with their village neighbours.

Among the four divisions of Mamprusi, in Janga only do the imam and the Muslims live in the chief's village. In the other three divisions the chief's village—Nalerigu, Wungu, and Pasinkpe—is separated from the Muslims' residence—Gambaga, Walwale, and Nabari, respectively. This may indicate reserved relations between chiefs and Muslims in Mamprusi compared with the intimate relations in Gonja, and the close association in Dagomba.

One case only was recorded of a chief's son taking a Muslim to the village when appointed chief.[2] Hence Mamprusi did not see the

[1] Information at Janga.

[2] The first chief of Nangmwango (south of the road from Walwale to Gambaga) was son of Nayiri Salifu and of a Muslim mother. He brought with him his

process of diffusing Islam in the countryside villages, which has been noted in Dagomba. As princes lived in the chief's village apart from the Muslims, the free and personal association with Muslims did not develop. Early in the history of Islam in Mamprusi a son of the Nayiri became converted. The office of *yarna* is said to have been created for a converted prince. Other individual cases may be discovered, but the impression is that there was no constant mobility from the chiefly estate, let alone from among the commoners, to the Muslim community.[1] The two important Muslim communities—Gambaga and Walwale—are characteristically of foreign origin. The 'estrangement' of Muslims in Mamprusi as compared with Dagomba is illustrated by Binger, who found it appropriate to denote Muslims in Mamprusi as 'Dagombas'.

Muslim maternal cousin, the ancestor of the only Muslim family in the village (information at Nangmwango).

[1] The reigning Nayiri (1964), Abdulai Shirga, has recently been converted by a certain *walī* ('a holy man'). This should be looked at as part of the contemporary scene, which is outside the scope of the present study.

CHAPTER VIII

Islam in the Country of Stateless Peoples

(a) *Wa—A Stronghold of Islam*

In the north-west of Ghana, amid stateless societies, the kingdom of Wa was founded by chiefs of Dagomba origin, probably in the middle of the seventeenth century.[1] Not long after the foundation of the kingdom, in the reign of the third Wa-Na, Pilpu (son of Sorliya, the founder), came the first imam, Ya'umaru ('Umar) Taraore. He was not, however, the first Muslim in the region of Wa, having been preceded by Muslims who had settled in three villages: Nasa, Vise, and Palwogho.[2]

Nasa, the only village of the three which still exists, is an autonomous Muslim village. Its headman, the *yarna* (a Muslim title current in other Mole-Dagbane states), is comparable in status to a *tengdana*, the traditional authority in chiefless societies.[3] This suggests that Nasa had been founded by Muslims independently of the chiefs of Wa, and probably before the latter assumed authority, or before the seventeenth century.

Opposite Wa, across the Black Volta river, are the Lobi gold-fields. The 'silent trade' in gold as described by al-Mas'ūdī and Ca da Mosto takes place on a river, where traders from the north exchange salt for gold brought by primitive people living across the river.[4] This stereotyped description may apply to more than one place in West Africa; among others also to our area. The Lobi may have been the primitive people of such accounts, while the Black Volta river could have marked the frontier, where northern traders had to stop for their trade with the Lobi gold-fields.

A Dagomba drummer at Wa related a tradition that Na Zokuli of Dagomba left Yendi in search of gold. Discovering gold at Dolma (Dorimon?) he decided to stay there and did not return to Dagomba.

[1] See below, pp. 201–3.

[2] 'History of the kingdom of Wa and its Muslims', IAS/AR-152; also IAS/AR-151.

[3] I. Wilks, personal communication. Professor Wilks's study of Wa may throw new light on its history.

[4] Al-Mas'ūdī, 1861–77, iv. 92–93; Ca da Mosto, 1895, pp. 57–58.

The Dagomba Drum History recalls the same episode in telling that Na Zokuli set out in search of gold. As he did not return his people went out to look for him and found that he had been transformed into a crocodile.[1] These traditions, as well as the claim of the Muslims of Zangbeyiri (the Hausa ward at Wa) that their ancestor came in search of gold, suggest that Wa was closely associated with gold. Soon after the foundation of their kingdom, at the beginning of the seventeenth century, the chiefs of Buna brought Nafana specialists from Banda to work in the neighbouring gold-fields.[2] Under the control of the Buna chiefs production of gold may have increased, but in all probability the Lobi had already extracted gold earlier. Indeed, it is quite possible that the Dagomba founders of the Buna and Wa dynasties were attracted to this area by the prospects of the gold. If an active trade in gold had existed prior to the foundation of the kingdoms of Buna and Wa, then the Wanagara, the ubiquitous traders in gold, may have already been in the region of Wa before the arrival of the chiefs.

The traditions say nothing about the relations between these early Muslims and the chiefs before the arrival of the first imam, Yaʿumaru. The latter, however, was introduced before the Wa-Na by the *yarna* of Nasa. Yaʿumaru, like the Nasa Muslims, was of the Taraore patronymic group. He was a learned Muslim, carrying with him the high prestige of Dia, whence he is said to have come.[3] Dia is described by Marty as 'la métropole islamique du Macina . . . la cité sainte et lettrée'.[4] It is said of Yaʿumaru that he 'came with the teaching of Islam'.[5] Although not the first Muslim, Imam Yaʿumaru is credited with introducing Islam as a religious force to Wa.

Arriving in the region of Wa, Yaʿumaru was introduced before the Wa-Na by the *yarna* of Nasa. Here again is a pattern known from Dagomba and Mamprusi, comprising two phases in the planting of Islam. Early Muslims who had come to the area for trade prepared the ground for a more intensive Islamic influence.

Wa, however, is different from Dagomba and Mamprusi in that both Muslim groups, the forerunners and those who followed, were

[1] Tait's manuscripts, text A.

[2] Labouret, 1931, p. 22; Person, 1964, p. 330.

[3] 'The History of the Kings and Imams of Wa', by Karamoro Fanta Siḍḍīq, IAS/AR-151.

[4] Marty, 1920, ii. 163–4. Ibn-Baṭṭūṭa (1920, iv. 179) described Dia as an autonomous Muslim town in the mid-fourteenth century.

[5] IAS/AR-152.

Wangara. In Dagomba, Hausa Muslims superseded the Wangara, leaving the latter in the shadow. In Wa, the *yarna*'s group together with the imam's group became integrated into the social and political life of the kingdom. In Dagomba, the *yarna* lost his status as 'the chief of the Muslims', while the *yarna* at Wa is still regarded as the head of the community, and he is known also as *Shaykh al-Wangara.*

In Wa, the Hausa Muslims are a small minority only, and the community is predominantly Wangara. The Wala Muslims were in contact with Dyula communities to the west; Kong having been the celebrated centre of Islamic learning. In the first half of the nineteenth century Imam Saʿīd of Wa went to Kong. On his return he infused a new spirit of learning at Wa, and he is regarded as a *mujaddid*, a restorer of Islam.[1]

The Muslim community of Wa presents an interesting case for the distinction, noted earlier, between the Voltaic zone of Islam (comprising Gonja and the Mossi-Dagomba states) and the Dyula zone, physically divided by the Black Volta river.[2] In its origin, style, scholastic genealogies, and other characteristics, the Wa community is part of the Dyula zone. Yet, unlike the Dyula, west of the Black Volta, the Wala Muslims have adopted the local language and have been integrated into the state, in the way typical of the Voltaic zone. In Buna, just across the river, the Muslims speak their own Dyula dialect, and retain their own ethnic and cultural identity *vis-à-vis* their neighbours. The chiefs of Buna claim Dagomba origin, but they became culturally assimilated in the local Kulanga, and lost all affinity to Dagomba. On the other hand, Wa remained historically as well as culturally part of the Mossi-Dagomba group of states. It had, in common with these states, the aptitude for integrating the Muslims.

When the Dagomba founders of the Wa kingdom came to the area they settled among the Dagaba peoples speaking the Mole-Dagbane dialect of an earlier migration.[3] Some of the Dagaba became subjects of the rulers of Wa, while others remained outside the kingdom. Yet even the Dagaba within the kingdom have not been fully integrated, as was seen by Dr. J. Goody:

In Wa there is a structural dichotomy between the chiefly lineages of the later invasion and the commoner clans who had come first and expelled or

[1] 'History of the Muslims in Wa', by al-ḥājj Ṣiḍḍīq Taraore, the Friday imam of Wa, IAS/AR-18.

[2] See above, p. 13.

[3] The traditions of the two migrations are told in IAS/AR-152.

absorbed the Lobi-speaking peoples. The names *Wala* and *Dagaba* conceptualize this cleavage from the actor's point of view. Although all the inhabitants of the area under the dominion of the state of Wa refer to themselves as *Wala* in opposition to *non-Wala*, the members of the commoner clans are spoken of as *Dagaba* by the dominant group. I have also heard them referred to as *Black Wala*, but it is not so readily applied to themselves by the politically inferior clans. The names *Wala* and *Dagaba* also refer to the distinction between Muslim and Pagan, which in some contexts is quite independent, although the chiefly lineages or the *White Wala* are in general Muslim. People outside the orbit of the state of Wa refer to themselves as *Dagaba*. In this area no pejorative significance is attached to its use.[1]

In Wa, as in the other Middle Volta states, the chiefs occupy a central position between the other two estates; the commoners and the Muslims. Peculiar to Wa, however, is the tendency to regard the chiefs as Muslims. 'At the present day', a British commissioner wrote in the 1910s, 'all the Wala chiefs and men of any standing at all in the country follow Mohammedanism, while the poorer classes remain pagans.'[2] Yet the situation was probably not as simple as that, for even in 1916 the Muslims complained that Wa-Na Dangana Tahuna (1908–19) had sent away Muslims who had come to pray for him in Ramaḍān.[3] Chiefs in Wa, a respectable Muslim elder said, had for a long time been Muslims only in name. The first real Muslim, he added, was Na Saidu Takora, the Wa-Na deposed by the British in 1896.

It is likely that Islamic influence on the chiefly estate increased in the second half of the last century. Chiefs succeed to the paramountcy of Wa from the three 'gate'-villages of Busa, Sing, and Pirisi. At Busa the first imam, said also to have been the first resident Muslim, was appointed not long before Babatu's raid on Wa in the late 1880s.[4] If Muslims did not live in the 'gate'-villages before, Islamic influence had reached the chiefs there indirectly only, through visits by Muslims from Wa, when attending state ceremonies, or after accession to the paramountcy.

Muslims now living in villages east of Wa settled there only three generations ago. They left Wa, with 'Grunshi' slaves bought from the Zaberma, to cultivate land in the villages.[5]

This scanty evidence may suggest that until quite recently, less than

[1] Goody, 1954, pp. 14–15. [2] Read, unpublished manuscript.

[3] Wa District Records, NAG, Accra, 119/54.

[4] Information at Busa, where the present imam (Adam) is the great-grandson of the first imam, 'Uthmān.

[5] Information at Guropisi, Bellung, and Tamina.

a century ago, Wala chiefs had not attained a degree of islamization higher than that of chiefs in the other Middle Volta states. However, the smallness of the state and the vitality of the Muslims community contributed to the influence of the Muslims in the cultural, social, and political life.[1] Chiefs and Muslims, both representing ideas and institutions alien to the local segmentary society, found mutual support in each other. The influential status of the Muslim, and their high proportion in the town's population, gave Wa its character as a stronghold of Islam amid pagan stateless peoples.

(*b*) *The Kantosi*

North of the organized states of Gonja, Wa, Dagomba, and Mamprusi, and south of the Mossi kingdom, several stateless tribes occupy the country astride the border between Ghana and Upper Volta. These tribes are referred to by the Dagomba and the Mamprusi as 'Gurense'. The Nankanse, and probably also the Kasena, willingly accept this name, but other tribes to whom it is often applied—such as the Isala, the Awuna, or the Tallensi—reject it 'as having a disparaging and derogatory significance. *Gurense* (*angl.* Grunshi) is very much the equivalent of the word "Kaffir"—unbelievers, eaters of dogs—as bestowed by the Mohammedans on those who do not follow the Prophet'.[2] For the purpose of the present study, looking at these peoples from the Islamic point of view, the term 'Grunshi' will be used. This may be justified also in the absence of any other term to designate all these tribes, and because it has so often been used by modern authors as well as in pre-colonial European sources.[3]

The 'Grunshi' together with other stateless tribes may be regarded as more pagans than the non-Muslims among the Dagomba, Mamprusi, or Wala. No Islamic elements have penetrated their culture, and they even rejected such aspects of civilization, associated in this area with Islam, as clothing and circumcision. Because of the absence of chiefs among these peoples, Muslims could not find the more communicative element in the local population, as they did in the organized states. Muslim individuals or small groups who had settled among stateless peoples eventually abandoned Islam.

[1] Reports of the administration show the involvement of Muslims in the political affairs of Wa (Wa District Records, 1915–46, NAG, Accra, 119/54, 134/54, 136/54).

[2] Rattray, 1932, i. 232; also pp. 374, 398, 538.

[3] Bowdich, 1819, p. 208; Koelle, 1854, pp. 6–7; Barth, 1857, iv. 551.

At least three such cases have been recorded among the Konkomba. Demon is one of the outpost chiefdoms of Dagomba in Konkomba land, where the chief and the elders are Dagomba, but the majority of the villagers are Konkomba. A tradition recorded from a drummer at Demon says that a Muslim settled at Demon at the same time that the *yarna* of Sabali and Kamshe-Na came to Dagomba. The people of Demon gave this Muslim a wife. His descendants lived there with their maternal family and eventually abandoned Islam. They kept sacred their ancestor's praying-place, calling it *jingli*, 'a mosque'. To this day they treat it as a shrine, where libations of milk (*sic*) are poured and chickens slaughtered when the aid of this Muslim's god is invoked. Similar traces of Islam are reported from the village of Yaoyili, near the Togolese border, where there are remains of an old mosque, and the village chief is supposed to fast in *Ramaḍān* and not to drink alcohol.[1] Among the Konkomba of Namon (in Togo), people, not Muslim any more, worship a praying-place their Muslim ancestor left behind.[2] Another example of apostasy, this time among the Brong, has been recorded at Njau, three miles south-west of Nsawkaw. The people there claim to be of Gonja origin, and say they were formerly Muslims, but abandoned Islam as they changed, to be like their Brong neighbours. Only one old man, referred to as *adiman* (*al-imām*) still prays. They buried the Koran, inherited from their ancestors, and erected a shrine above it to be worshipped.

Were the Gonja ancestors of Njau really Muslims, or were they 'islamized' Gonja only? The same problem arises in the case of some clans among the Isala who claim origin from Mamprusi. Our ancestors, they say, were long ago Mohammedans and circumcised, but 'we no longer circumcise or practise Mohammedanism'.[3] Whether real Muslims or 'islamized' Mamprusi, the fact remains that once people became assimilated in the land of 'Grunshi', Islamic practices were discontinued.

The 'Grunshi', however, have their own Muslims, known as *Kantosi*, a name said to have been given to them by the Dagomba and the Mamprusi. The Awuna call them *Yare* or *Yara* (of the same origin as *Yarse*), and the Isala call them *Nyele*.[4] These names may be used for

[1] Information from Demon-Na Bukari.

[2] Information at Bapure (Togo), where another branch of the same family survived as Muslims, probably because they lived on a trade-route.

[3] Rattray, 1932, ii. 472–3, 476.

[4] Tauxier, 1824, pp. 119–20. Rattray (1932, ii. 473, n. 1) says: 'In Challe, Samtie, Gyigyen, Sakalo, Dolbezan, Halembalea, Katoa, and Kosale, *Mallamai* are

all Muslims, and particularly for the Mande Muslims. The latter call both the Kantosi and the Wala Muslims by the hyphened name of *Dagara-Dyula* (that is, the Dyula who settled among the Dagara, more correctly Dagaba). Indeed, the Kantosi often refer to themselves as *Wala*, but the Wala call the Kantosi *Samunu*. The names are confusing, but may become more significant when the history of the Kantosi is reviewed. For their early history, reference should be made to the history of Wa, as narrated in a manuscript written in 1922:[1]

The first among them [the Wala Muslims] came from Mande. . . . They divided into three; some settled at the village of Palwogho, others at Vise and Nasa. Those who settled at Palwogho were of three clans: Senu, Dao, and Juna. Those who settled at Vise belonged to one clan, Kunate. Those who settled at Nasa also belonged to one clan, Taraore. These were the first Muslims in the country of Wa.

[Then came the second group of Muslims with Yaʿumaru the first imam.] The early Muslims, those of Palwogho and Vise, were involved in an internal dispute. They fought each other, and scattered. Some of them moved to Wa, others went to the country of Kassena Grunshi.

Among those who came to Wa, Kunate, Juna, and Dao are in the Kabanya ward, while Sambaleyiri is the ward of the Senu.

All the Muslims of Palwogho and Vise, those now in 'Grunshi' land (the Kantosi) and those at Wa, are called *Samunu* by the Wala. *Samunu*, it is said, means 'the people of the east', because these people had lived east of Wa. It is in this direction, presumably, that the sites of Palwogho and Vise are to be looked for.

All the patronymics—Kunate, Dao, Senu, and Juna—mentioned in the History of Wa (quoted above) for the people of Palwogho and Vise occur also among the Kantosi. There are, however, also Taraore among the Kantosi, suggesting that the division of the 'clans' between Nasa and the other two places was not as clear as is related by the written tradition. Indeed, in Nasa itself the imam is a Kunate.[2] In the two largest Kantosi communities—To and Koho—the imams are also Kunate. One may suggest that the Kunate was the 'clan' of the *'ulamā'* among these groups.

The Wa History (AR/152), in counting the patronymic groups, reflects the present composition of Wa. All the groups now at Wa are

to be found; the Isala in fact sometimes refer to the inhabitants of these towns as *Yalea* (Mohammaden scribes)'.

[1] IAS/AR-152.

[2] I. Wilks, personal communication.

mentioned, but there are other patronymic groups among the Kantosi not now represented at Wa, and therefore not mentioned by the History. Kulibali, for example, is one of them. That the Kulibali had been with the Kantosi before they left the region of Wa is suggested by the existence of a Kantosi group at Walwale of the Kulibali patronymic group. The title of its headman is *Vise-Naba*, undoubtedly associated with the old Vise of the Wala-Kantosi. It is said that their ancestor Wuni set out from Wa and waged war as far as Walwale. In Mamprusi he helped the Nayiri in war, and was appointed, in reward, chief of all the Kantosi in Mamprusi.[1] Other Kantosi also assumed offices in Mamprusi: a Kantosi holds the office of *kpanalana*, 'the custodian of the spear';[2] 'the chieftainesses of the women', *magajia*, in the two principal towns—Gambaga and Walwale—are two Kantosi sisters.[3] Some wandering Kantosi were appointed imams in Mamprusi and Dagomba.[4]

The Kantosi in 'Grunshi' land are concentrated mainly in the territory of one tribe, called Awuna or Nouna.[5] Fewer Kantosi live among the Builsa, Kasena, and Isala. The Kantosi are scattered in many villages, two or three compounds in the margins of a village. Dispersed as they are, the Kantosi say that they always had one important centre. Judging from the present one at To, this centre accommodated a considerable number of Kantosi. Separated from the local Awuna village, the Kantosi's section may be regarded as a village in itself. The first such centre remembered was at Dabiu (five miles north-west of Leo); it then moved to Nabon (thirty miles north of Leo), and later to the present centre at To (twenty-five miles north of Leo).[6] In the middle of the nineteenth century, when al-ḥājj Maḥmūd of Wahabu started his *jihād*, the Kantosi centre was at Nabon. As this was their second centre, after Dabiu, it is likely that the Kantosi had already been in 'Grunshi' land earlier.

It is difficult to tell when the Kantosi came to 'Grunshi' land from the region of Wa. They must have stayed in their former residence long enough to adopt Wale as their first language, which they still

[1] Information from the Vise-Naba at Walwale. It is significant that Kantosi Muslims at Wa knew nothing about this Vise-Naba.

[2] Information from Kpanalana Yūsuf at Nalerigu.

[3] Mrs. Drucker-Brown, personal communication.

[4] Imam Ya'qūb at Nabari (see above, p. 137), and Imam Muṣṭafā at Savelugu.

[5] Awuna is the name used by Rattray (1932, ii. 525); Nouna is used by the French: *Carte ethnique d'Haute Volta*, dressée par G. Le Moal, *IFAN*, Ouagadougou, n.d. Tauxier (1912) calls this tribe Nounouma.

[6] Information at To and Koho.

speak. That a later rather than an earlier date is to be preferred is suggested also by the strong relations which still exist between the people of Palwogho and Vise in their dispersion, in 'Grunshi' land and at Wa. Genealogies recorded are of little use, as these vary from three to seven generations back to the departure from Palwogho and Vise. This event, however, may tentatively be dated to the eighteenth century.

The three successive Kantosi centres, as well as other smaller Kantosi communities, were lined along an important trade-route from Kumasi and Buipe, over Boromo and Safane, to Jenne.[1] The Kantosi were engaged in a short-distance trade in salt and kola.[2] Their commercial activities covered, therefore, that tract of country between the Marka and the Dafing in the north and the Muslim communities of the Middle Volta states in the south. One wonders whether an internal dispute in the region of Wa was all that caused them to migrate from their former residence, or whether they also responded to the need for small trading communities in 'Grunshi' land. If so, their dispersion was not one single act, but a longer process during which Wala Muslims moved northward.

In their former residence, in the region of Wa, the Kantosi lived among stateless tribes. This past experience may have prepared them for residence among the 'Grunshi'. The Kantosi traded with their 'Grunshi' neighbours, and also rendered them some religious services (amulets, charms, and prayers). This contact, however, has never been institutionalized as in the organized states. For the Kantosi it was not a question of integrating into the local society, but rather one of survival as Muslims in an area so unfavourable to Islam. The 'Grunshi' tolerated the Kantosi as peaceful traders and residents, but the latter were ready to bring about a radical change in the position of Islam in that area. In the second half of the nineteenth century they became involved in two militant movements led by Muslims: the *jihād* of al-ḥājj Maḥmūd of Wahabu and the raids of the Zaberma.

The Zaberma raided 'Grunshi' land itself, and this will be dealt with later. Al-ḥājj Maḥmūd of Wahabu fought his *jihād* in Dafina, within the Black Volta upper bend, which is outside our area. Yet the involvement of the Kantosi in his wars together with his link with the Zaberma call for a brief study of this *jihād*.[3]

[1] Route described in manuscript, No. 8, Dupuis, 1824, cxxxi–cxxxii.

[2] Tauxier, 1912, p. 415.

[3] Tauxier (1912, pp. 410–11) studied the traditions of this *jihād* at the beginning

The Muslim Dafing and Marka lived for a long time in peace among the pagan Bobo and Ko, 'tribes without rulers'. Dafina is an extension of the more islamized region of Jenne, on the route leading south-eastward to the Middle Volta Basin. It is already part of what is known in our area as 'Wangara'. Safane was a celebrated centre of Islamic learning in this area.[1]

Maḥmūd was born at Douroula (twenty miles north-east of Dedougou), whither his father had come from a village near Jenne. Maḥmūd studied with his father, Sidi Muḥammad Karantao,[2] and later also at Safane. During his pilgrimage, it is said, he vowed to fight for the cause of Islam. Back from Mecca, after his father's death, he stayed for some time at Douroula and Safane before departing with his students to establish his own school away from the Muslim scholars of Safane, with whom he was in disagreement. He settled first at Poura (thirteen miles south-east of Boromo), and then at Dumakoro, eight miles away. It was from Dumakoro, facing the pagan town of Boromo, that al-ḥājj Maḥmūd launched his *jihād*, claiming that the pagans wanted to drive him away.[3]

When preparing for the *jihād*, al-ḥājj Maḥmūd sent to Muslims in different directions, calling upon them to join him. Some Marka-Dafing Muslims from villages around Safane responded. A group of Muslims from Ouahigouya came under the leadership of Yaḥyā Gira, father of the present chief of Boromo. Three hundred Kantosi (or Dagara-Dyula as they are known by the Marka) came from Taslima and Bredie, led by Mahamma Dagari.[4] Taslima, it is said, was the Muslim name for the Kantosi settlement at Nabon.

According to genealogies collected at Boromo, Wahabu, and Koho, those who joined the *jihād* were either fathers or grandfathers of the informants. Yaḥyā Gira, for example, one of the first supporters of al-ḥājj Maḥmūd and the first Muslim chief of Boromo,

of the century, when people who had taken part in the *jihād* were still alive. Tauxier's account has been collated with four Arabic manuscripts (IAS/AR-66, 77, 348, and 349) of recent composition. I have collected oral information at Boromo, Wahabu, Koho, Douroula, and Safane.

[1] Early in the nineteenth century Safane is described as 'a great town with a Friday-mosque' (Dupuis, 1824, manuscript No. 8).

[2] Two *ijāzas* (IAS/AR-232 and 339) include al-ḥājj Maḥmūd in its scholastic genealogies, and in both he appears as the disciple of his father.

[3] Dupuis (1824, p. xcv) says: 'it is usual for the traveller to stop several days at a city of some magnitude, called Borma from the island on which it is seated.'

[4] The Arabic manuscript IAS/AR-66 tells the story of the *jihād* from the view-point of the Dagara-Dyula (Kantosi).

died only in 1914.[1] It is likely, therefore, that the *jihād* started in the middle of the nineteenth century.[2]

The *jihād* started by attacking Boromo; the town was conquered, and its Ko inhabitants driven away. Boromo, re-named Dar al-Salam, was given to Yaḥyā Gira and his Mossi followers, joined by some of the Dagara-Dyula (Kantosi). Al-ḥājj then conquered villages along the river, due north of Boromo. Coming back to the neighbourhood of Boromo, he expelled the Bobo of M'pehom, a nearby village, changed its name to Wahabu (*wahaba 'llāh*), and made his residence there. At Koho, two miles from Wahabu, al-ḥājj Maḥmūd settled his Dagara-Dyula followers, and the village was named *Shukr li-'llāhi.*

Al-ḥājj Maḥmūd was succeeded by his nephew, Karamoro Mukhtār, who carried on the *jihād*.[3] Mukhtār first tried to conquer the region south of Boromo; he reached Diebugu, where he encountered firm resistance and retreated to Wahabu. By that time the peoples conquered by Al-ḥājj within the river bend renewed their resistance. Unable to reconquer this area himself, Mukhtār joined forces with the Zaberma leader Babatu, who came up from Sati. The two armies advanced north, destroying villages on their way. But just before Safane they encountered a united front of Bobo, Ko, and Awuna which defeated the Muslim force. Babatu retreated during the night across the Volta river back to Sati.[4] Mukhtār retreated to Wahabu, but was ambushed and beaten by the Marka of Da, a village between Safane and Wahabu. Thus ended the military activities of Mukhtār. When Binger visited Wahabu, in 1888, the state founded by al-ḥājj Maḥmūd included only the villages of Boromo, Wahabu, Koho, and Nouna, all inhabited by his followers. Tauxier says that when the French occupied the country, about thirty villages of Bobo were paying annual tribute in millet to the chief of Wahabu.[5]

The Marka attack on Mukhtār was inspired by a Muslim, and

[1] 'Carnet du chef de canton Boromo' in the files of the *Boromo cercle* office, written after 1932 (when the present chief already held office).

[2] Tauxier (loc. cit.) dates the beginning of the *jihād* to 1840. He may have relied on Binger (1892, i. 416) who said that the *jihād* had been launched about fifty years before his visit (1888).

[3] Mukhtār is sometimes referred to as al-ḥājj Maḥmūd's son, but Binger (loc. cit.) who met Mukhtār says that he was Maḥmūd's nephew. It is possible that al-ḥājj Maḥmūd was still alive *c.* 1874, when Mūsā of Sati sought his blessing before the battle against the Dagomba (see below, pp. 152, 154).

[4] This episode is recorded also in the traditions about the Zaberma (Tamakloe, 1931, p. 51; Krause manuscripts, No. 30).

[5] Binger, loc. cit.; Tauxier, loc. cit.

reflects the attitude of the old Muslim communities of Dafina to the *jihād*. Al-ḥājj had some Marka among his followers, and some Marka villages, like his natal village, Douroula, were his allies. But most Marka Muslims seem to have resented the *jihād*. Informants at Safane blamed al-ḥājj Maḥmūd for fighting Muslims and pagans indiscriminately.[1] Birifor, where Muslims were the majority, was attacked and devastated. The *jihād* interfered with the long peaceful co-existence of the Muslims with their pagan neighbours. At Bobo-Dyulaso and Kotedougou Binger met Muslim familes from Dafina, refugees of the *jihād*.[2]

The *jihād* of al-ḥājj Maḥmūd was one of the nineteenth-century Islamic militant movements. Although the traditions say that he was inspired during his pilgrimage, there is little doubt that Maḥmūd was influenced by the *jihād* of Shekhu Ahmadu in Massina, which had reached the northern end of the Black Volta upper bend. Within the river bend al-ḥājj Maḥmūd tried to extend the frontiers of *Dar al-Islām* by exploiting the relative weakness of the stateless tribes. His limited military resources had been enough to break through, but as the local peoples united under his pressure, their resistance put an end to al-ḥājj's military exploits. Although his original ambitions were not realized, and only a few prisoners became converted, al-ḥājj Maḥmūd succeeded in establishing a miniature Muslim state amid pagan stateless tribes, an enclave of *Dar al-Islām*. It survived within its narrow frontiers through the policy of colonization pursued by al-ḥājj Maḥmūd. He fortified his conquest by settling his warriors in a cluster of villages.

The inhabitants of these villages still represent the three elements of al-ḥājj's followers: Boromo is inhabited by Yarse-Mossi and some Dagara-Dyula; Wahabu by Marka-Dafing; and Koho is a Dagara-Dyula (Kantosi) settlement.[3] Three groups of Muslims of Mande origin (Wangara), with differing histories, joined together on the

[1] Information at Safane. According to the Arabic manuscript IAS/AR-77, there was tension between al-ḥājj Maḥmūd and the Muslims of Safane, going back to the period before his pilgrimage, when Muslims abused him by refuting his evidence on the first moon of Ramaḍān.

[2] Binger, 1892, i. 369, 380, 416. Binger says that these families left Dafina about fifteen years before his visit.

[3] Binger (1892, i. 416) referred to the people of Koho as 'Mande du Dagomba'. Tauxier (1912, p. 410) called them 'Dagara-Dyula from Wa'. Elsewhere (ibid., pp. 441–2) Tauxier called the Kantosi 'Yarse of the Grunshi' who came from Mossi. The author of IAS/AR-77 made al-ḥājj Maḥmūd pass through Wa, in order to explain his Wala (Dagara-Dyula) followers.

fringes of 'Wangara' to launch a *jihād*. Of these three, the Kantosi came the longest way, from the Niger southward to Wa; then again north to 'Grunshi' land and to Koho.

(*c*) *The Zaberma*

The organized states regarded the stateless tribes as fair game for slave-raiding. Slaves made up the main part of the tribute Gonja and Dagomba had to pay to Ashanti.[1] Occasional slave-raids were, therefore, a common feature in the history of this area. Raids came upon the victims like a storm which passed away, leaving scars which had hardly healed before the next raid. The situation became worse in the last quarter of the nineteenth century, when instead of occasional raids from the outside, Zaberma warriors carried out a series of continuous slave-raids. Their activities covered the country from Wa and Daboya in the south to the frontiers of Mossi in the north; from the Black Volta in the west to the Red Volta in the east.

A detailed history of the Zaberma in this area is too long to be included in this study; here only the Islamic aspects of this history will be dealt with.

Zabermawa (*angl.* Zaberma) is the Hausa name for the Jerma (or Zerma) people speaking a Songhay dialect in the region of Niamey and Dosso on the banks of the Niger (the republic of Niger). For many centuries the Zaberma resisted Islam, and remained pagan. In the first half of the nineteenth century they stood up against an invasion of the Fulani of Sokoto and Gwandu, in their attempt to spread the *jihād* westward. From 1830 to 1849 the Fulani were victorious. Then the scales turned; a successful revolt of the Zaberma, aided by people from Kebbi and Dendi, drove the Fulani out of the country about 1860.[2]

The Muslim Fulani were finally expelled, but it was during these forty years of fighting against the Muslim threat that Islam made progress among the Zaberma. The Zaberma, who had been completely pagan when they came to that region in the sixteenth century, had become predominantly Muslim by the middle of the nineteenth century. The new religion, however, did not completely destroy the old one; local beliefs are still alive in the culture of the Zaberma.[3]

[1] See above, p. 41.
[2] Rouch, 1953, pp. 226–9; Périé et Sellier, 1950; Barth, 1857, iv. 203, v. 275.
[3] Rouch, 1953, p. 229.

The confrontation with the Fulani caused an upheaval among the Zaberma. Their land devastated and themselves islamized, the Zaberma began to leave their country, some for trade, others for adventure. In the second half of the nineteenth century Zaberma warriors appeared as mercenaries in the service of chiefs in Kotokoli, in northern Dahomey, and in Dagomba.[1]

A group of Zaberma came to Dagomba to sell horses, during the reign of Na Abdulai (d. 1876). As payment was delayed they waited there, until they met a Zaberma Mallam, Alfa Hanno, who became their leader.[2] Being idle, the Zaberma were invited by Adam, chief of Karaga, to join the Dagomba slave-raids in 'Grunshi' land. Starting as mercenaries the Zaberma decided to leave the service of the Dagomba and to stay behind in 'Grunshi' land. There they offered their services to local petty chiefs in their internal disputes, and in this way established themselves firmly in the country.

Alfa Hanno led the Zaberma in 'Grunshi' land for about four years.[3] By the time he died the Zaberma power had reached a stage which alarmed the Dagomba, who still regarded themselves as masters of the Zaberma warriors. Andani, son of Na Yaʿqūba, then chief of Savelugu, set out to stop the Zaberma activities, and to bring them back under Dagomba authority. It was regarded as a suitable opportunity because the old leader, Alfa Hanno, was dead, and his successor Gazari had not yet consolidated his leadership. In the first engagements the Dagomba were victorious, and the Zaberma had to retreat. But this initial success turned into defeat when the Zaberma recruited the support of a local chief, Mūsā of Sati. Na Andani retreated to Dagomba, leaving behind many casualties and captives. Not long after—one tradition says two years[4]—the Ya-Na Abdulai died and Andani succeeded his brother to the paramountcy. As Na Abdulai's death is safely dated to 1876,[5] one may calculate dates

[1] On the Zaberma in Kotokoli, see below, p. 179; in Dahomey, Cornevin, 1962*b*, p. 64. On adventures of Zaberma warriors as far west as the Ivory Coast, see Rouch et Bernus, 1959.

[2] Krause manuscripts, No. 30; reproduced in Olderogge, 1960, pp. 175–6 (translated by T. Muṣṭafā at IAS, Legon). This account was written while the Zaberma were still raiding in 'Grunshi' land.

[3] Mallam Abu (Hausa manuscript at S.O.A.S., London) suggests two years; Tamakloe (1931, p. 46) six years; the Zaberma headman at Yendi (in an interview) said three years.

[4] Mallam Abu, op. cit.

[5] R. Johnson was sent by Dr. Gouldsbury to Yendi. He commenced his way back to the coast in July 1876, after he had been detained for six weeks, as the roads had been closed because of the death of the king of Yendi. (D.C. Accra to

back; Alfa Hanno died *c.* 1874, and the Zaberma adventures in 'Grunshi' land, independent of the Dagomba, started probably *c.* 1870.[1]

The Zaberma built up their power in 'Grunshi' land gradually. In the earlier stage they depended to a large extent on local chiefs. At first they were called to fight in the cause of such chiefs as those of Dolbizan and Nebiewale, and later it was another chief, Mūsā of Sati, who saved them from defeat. These and some other chiefs were of the Isala, among whom a new pattern of authority emerged, presumably in the nineteenth century.[2] This is explained by Rattray:

> The word used for chief in the Isalen language tells its own story. *Koro* . . . meant, originally, any man of wealth or substance in a clan. Anyone with more cattle or larger farms or more sons and kindred than his neighbours was a *koro*. As such, he was accorded a certain respect and occupied a position of minor authority among his neighbours. A *koro* had not, however, any administrative, executive, or religious power. All such were vested in the hands of the *Tinteintina* [*Tengadana* in other languages]. . . . The jumbling-up of clans, and the germ of conception of territorial, as opposed to clan groupings, had no doubt begun to manifest itself shortly before the advent of Europeans. Men of wealth and outstanding ability had already arisen in some of the clan settlements, and in the turmoil and chaos resulting from the depredations of the Zaberma, mixed clans had sometimes rallied around such natural leaders for protection and leadership.[3]

The emergence of such small polities could also have been stimulated by the trade-route from Wagadugu to Wa, which passed Isala settlements where some of the early chiefs appeared.[4] The new pattern brought new tensions, not only within the groups, between Earth-priest and secular chiefs, but also between two claimants to a chieftaincy or two neighbouring chiefs competing over spheres of influence. Such tensions caused disputes in which the Zaberma warriors were called to intervene.[5]

Ag. Colonial Secretary, 28 August 1876, enclosure in a dispatch to Lord Carnarvon, PRO, CO. 96/118, No. 186.)

[1] Tamakloe (1931, p. 45) says the Zaberma joined the Dagomba expedition of 1858, but this is too early a date for an event in Na Abdulai's reign, who succeeded only in the 1860s (see below, p. 198). Tauxier (1912, p. 183) dates the beginning of the Zaberma raids as an independent force to 1872.

[2] This is suggested from lists of local chiefs given by Rattray, 1932, i. 468–71.

[3] Ibid., p. 486.

[4] Cf. Goody, 1956, p. 13.

[5] In Nebiewale the Zaberma were called to beat a claimant to the chieftaincy. Other disputes—Dolbizan v. Navarro, Pien v. Kwapo, Prata v. Tasian—were between two neighbours (Tamakloe, 1931, pp. 46–47).

Significantly, the emergence of the small chieftaincies gave new access to Islamic influence. Mūsā, chief of Sati, had been a Muslim before his contact with the Zaberma. Indeed, he may have supported the Zaberma because he regarded them as fighting for the cause of Islam. The concept of a *jihād* was known to Mūsā of Sati because there is evidence to suggest that he had been converted by al-ḥājj Maḥmūd of Wahabu.[1] At a certain stage in his career al-ḥājj Maḥmūd extended his influence over parts of 'Grunshi' land: an Arabic manuscript from Boromo says that al-ḥājj advanced to Leo and then to Sati,[2] whereas Binger heard from the chief of Koumoulou (Coumbili, about forty-seven miles east-north-east of Leo) that he had obtained the protection of 'le marabout de Ouahabou'.[3] Mūsā's contacts with Wahabu continued, for it is said that before the decisive battle against the Dagomba (*c.* 1874), Mūsā had sent to seek the blessing of al-ḥājj Maḥmūd.[4]

The Zaberma had reason to be most grateful to Mūsā of Sati, because to him they owed their survival in 'Grunshi' land. A treaty of alliance was made between Mūsā and the Zaberma leader, Gazari. The latter withdrew from Sati and pitched his camp at Kassane (about fourteen miles north-east of Tumu). Mūsā of Sati took part in some of Gazari's raids.[5] The alliance of the Zaberma with Mūsā was broken when Babatu, Gazari's successor, attacked Sati and killed Mūsā. Babatu transferred his headquarters to Sati, which had already been fortified by Mūsā. This was shortly before 1887.[6]

According to Tamakloe, Sati was attacked because Mūsā had supported Ali Giwa, one of the Zaberma captains, in a dispute with Babatu.[7] Another version says that Mūsā provoked Babatu by building a wall around his village with the intention of getting rid of the Zaberma.[8] Before the attack, Mūsā sent a Kantosi Mallam to Babatu in an attempt to prevent the war. Mūsā mentioned his contract with Gazari but Babatu denied any obligation.[9] Babatu was a more ruthless

[1] This was said explicitly by one informant only, Imam Ṭāhir of To. Savonnet (1956) says: 'Moussa Kodoi, fils de chef du village Sissala de Sati, récemment islamisé à Ouahabou. . . .' That Mūsā had already been a chief's son is attested also by Tamakloe (1931, p. 47), saying that he 'was then acting as chief for his senile father Boi'.

[2] IAS/AR-348.

[3] Binger, 1892, ii. 39.

[4] Mallam Abu, op. cit.

[5] Ibid.

[6] Krause (1887), passing through Sati in February 1887, found the Zaberma already there. Binger (1892, i. 428) says that the Zaberma conquered Sati not long before his visit (1888).

[7] Tamakloe, 1931, p. 54.

[8] Savonnet, 1956.

[9] Mallam Abu (op. cit.), who generally sympathizes with Babatu.

warrior than both Alfa Hanno and Gazari, and it was under his leadership that the Zaberma attacked Muslims. Mūsā of Sati was one example, Wa was another.

Shortly after the arrival of the Zaberma in 'Grunshi' land, Mahama, son of Imam Siḍḍīq of Wa, came to see them. Alfa Hanno sent a cow and two slaves with him to Wa, as a gift of friendship. Later the people of Wa sent fifty-seven guns to the Zaberma.[1] Following the cordial relations between Wa and the Zaberma, the two co-operated in a raid on the Dagaba. During this raid the Wa-Na's son, Bazore, quarrelled with Babatu, left the raid, and returned to Wa. Babatu went on raiding the Dagaba. Some of the attacked villagers sought refuge in Wa, and Babatu demanded the surrender of these refugees. This the Wa-Na refused, and Babatu decided to attack Wa. The Wala, including their Muslims, set out to meet him at Nasa, but were routed. 'Babatu then attacks Wa and burns it, is fired on by a lot of people who are occupying the mosque. The mosque is burnt, which gives Babatu a bad name with many Mohammedans in the Hinterland.'[2] Many men and women, including Muslims, were taken prisoner, others sought refuge at Buna.

On his way back from Wa, Babatu turned to Walembele, which accommodated an important Muslim community, one of the very few among the Isala. Walembele was on the trade-route from Mossi and Dafina to Wa. Its Muslims, of the Sisse patronymic group, came to Wa via Kong and Bole, and thence moved to settle in two villages: Walembele (among the Isala), and Nandaw Wala (among the Dagaba).[3] At an earlier stage, Babatu spared Walembele after its Muslims had accepted his protection in return for tribute.[4] The chief of Walembele, it is said, refused to send his people to help Babatu in his attack on Wa. Babatu came to punish him, and made excessive demands which the Walembele people could not accept. Instead of replying they secretly evacuated the town, fleeing to Kundugu, about thirty miles away in the direction of Daboya. Babatu pursued them but was repelled.[5]

[1] A History of Wa in Hausa (IAS/AR-22).

[2] 'Report on Wa', by Captain Mackworth, 6 June 1898; enclosure 1 in No. 382, *African* (*West*), No. 549, PRO, CO. 879/52. Accounts of the attack on Wa, in Mallam Abu, op. cit.; Tamakloe, 1931, pp. 52–53; and from informants at Wa.

[3] They settled there four or five generations ago, probably in the early nineteenth century. Information at Walembele and Nandaw-Wala.

[4] Mallam Abu, op. cit.

[5] Tamakloe, 1931, p. 53. The Zaberma later returned to Kundungu when they intervened in the Civil War of Daboya (see above, pp. 71–72).

Hence, towards the end of his career Babatu came into conflict with the three Muslim elements—Mūsā of Sati, Wa, and Walembele—which had supported the Zaberma earlier. Only the Kantosi Muslims remained faithful to Babatu until the very end of his campaigns. Kantosi were among the Mallams of the Zaberma, others having been Hausa, Fulani, and Wangara.[1] Mallams offered prayers, were consulted to choose the appropriate day for a raid, and advocated prudence to the Zaberma warriors in the frequent internal disputes.[2]

Only a few Zaberma had initiated the raids in 'Grunshi' land, but these were soon joined by other fellow countrymen, by Hausa, and by other Muslims, who came to share the abundant booty. But all these were only a minority in the so-called Zaberma troops, which swelled by recruiting local people, some as volunteers, many as captives. Local people were promoted in the service of the Zaberma and reached the rank of lieutenants to the Zaberma captains. These local troops took part in raids on villages of their own peoples. It was only natural that there should be much discontent among these warriors, who felt that they could do little against their foreign superiors, the latter being horsemen and better armed. The growing discontent among the local troops exploded when one of the 'Grunshi' lieutenants, Amariya, having been himself maltreated, declared an open revolt against the Zaberma, in 1893 or 1894.[3]

Many of the 'Grunshi' in the Zaberma army joined Amariya, who had the support of most of the villages.[4] Babatu failed in his attempt to subdue the revolt, and a series of engagements between the Zaberma and the 'Grunshi' were inconclusive. In August 1896 Samori's son came east of the Black Volta, and tried to bring the two sides together for arbitration. But then news of the French arrival in Wagadugu reached Amariya. On 19 September 1896 Amariya signed a treaty of protectorate with the French, styling himself 'king of Grunshi'. Babatu had now to stand against a combined force of Amariya and the French. Babatu retreated southward, still raiding villages on his way, until he encountered the British at Yagaba. At the end of 1897 he withdrew to Dagomba, first in the British territory, and later in the

[1] Names of Mallams are mentioned in the Krause manuscripts (No. 30) and by Mallam Abu, op. cit.

[2] Mallam Abu, op. cit.

[3] Cf. Hébert, 1961, pp. 13–14. This is a reproduction of an article by H. Labouret, first published in *Renseignements Coloniaux*, 1925, pp. 341–55.

[4] Tauxier, 1912, p. 234.

German. There he settled at Yendi, where he died, and where descendants of his companions still live.[1]

Amariya settled at Leo, whence he tried to impose his rule as 'king of Grunshi' under the French protectorate. The French, in their turn, were at first interested in confirming Amariya's status as 'king', in order to validate their treaty with him, but later realized that he was not a 'king'. A native of Kanjaga of the Builsa tribe, Amariya had been captured by the Zaberma as a young boy. He grew up in the service of Gazari to become a commander in the Zaberma army.[2] Under the influence of the Zaberma he became a Muslim, and remained so until his death. Amariya's son, Ibrāhīm, is the present (1964) imam of Leo.

The main results of the Zaberma raids were devastation, depopulation, and loss of property, in particular livestock.[3] Another outcome of the Zaberma period was the beginning of the spread of Islam among the pagans of this area, and mainly among the Isala. Local recruits to the Zaberma troops learned to pray, but only the more important commanders among them became real Muslims. Others stopped praying once they went back to their villages. Thousands of people were sold as slaves by the Zaberma, and were taken to Mossi, Jerma, Wa, Ashanti, the coast, and elsewhere. In their slavery some of the captives came into contact with Islam, through their masters or neighbouring Muslim communities. When they came back to their villages some abandoned the new faith they had adopted, others remained Muslims.[4] These were among the first 'Grunshi' Muslims, whose number increased during the colonial period through service in the British auxiliary forces, and during seasonal migrations to the south.

Yagbon, headman of the Isala village of Gwolu (twenty-one miles

[1] Hébert, 1961, pp. 14–18; Captain Voulet, 1898; Chanoin, 1898; reports by British officers in *African* (*West*), No. 549, PRO, CO. 879/52.

[2] 'Fiche de Renseignement—Hamaria' and 'Histoire de Leo' in the archives of the 'Cercle de Leo'. Amariya was deposed from his 'kingship' in 1916. The British were busy collecting evidence about Amariya in January 1898 to prove that his claim over 'Grunshi' land was invalid (see enclosure 1 in No. 185, *African* (*West*), No. 549, PRO, CO. 879/52).

[3] Tauxier, 1912, pp. 59, 88, 94, 111, 139, 161, 347; Hilton, Ph.D. thesis, London, 1956.

[4] To mention only two examples: A Dagaba from Topari (near Lawra) was born at Sarabatenga (a Yarse village south of Wagadugu), where his father had been sold as slave; a man from the village of Nawia (about twenty-two miles north-east of Lawra) had been sold by the Zaberma to Buna, where he became a Muslim. See also Tauxier, 1912, pp. 332, 359.

north-west of Tumu), entered into alliance with the Zaberma through his neighbour, Mūsā of Sati. Yagbon was succeeded by his son, Tangia, who increased his power by taking under his protection neighbouring Isala clans. Tangia's brother, Mūsā, was sent to stay with the Zaberma, where he became a Muslim. Babatu's attack on Sati alienated Tangia from the Zaberma, and he hastened to build a wall around his village. Babatu, however, did not attack Gwolu. Tangia was succeeded by his Muslim brother, Mūsā, one of the first Muslim chiefs among the Isala.[1]

The Zaberma were the masters of 'Grunshi' land in the sense that they roamed about the country raiding, destroying villages, and capturing people. The list of their raids, which appears to be in temporal sequence, shows that they raided one area, moved to others, and then back to an area already raided.[2] Villages which agreed to pay the heavy tribute in slaves and cattle imposed by the Zaberma were spared, others were attacked. Some villages had to be besieged for many months before they were conquered, but none seems to have been strong enough to withstand a Zaberma attack. Conquered villages were divided among the Zaberma captains who levied tribute.[3]

The Zaberma were unsuccessful in their attempt to push northward. Gazari was killed in an attempt to enter the country of the Kiprisi (between Mossi and Boromo) and Babatu suffered a defeat at Safane when he fought there together with Karamoro Mukhtār. With the Moro-Naba of Mossi Babatu exchanged gifts, and it was after a notice from Wagadugu that Babatu refrained from attacking three villages, where the chiefs were related to the Mossi.[4] Dagomba had ambivalent relations with the Zaberma. The latter started as Dagomba mercenaries, but later twice defeated their former masters; first when Andani was defeated by Gazari and Mūsā of Sati, and then when Mahama, chief of Savelugu, came to help the chief of Dolbizan, and was routed by Babatu. Yet when the Zaberma had to leave 'Grunshi' land they were welcomed in Dagomba.

The Zaberma raids stimulated economic activities not only in 'Grunshi' land but further afield. Kassane, Gazari's camp, became a commercial entrepôt. 'Men from the four quarters made their abode

[1] Rattray, 1932, ii. 471–2; information at Gwolu. Remains of the wall are still seen at Gwolu.

[2] Mallam Abu, op. cit.; Tamakloe, 1931; Tauxier, 1912, pp. 285–6, 319.

[3] This one can learn from disputes among the Zaberma leaders over conquered villages (Mallam Abu, op. cit.).

[4] Tauxier, 1912, pp. 224–5.

in Kasana for the purpose of the slave trade, and every kind of commodity was to be found there.'[1] 'It is stated that it was the largest market in the western Sudan, at that time. . . . To this day ruins can be seen at Kassane showing what a large place it was.'[2] On his way through 'Grunshi' land, Binger noted much trade carried along the routes leading to the Zaberma camp. Yarse and Mande traders settled on the northern frontiers of the Zaberma dominions, and supplied millet, salt, and horses to the Zaberma in exchange for slaves.[3] In 1892 Ferguson found a flourishing market at Yagaba, on the southern fringes of 'Grunshi' land, where guns, gunpowder, kola, and horses were traded for slaves, some ivory, and gold.[4] The market of Bawku, further to the east, developed at that time, because the great caravans from Hausaland and Mossi stopped there and in Tenkodougou to trade with the Zaberma, sending them horses and fine gowns in exchange for slaves.[5] The slave market at Salaga, already established, shared the prosperity of the slave trade with Kintampo, Kete-Krachi, Wa, and Bole.[6]

As a result of the ample supply of slaves, their price dropped considerably, and more people could afford to buy slaves. One may notice a new pattern of settlement developing at that time among Muslims. Binger found that many of the Muslims of Salaga had slaves, who farmed for their masters in small villages around Salaga.[7] Taraore Muslims from Wa then moved to the outlying villages employing slaves for farming.[8] Mahamma, imam of Larabanga (Gonja), had bought 'Grunshi' slaves whom he settled at a nearby village, Nabori, to work for him. Under the influence of Larabanga the people of Nabori, many of them descendants of slaves, became Muslims.[9]

Slaves were in great demand for agricultural and domestic work. To the north slaves were exchanged for horses, to the south for arms. The constant supply of horses and arms enabled the Zaberma to maintain their ascendancy in 'Grunshi' land. Free supplying of arms to the north became possible in the last quarter of the nineteenth

[1] Tamakloe, 1931, p. 48.

[2] Whitall, unpublished manuscript.

[3] Binger, 1892, ii. 2.

[4] Report by Ferguson, 12 December 1892, enclosure 3 in No. 28, *African* (*West*), No. 448, PRO, CO. 879/38.

[5] Syme, unpublished manuscript.

[6] Binger, 1892, ii. 54, 101, 116, 142. See above, p. 41.

[7] Ibid., ii. 85. Dogon-Kade, twelve miles north of Salaga, was inhabited by slaves at that time.

[8] See above, p. 142.

[9] Information at Larabanga.

century only, after Ashanti had ceased to prevent direct communication with the coast. The trade in slaves for arms may be looked at as a replica of the eighteenth-century slave trade, with similar devastating results, but also with the same prospects of building up a new local African power.

That this new power might have been a Muslim one was presumably conditioned by the *jihād* movements in the northern belt of the Sudan. The Fulani *jihād*, it has been noted, stimulated the mobility of the Zaberma, who then became Muslims. The *jihād* of al-ḥājj Maḥmūd of Wahabu, itself probably influenced by that of Massina, prepared the way for the Zaberma in 'Grunshi' land, as is seen from the essential support accorded to the Zaberma by Mūsā of Sati, a follower of al-ḥājj Maḥmūd.

The Zaberma adventures were brought to an end by the intervention of the European powers. In this, they shared the fate of their great neighbour to the west, Samori. Their northern neighbour—Mukhtār of Wahabu—survived the colonial occupation because he had consolidated a miniature state, which ceased to be aggressive, before the advent of the Europeans.

For the history of Islam in the Middle Volta Basin it should be noted that all three—al-ḥājj Maḥmūd, Samori, and the Zaberma—brought the new idea of a militant Islam to an area where Islam had hitherto been represented by peaceful traders and Mallams.

PART III

PATTERNS OF ISLAMIZATION

CHAPTER IX

Islam in Mossi (Wagadugu)

THE detailed study of Islam in the Middle Volta states suggested patterns for the process of Muslim settlement, their integration into the socio-political system, the infusion of Islamic elements into the local culture, and finally conversion among the local population. All these, common to all the states, varied in degree and intensity according to the historical, social, and political conditions of the different states. Towards the end of this work the patterns of islamization in the Middle Volta states will be restated in a comparative study.

The concept of islamization as conceived, empirically, through the study of Islam in the Middle Volta states, may be tried in re-evaluating the position of Islam in other West African polities. Here documentary evidence and secondary sources will be only partly supplemented by my own field-work.

The Mossi states of the Upper Volta Basin are linked by traditions of common origin, linguistic affinity, a comparable political structure, and a similar economic basis with the states of the Middle Volta Basin to the south. The country to the north, on the other hand, was different in all these respects. When the Mossi states consolidated, in the fifteenth century, there was also a religious dichotomy, because the north was represented by the islamized Mali and Songhay.

The decline of Mali at that period created a political vacuum on the Niger, which attracted the Mossi, then in an expansionist mood before their political frontiers became stabilized. In the 1470s the Mossi invaded Massina, and advanced as far as Walata (1480).[1] The Mossi invasion to the Sahel was bound to be ephemeral because of the rising power of Songhay. In 1483 Sonni ʿAlī defeated the Mossi and drove them back to their country.[2]

The confrontation between Mossi and the northern states of the

[1] Al-Saʿdī, 1900, pp. 68–70, 186; translation, pp. 112–15, 284. Kaʿtī, 1913, pp. 46–48; translation, pp. 89–93. Earlier references to Mossi invasions into the Middle Niger as far as Timbuktu and Gao (Al-Saʿdī, 1900, p. 8; translation, pp. 16–17; Deuxième appendice in Kaʿtī, p. 333) need a new critical study in the light of the new chronology of Mossi (cf. Fage, 1964, pp. 178–9).

[2] Al-Saʿdī, 1900, p. 70; translation, p. 115; Kaʿtī, 1913, pp. 46–48; translation, pp. 89–93.

western Sudan had, therefore, been hostile from the beginning. The eruption of the Mossi into the Sahel was regarded in Timbuktu as a threat to Islam from the pagans of the south. Once the political authority of Songhay had been established, and its Islamic character reinforced by Askiya Muḥammad, the latter turned to deal with the Mossi, who represented a threat both to his empire and to Islam.

Askiya's war against Mossi, in 1498, was proclaimed a *jihād*, a holy war. This is related by al-Saʿdī, who adds: 'there has been no other *jihād* in this region except this expedition [against Mossi].'[1] Other expeditions against pagan peoples are on record, but these were not regarded as *jihād*s; it was on the front with Mossi that the confrontation between Islam and paganism was regarded as the most crucial. The *jihād* was conducted according to the Islamic law; Askiya had first sent an ultimatum to the Mossi king, calling him to accept Islam. After consulting his ancestors the Mossi king rejected the ultimatum. Askiya Muḥammad invaded Mossi country, destroyed towns, and took prisoners (who became Muslim).[2] Mossi, however, had not been subjugated, for three later expeditions against Mossi, between 1549 and 1578, are reported.[3]

This documented resistance of Mossi against an Islamic holy war gave it in history the attribute of 'the successful champion of paganism'.[4] Indeed, Mossi blocked the expansion of the islamized empire of Songhay southward, and so did Gurma and Borgu. But, in rejecting Askiya's ultimatum, the Mossi rejected not the religion of Islam *per se*, but Islam as the religion of the northern powerful neighbour, acceptance of which might have implied political submission. The country which had warded off an Islamic aggression was nevertheless open to peaceful Muslim traders of Mande origin, known in Mossi as *yarse*.[5]

The first group of Yarse came to Mossi in the reign of Naba Kundumie, the sixth Moro-Naba, probably at the beginning of the sixteenth century.[6] The first Muslim is said to have been Bukari Sakande, who settled at Zoghna, the old Yarse ward of Wagadugu. He was

[1] Al-Saʿdī, 1900, p. 74; translation, p. 123.

[2] Ibid.

[3] Ibid., pp. 102, 106, 110; translation, pp. 168, 173, 179.

[4] Barth, 1857, iv. 603. Barth was the first European to consult al-Saʿdī's work.

[5] On trade and routes in Mossi, see Barth, 1857, iv. 288–99, 558–64; Binger, 1892, i. 478–506; Marc, 1909, pp. 170–6; Skinner, 1964, pp. 110–18.

[6] Tauxier, 1912, pp. 464–6; Tiendrebeogo, 1963, p. 15; Ilboudo, 1966, p. 49; information at Wagadugu. On the date, see below, p. 201.

joined by Famare Koanda, who settled at Ghonsin, near Zoghna. Koanda was created *yar-naba*, 'the chief of the Yarse', an office still held by his descendants.[1]

After this the number of Yarse in Mossi increased. By the end of the last century there were Yarse communities in almost every village with a big market, mainly along the caravan routes. The Yarse lived in separate wards, or in exclusively Yarse villages. They lived in the districts of La, Mane, and Kaya to the north of Wagadugu, as well as in Kombissiri, Sarabatenga, and Dakaye, south of Wagadugu. The important market village of Putenga, near Kupela, also had an important Yarse community.[2]

Through their long residence among the Mossi, the Yarse abandoned their Mande dialect and began to speak More, the language of the Mossi. They also adopted some of the Mossi customs. The definition of the term *Yargha* (singular of Yarse) in G. Alexandre's dictionary reflects the Mossi point of view: 'Fraction du peuple Mosé [Mossi], d'origine Mandé, mais actuellement assimilée au reste des Mosé, dont elle ne se distingue que par ses occupations commerciales plutôt qu'agricoles et sa religion, *souvent musulmane*.'[3]

Here the distinct religion of the Yarse comes only after their Mande origin and commercial occupation, and even then with the qualification 'souvent musulmane', implying that not all the Yarse are necessarily Muslim.[4]

The same image of the Yarse is conveyed by a remark of one of the senior ministers of the Moro-Naba when interviewed: 'Les Yarse font le salam, mais ils ne sont pas croyants; ils sont commerçants et voyageurs.' He insisted that Islam had been introduced to Mossi during the reign of Naba Dulugu only. For him Islam is represented by the imam and his followers, not by the Yarse (although the imam himself is ethnically a Yargha); by the clerics and not by the traders.

The creation of the imamship and the building of the first mosque in Wagadugu by Moro-Naba Dulugu, in the second half of the

[1] Sakande is the same patronymic as Saghanogho, Koande as Kunate. Information at Wagadugu. The *yar-naba* is called also *Zouagn'yars'naba*, after the name of his ward (Kabore, 1966, p. 57).

[2] Marc, 1909, p. 112; Tauxier, 1912, p. 429; Randau, 1934, p. 325.

[3] Alexandre, 1953, ii. 465; my italics.

[4] See also Tauxier, 1912, p. 445; Delbosom, 1934, p. 327. A Yargha from Pissy (on the Wagadugu-Po road) said that his grandfather, though Yargha, had not been a Muslim, and only his father became a Muslim.

eighteenth century, marked the official introduction of Islam to the Moro-Naba's court. The impact of Muslims on the Mossi rulers had, however, begun earlier in the eighteenth century, in the reign of Naba Kom I. This ruler is said to have been the son of a Yargha woman.[1] To him the tradition ascribes the introduction of circumcision. His Yargha mother had him circumcised together with the Yarse children (the Moro-Naba's sons grew up with their mother's patrilineage).[2] When he became Moro-Naba he ordered all the Mossi princes and their followers to be circumcised. Only the autochthons (*Ninissi*) and the blacksmiths were exempted.[3] Though the origin of circumcision in Mossi needs further investigation, the tradition itself regards it as an Islamic custom.

In the reign of Naba Kom, Yarse settled also south of Wagadugu. They came to Kombissiri, and established a new village at Dakaye. The Yarse of Dakaye sent one of their number to study at Yambere (in Ghana), and he became the first great cleric of a lineage which is still influential in the region of Dakaye.[4] The Yambere of this Dakaye tradition is Gambaga;[5] an independent tradition recorded there says that a Muslim from Dakaye came to study Koran with Maḥmūd, the first imam of Gambaga.[6] The settlement of Muslims south of Wagadugu may have been associated with the increase of trade between Mossi and the south, over Mamprusi. Islamic influence from Mamprusi along these trade-routes is attested also by the fact that the first imam of Nobere came from Walwale.[7]

The tradition that the chiefs of Mossi are descendants of the daughter of the Mamprusi king is a living one. On the death of the Moro-Naba, the news is immediately sent to Gambaga.[8] The Mamprusi chief is regarded as the 'father' of the Mossi chiefs. Sons, one tradition says, imitate the father; so when Moro-Naba Dulugu heard that the Mamprusi chief had an imam besides his other ministers, he

[1] Tiendrebeogo, 1963, p. 26; Bichon, 1962, p. 82; Frobenius, 1913, p. 516.

[2] Skinner, 1964, pp. 46, 49.

[3] Tiendrebeogo, 1963, pp. 26–27; his account of the traditional history follows the Drum History.

[4] Bichon, 1962, pp. 82–83.

[5] Yambere may be Yab'yiri, 'the natal place', as Gambaga is known in Mossi (cf. Kabore, 1966, p. 21).

[6] Information at Gambaga, see above, p. 129. Close relations are said to have been maintained between the descendants of Imam Maḥmūd of Gambaga and the Muslims of Dakaye. The Dakaye Muslim took with him a Koran from Gambaga, still kept at Dakaye, where it is called *Zangbeghi* ('the Hausa'), after the Hausa imam of Gambaga.

[7] Information at Nobere, on the Wagadugu-Po-Navrongo road.

[8] Kabore, 1966, pp. 21, 55.

wished to have an imam in his court as well. He therefore invited a Muslim from Zitenga, and made him the first imam.[1]

This Muslim, Muṣṭafā Baghayogho, was a member of a family of Timbuktu origin, who had first settled at Mane, and then at Zitenga, both in Mossi. The Baghayogho were *'ulamā'* rather than traders.[2] If the tradition above, recorded by Delbosom, a member of the chiefly estate, is of any significance, the arrival of Muslim *'ulamā'* from the north had not been enough to open the Moro-Naba's court, and the imamship was created under Mamprusi influence. Islam had been introduced to Mamprusi during Na Atabia's reign early in the eighteenth century, over half a century before Naba Dulugu's reign. Facing the brutal challenge of the islamized empire of Songhay, the Mossi may have been suspicious of Islamic influence coming from the alien north. Once Islam had been accommodated in the sister states to the south, Dagomba and Mamprusi, without undermining the political structure, it was presented in a way acceptable to the Mossi.

In Dagomba, Na Zangina is credited with the introduction of Islam, but close contact between chiefs and Muslims started at least one generation earlier.[3] The same seems true of Mossi where the nominal conversion of Naba Dulugu was the product of at least one generation of association between chiefs and Muslims. Dulugu, it is said, was sent together with his brothers, by their father, Moro-Naba Sagha, to study Koran with Muslims. Two of Naba Dulugu's brothers, Ngadi and Sigiri, also became Muslims and as village chiefs laid the foundation of the Muslim communities in Nobere and Nobili respectively.[4]

There were other Mossi chiefs regarded as Muslims, and most of the converted Mossi Muslims (as distinguished from the Yarse) in the pre-colonial period were sons or descendants of chiefs.[5] In Mossi, as in the other states studied, Islam reached the chiefs before the commoners. This would appear inconsistent with what has been said about the resistance of the Mossi to Islamic influence. One of the reasons given is that the religious character of the *nam* (chiefship), based on a

[1] Delbosom, 1932, pp. 204–5.

[2] Cf. Marty, 1920, ii. 20–21; al-Saʿdī, 1900, pp. 43–47; translation, pp. 71–77.

[3] See above, p. 91.

[4] Information at Nobere and Nobili; on the latter see also *Fiche de village Nobili*, archives of the Ministry of the Interior, Wagadugu. See also Skinner, 1966, pp. 357–9.

[5] Bichon, 1962, pp. 83–85; Delbosom, 1932, pp. 209–11; files of Muslims in the archives of the Ministry of the Interior, Wagadugu.

ritual bond between the living chief and his ancestors, is incompatible with Islam. Conversion means abandoning the rites which support the political system.[1] Skinner points to a compromise in meeting this dilemma: 'although the rulers permitted their younger sons to adopt Islam, they themselves and the heirs to the throne remained pagan in order to maintain the bonds with the ancestors.'[2] A survey of the history of the Moro-Nabas since Naba Dulugu does not prove this rule, but indicates a certain tension (probably raised by the more conservative elements in the court, representatives of the traditional religion), and a concern to avoid the interference of Islamic influence in the functioning of the political system.

Naba Dulugu, himself regarded as a Muslim, is said to have sent away his son Sawadogo for being too favourable to Islam. For the same reason he deposed Naba Pouanda, the first Muslim chief of Kombissiri. Nevertheless, Sawadogo succeeded his father as Moro-Naba, and even restored the deposed chief of Kombissiri.[3]

During the reign of Naba Sawadogo the Yarse village of Sarabatenga was founded north of Dakaye, and became another centre for the diffusing of Islam.[4] Moro-Naba Sawadogo sent his son, the future Naba Kutu, to a Koranic school at Sarabatenga. Moro-Naba Kutu is the only paramount chief of Mossi regarded as a real and devoted Muslim. He is said to have delegated judgement according to the customary law to his ministers.[5]

But even this Moro-Naba, more devoted to Islam than any of his predecessors and successors, was confronted with the dilemma of the continuity of the dynasty under the impact of Islam. About him it is said that he sent most of his sons to Koranic schools, but not his first-born son, who succeeded him as Moro-Naba Sanum. The other sons, however, did not take Islamic studies seriously because they all looked forward to being Nabas.[6] In 1888 Binger met two sons of Naba Kutu (*alias* Hallilou): the reigning Moro-Naba Sanum (*alias* Alassane) and his brother, Naba Bukari Kutu. This is what Binger had to say about their religion:

> Hallilou, le père d'Alassane et de Boukary, était musulman et savait même lire et écrire. Je crois que ses deux fils ne sont rien de tout, c'est-à-dire musulmans non pratiquants.

[1] Skinner, 1964, pp. 126–7; Ilboudo, 1966, p. 46; Kabore, 1966, p. 120.

[2] Skinner, 1958, p. 1105.

[3] Bichon, 1962, p. 84.

[4] 'Histoire sommaire du village Sagabatinga-Yarce', archives of the Ministry of Interior, Wagadugu.

[5] Delbosom, 1932, p. 209; Tiendrebeogo, 1963, p. 34.

[6] Delbosom, loc. cit.

> Les Mossi musulmans disent qu'Alassane est musulman et qu'il fait ses prières à l'abri du regard de ses sujets; les fétichistes, eux, disent le contraire et parlent avec orgueil de leur naba, qui boit du dolo comme eux.[1]

Here is the dualism of Islam and paganism, which remain in dichotomy in Mossi, where the process of adapting the local culture under Islamic influence has not gone the same way as in Dagomba. In Dagomba, Mamprusi, and Gonja the Muslim festivals became national feasts, celebrated by non-Muslims in a way which left little of the Islamic character, but, on the other hand, these festivals replaced local ones and became part of the social and political life. In Mossi the more important national festivals are anchored in the traditional religion, without any apparent Islamic influence.[2] Of the Muslim festivals only the Muslim New Year (*Zambende* in More) is officially celebrated in Mossi. In the two principal Muslim festivals—*'īd al-fiṭr* (*Nolokre*) and *'īd al-aḍḥā* (*Kibsa*)—the Moro-Naba and his entourage take part in the communal prayer, becoming Muslim for the occasion. The Moro-Naba is expected to fast in *Ramaḍān*, but instead of fasting himself, it is said, he hires someone else to fast for him.[3] His own fast is a ritual fiction; the Muslims usually flattered him and the other chiefs by pretending to believe that they observed the fast. During the *Ramaḍān* Muslims greet the chief: 'I greet you who are fasting.'[4]

Various Muslim groups in Mossi have integrated in differing degrees into the socio-political system. The least integrated group seems to be the Fulani, called *Silmisi* (sing. *Silmiga*) by the Mossi. The Fulani are herdsmen, tending their own cattle as well as the cattle of the Mossi. In Mossi, as in Borgu, the pastoral Fulani are despised by the sedentary population.[5] Their contribution to the propagation of Islam among the Mossi was insignificant.[6]

The traditional history records two cases of Fulani involvement in Mossi political affairs. Moro-Naba Motiba (twelfth ruler back from *c.* 1900) is said to have been a Fulani usurper. He had been a close counsellor of Moro-Naba Wubi, and after the latter's death Motiba seized the chieftaincy for seven years, until replaced by the legitimate heir, Naba Warga.[7]

[1] Binger, 1892, i. 461–2.

[2] Cf. Skinner, 1964, pp. 126–7, 133–4.

[3] Delbosom, 1932, pp. 203, 206–9.

[4] Skinner, 1964, pp. 135–6.

[5] Ibid., p. 210, n. 26; Lombard, 1965, pp. 36–37, 130–6.

[6] Mathieu, unpublished manuscript; Bichon, 1963, p. 82. The latter's reference to the Fulani south of Wagadugu may be relevant to other parts of the country.

[7] Tiendrebeogo, 1963, pp. 18–19; also, the Arabic history of Mossi by al-ḥājj Mūsā Kongo; manuscript in possession of the author.

In the first half of the nineteenth century a Fulani, remembered as Wali, attempted to force the chief of Boulsa to accept the law of Islam. The Naba refused and Wali rebelled, supported by Fulani, Yarse, and a good number of Mossi. The revolt was suppressed, Wali ran away, and many of his followers were executed.[1] In the nineteenth century Mossi had militant Fulani concentrations near the frontiers, from Massina in the north to Dori in the north-east. This attempt by the Fulani, a reminder of the beginnings of more successful Fulani *jihād* movements, shows the potential danger the Mossi faced from the Fulani herdsmen. The control over these and other strangers in Mossi seems to have been effective enough to avoid a successful Islamic uprising.

The long residence of the Fulani among the Mossi led to the creation of a peculiar group, the *Silmi-Mossi*. These are Fulani who have been assimilated by the Mossi, having more Mossi customs than Fulani, and speaking More.[2] They changed from a pastoral to a sedentary way of life. The Silmi-Mossi are generally regarded as Muslims.[3]

The Yarse form the principal group of Muslims in Mossi, both in numbers and in their contribution to the propagation of Islam. They remained a distinct group in Mossi because of their different origin, occupation, and religion. The Yarse come under the authority of the Rasum-Naba, the minister in charge of the treasury. They did not pay regular tribute (apart from market and caravan tolls), but were expected to offer occasional presents to the chiefs.[4]

Tauxier says that the *Yar-naba*, headman of the Yarse, was one of the most influential elders in Mossi, and ranked next to the five senior ministers of the Moro-Naba.[5] At present the *Yar-Naba* does not seem to be more than the headman of the old Yarse wards of Zoghna and Ghonsin. He comes with his followers to greet the

[1] Cheron, 1924, p. 653. The revolt occurred in the reign of Naba Pyogo, the twentieth chief of Boulsa on Cheron's list. The twenty-second chief was executed by Naba Sanum. The latter succeeded *c.* 1870. Hence the revolt may be dated to the first half of the nineteenth century.

This Fulani revolt is recorded also in Mallam Alhasan's *The Moshi tribe*, translated by J. Withers-Gill (Accra, 1924).

[2] Alexandre, 1953, ii. 360.

[3] Mathieu (unpublished manuscript) counts the Silmi-Mossi together with the Fulani as Muslims. Silmi-Mossi appear as Muslims in the files in the archives of the Ministry of the Interior, Wagadugu. Kabore (1966, p. 26) says that the Silmi-Mossi are pagans (?).

[4] Randau, 1934, p. 325.

[5] Tauxier, 1912, p. 569.

Moro-Naba on Fridays and on other ceremonial occasions, but then there is also another group of Muslims, led by the imam.[1]

The Mossi distinguish between the terms *yarse* for the ethnic group, and *mwemba* (sing. *more*) for what they regard as proper Muslims.[2] The section of the *mwemba* at Wagadugu is Moeme, where the imam and his followers live. These are the Muslims who render the religious services to the Moro-Naba. The imam is primarily an elder of the court, and has to swear by Allah and the Prophet to be faithful, obedient, and helpful in times of need.[3] Since the time when Islamic influence found its way to the Moro-Naba's court, Muslims have always been in presence around the ruler. Muslims were among the idle courtiers of the Moro-Naba; they had no definite titles or functions, they were there to praise the ruler and to add to the grandeur of the court, living on the chiefs' generous donations. They had the privilege, as in the other Middle Volta states, of entering before the chief with their headgear and sandals on. They often wandered about in the country, either as traders or as clerics, visiting local chiefs. The latter were careful to give them ample presents, not only in reward for the Muslims' blessing and amulets, but also because these Muslims used to report to the Moro-Naba what they had seen in the country.[4]

Evidence from the late nineteenth century indicates that the imam rather than the *yar-naba* was influential in the court. The communication of the Muslims with the outside world made the imam and his followers most suitable to serve as hosts to European travellers. Binger, who visited Wagadugu in 1888, was sent to lodge with the imam. Like his countrymen after him, Binger encountered difficulties in dealing with the Moro-Naba, but his relations with the imam were amicable.[5]

Two years later, the Frenchman Crozat visited Wagadugu and had apparently even greater difficulties. To him the Muslims looked very powerful: 'I already knew from experience what sort of influence these men exercised over the chiefs. As a counsellor of the chief, the imam is overtly acknowledged as the second official in the village, but in reality he often commanded it.'[6] The Muslims' influence

[1] Kabore, 1966, pp. 57, 62.

[2] Alexandre, 1953, ii. 257, 465. The word *more* is of Mande origin (cf. Delafosse, 1955, ii. 512–13).

[3] Delbosom, 1932, p. 205; Skinner, 1964, p. 134.

[4] Kabore, 1966, pp. 46, 57; Ilboudo, 1966, p. 38.

[5] Binger, 1892, i. 458, 466.

[6] Crozat, 'Rapport sur une mission au Mossi (1890)', *Journal de la République Française*, 5–9 octobre 1891. Quoted by Skinner, 1964, p. 135.

derived, according to Crozat, from the fact that the king 'spent his time consulting holy men who had him under their control'.[1]

A similar description is given by Monteil, who came to Wagadugu a year after Crozat, in 1891.[2] Of his relations with the imam, Crozat says: 'I succeeded in so far as the imam was not hostile to me, but he did not help me as he might have.'[3] Monteil had a more difficult experience, saying: 'I could do nothing against the influence of the Almamy [imam] and his son Tedlika.'[4]

Their evidence on the powerful position of the imam is not convincing beyond doubt. The reluctance of the Moro-Naba to co-operate with the Europeans was clear at the time of Binger, who was on good terms with the imam. Crozat faced difficulties although he succeeded in neutralizing the imam. Was the imam really the prime cause of Monteil's troubles? It is possible, however, that the Muslims, who knew about events elsewhere in the continent (the French fighting against al-Tijānī and Samori), became more aware of the European danger, both to Islam and to African independence. Although it is difficult to judge the extent of the Muslims' influence, the fact remains that by the end of the last century, Muslims in Mossi were a factor to be taken carefully into account.

The most integrated Muslim group in Mossi was, of course, the converted Mossi themselves. Conversion of chiefs' sons or descendants occurred also in Dagomba, but there the general pattern was that the converted moved from the chiefly to the Muslim estate. In Mossi, chiefs and princes who became Muslims remained within the chiefly estate. It is possible that in fact many of these so-called Muslim chiefs did not practise Islam more than the average Dagomba chief, but they were regarded as Muslims by contrast with other chiefs who declared themselves pagan. In Dagomba there is a dichotomy between being a chief and being a Muslim, but chiefs absorbed such Islamic influence as to be 'half islamized'. Islamic influence on the national culture of the Mossi was superficial, and the standard image of 'a half islamized chief' has not developed there as in Dagomba and Gonja. The attitude to Islam remained, more or less, the choice of the individual; hence, unlike Dagomba and Gonja, there are now in Mossi chiefs who are Muslims, while others are professed pagans or Christians.

[1] Crozat, in Skinner, 1964, pp. 145–6.
[2] Monteil, 1894, p. 137.
[3] Crozat, in Skinner, 1964, p. 135.
[4] Monteil, 1894, p. 136.

CHAPTER X

Islam in Borgu and Kotokoli

(*a*) *Borgu*

MOSSI and Borgu were regarded as being among the bitter enemies of the Songhay empire.[1] These two peoples checked the advance of Askiya Muḥammad to the south. At the beginning of A.H. 911 (1505) the Songhay army was defeated by the chief of Busa.[2] Fifty years later, in A.H. 963 (1555/6), Askiya Dawūd devastated Busa,[3] but as in the case of Mossi, a single victory was not enough to bring the country under the domination of Songhay.

Thus, early in their history the Bariba (as the people of Borgu are known) faced and resisted the aggression of an islamized empire. In Mossi the confrontation with Songhay did not leave its traces in the local traditions; and what about Borgu? Is there any association between the threat from Askiya Muḥammad, the Muslim ruler, and the tradition that one of the early rulers of Borgu succeeded in evading an attempt to convert him?

This is one of the traditions about Kisra, the ancestor of the Bariba chiefs, who is said to have come from the north-east, retreating from the threat of a rising Muslim force.[4] Later, not long after Kisra's descendants established the chiefdom of Busa, Muslim envoys came to the chief of Busa, and persuaded him to accept Islam. The chief refused, but conceded that he would pray twice a year, at the two principal Muslim festivals. He soon, however, regretted even this concession, mounted his horse, and ordered the drums to be beaten in defiance of Islam. This act is repeated every year when the chief is called out to see the first moon of the *Ramaḍān*.[5]

[1] Al-Saʿdī, 1900, p. 119; translation, p. 192.

[2] Ibid., p. 76; translation, p. 125; Kaʿtī, 1913, pp. 69, 71; translation, pp. 133, 137. Earlier, Sonni Ali failed in an attempt to conquer Borgu (al-Saʿdī, 1900, p. 65; translation, pp. 104–5).

[3] Ibid., p. 103; translation, p. 169.

[4] Hogben and Kirk-Greene, 1966, p. 577.

[5] Lombard, 1965, pp. 99, 224–5. Lombard adds that in Busa it is said the messengers came from an African king, probably from Gao. See also Hogben and Kirk-Greene, 1966, pp. 578–9.

This tradition reflects ambivalent attitudes towards Islam among the Bariba. On the one hand, there is a strong tradition about resistance to an Islamic pressure, for which there is historical evidence in at least two cases, namely, the Songhay invasion in the sixteenth century, and involvement in wars with forces of the Fulani *jihād* in the first half of the nineteenth century.[1] On the other hand, the Bariba chiefs came under a certain Islamic influence of resident Muslims, in the same way as in the Middle Volta Basin and other West African states. The aggression from the outside conditioned the inside impact; the Bariba have been reluctant to accept Islamic religious influence. In Dagomba chiefs willingly celebrate Islamic festivals and pray occasionally, whereas in Borgu the tradition insists that the chiefs pray twice a year *only*.

Muslim informants in northern Dahomey interpreted the name Bariba, applied to the people of Borgu, as having the connotation of 'unbelievers'.[2] It is therefore impossible, they said, to speak of a Muslim Bariba; a Bariba who becomes a Muslim is referred to as Dendi, a term which covers most of the Muslim residents (excluding the Fulani).

The Dendi, speaking a Songhay dialect, spread throughout northern Dahomey from their centre on the Niger in the region of Illo and Gaya.[3] They settled in centres on the caravan routes leading from Hausaland to Gonja, such as Djougou, Parakou, Nikki, Kandi, etc. These centres, as the history of Djougou suggests, were first settled by Hausa and Bornu Muslims who carried on the trade. But it was the Dendi Muslims who contributed to the growth of these communities, as described by Marty: 'c'est à eux que Ouangara [the Muslim section of Djougou], jadis simple "village des étrangers, au cœur de l'habitat Pila-Pila", s'est transformé en un grand centre commercial.'[4]

The cultural influence of the Dendi exceeded their proportion among the Muslim population; their language became the lingua franca of the Muslims in northern Dahomey. Hence, Dendi became

[1] On the engagements between the Fulani and Borgu, see Hogben and Kirk-Greene, 1966, p. 580.

[2] But see Lombard, 1965, p. 43, n. 1, where the meaning of the word 'Bariba' is discussed.

[3] On the Dendi, their country, and their history, see Perron, 1924; Marty, 1926, pp. 162–4; Cornevin, 1962*b*, pp. 63–64, 162–3, 214–15.

[4] Marty, 1926, p. 162.

synonym to Muslim[1] and antonym to Bariba. To the Muslims in the Middle Volta Basin northern Dahomey is known as Dendi.

The Bariba were notorious as robbers and murderers, their country being regarded as unsafe for passing caravans.[2] Yet the Hausa traders, engaged in the remunerative kola trade, ventured to pass through this territory. Raids on caravans did not stop entirely, but tolls paid to Bariba chiefs helped in achieving some security. It is likely that chiefs became better disposed to extend their protection to the caravans as their relations with the resident Muslims became closer.[3]

In analysing relations between chiefs and Muslims in Borgu distinction should be made between places where Muslims were in the minority, such as Nikki, and places where Muslims comprised the majority, such as at Parakou. Parakou was on two important routes, one leading westward to Gonja, and the other southward to Abomey. It is said that Muslim traders from Hausaland had settled at Parakou before the Bariba chiefs arrived there. The headman of the Muslim community, the *Baparakpe*, was at first appointed by the Earth-priest of Parakou, and only at a later period by the chief. It is the *Baparakpe* who appoints the imam. After his installation ceremony, the Bariba chief of Parakou retires for seven days to a house near the imam's residence, where, it is said, his ancestor, the first chief of Parakou, stayed for some time when he first came to the town. In the absence of the chief, or during an interregnum, the *Baparakpe* rules the town.[4] It is not surprising that in view of the autonomy enjoyed by the Muslims of Parakou, and their influence over the chief, Parakou was sometimes regarded as a small semi-autonomous state, 'the kingdom of the Gambari'.[5] Indeed, this is the impression one may get from comparing the small, enclosed, and quiet town of the chief with the larger, busy, and animated town of the Muslims.

In Nikki the scene is quite different. The main town is that of the Bariba chief, while the Muslim section, known as *Maro*, is a couple of miles away. At present it is only a small village of a few compounds. Parakou is still an important commercial centre, where the railway

[1] 'Dendi' as a term to cover all the Muslims in northern Dahomey was adopted by the French administration, and this could make it even more widely used (Lombard, 1957, p. 466).

[2] See above, p. 25, n. 1.

[3] Lombard, 1965, p. 225.

[4] Ibid., pp. 226, 228.

[5] Marty, 1926, pp. 178–9. 'Gambari' is the name given to Hausa traders in this region.

from the south meets the tarred road running north. Nikki, on the other hand, is now off the main road, affected by the division of Borgu between Nigeria and Dahomey. It is possible, therefore, that in the pre-colonial period Nikki had a larger Muslim community, but certainly not as large and influential as that of Parakou. Parakou, with its heterogeneous population (including an important Yoruba element besides the Muslims) was the least Bariba of the Borgu chiefdoms. Nikki, on the other hand, was second only to Busa in the traditional hierarchy of Borgu, and sometimes the most powerful of the Borgu chiefdoms.

In Nikki, as in other towns of Borgu, the *Baparakpe* was the head of the Muslim community. But in Nikki his political influence was limited; he acted as intermediary between the chief and the Muslims and between the chief and the imam. He collected the tolls from passing caravans. Having been closely involved in political affairs, dealing daily with the chief and his court, the *Baparakpe* was subject to Bariba influence. This is shown by some customs associated with his office. Upon his appointment his head was shaved; after his installation he retired for seven days, during which he was instructed by the *sobabe*, the chief of the society of the young. Another group of Muslims oriented towards the chiefs were the Gesere court poets ('griots'). These were Dendi Muslims of the Taraore patronymic, who lived at *Maro*, the Muslim section, but became attached to the chief through their professional activity. The imam's duties were strictly religious; he was the spiritual head of the Muslim community, but also came to pray for the chief's victory. Lombard observes a certain duality in the social structure of the Muslim community: those who maintain reserved relations with the chiefs—the imam at the head of the majority of the Muslim community, and those who are more closely integrated in the political and social life of the chiefdom—the *Baparakpe*, the court poets, and the few converted Bariba.[1]

Commoners in Borgu became involved in chiefly affairs, and had prospects of promotion, through giving daughters to members of the chiefly estate. In the political competition princes and chiefs had the support of their maternal families. Muslims remained outside this system, because they did not give their daughters to non-Muslims,[2] following the Muslim Law. Individual Muslims could, however, gain some influence through friendship with young princes, who used to consult old Muslims, both for advice and blessing, after their

[1] Lombard, 1966, pp. 139–41.

[2] Ibid., p. 119.

accession to political office. Bariba chiefs, however, did not become Muslims, and even their Muslim names are those given to them by the Muslim 'griots'.[1]

Another Muslim element in Borgu was the Fulani herdsmen. There are Fulani attached to many Bariba villages. But, as in Mossi, the Fulani have no social communication with the local sedentary population. Their contribution to the propagation of Islam among the Bariba was nil, but they could have been important in the case of a more successful invasion of the forces of the Fulani *jihād*.[2]

The Bariba are related to the Mossi-Dagomba group of states, both in their language, classified in the Voltaic group, and in their political structure. Among the similar features in the political system Lombard numbers a decentralized organization, with great autonomy for provincial chiefs, who are related to the paramount; collateral succession, and a rotation of the chieftaincy among several branches. There is also an historical association between the Mossi-Dagomba and the Bariba; the rulers of all these states may have been part of the Kisra complex, and were subject to southern Mande influence.[3] Following this comparison Lombard suggests that these states had reacted to Islam in a similar way. It seems, however, that Islam was accommodated in Dagomba more easily than in Borgu, the latter being closer to Mossi in this respect. Mossi and Borgu were bordered by Islamic territories, and were more aware of the political danger from the protagonists of Islam.

In states which showed resistance to Islam, a force both religious and political, the religious system and the political structure had to be interdependent. It is significant, however, that in analysing the interaction of politics and religion two different patterns were suggested for Mossi and Borgu. 'Religion and ritual', says Skinner, 'played an important role in supporting and preserving the political system.'[4] In Borgu, on the other hand, Lombard implies that the political authority had to be mobilized to maintain the superiority of the pagan beliefs over Islam. Lombard noticed a certain feeling of inferiority among the Bariba facing the religious and cultural superiority of the Muslims. The Bariba culture was influenced by the strangers' Muslim culture, more than the opposite.[5] What he is really

[1] Ibid., p. 229.
[2] On the position of the Fulani in Borgu, ibid., pp. 130–7.
[3] Ibid., pp. 94–95; Fage, 1964, p. 178.
[4] Skinner, 1964, p. 126.
[5] Lombard, 1965, pp. 50–51.

speaking of is the infiltration of Islamic elements into the local culture, a process known from other states.

(*b*) *Kotokoli*

In northern Togo, among stateless tribes, the confederated chiefdoms of the Kotokoli were founded by the Mola clan, of Gurma origin. According to genealogical evidence the Mola established their authority over the autochthonous population at the beginning of the eighteenth century.[1] The more important Kotokoli centres were located on important trade-routes from Hausaland to Gonja, and the foundation of the chiefdoms may have been associated with the growth of trade on these routes in the eighteenth century.[2]

Towards the end of the eighteenth century Muslims settled under the auspices of the Kotokoli chiefs, as traders and artisans. These Muslims came from Hausaland (the *Ture*), Bornu (the *Mande*), Djougou and Parakou (the *Taraore*, originally from Songhay), Gurma (the *Fofana*), as well as from Yendi (*Sisse*), and Gonja (*Kamaghte* and *Kaute*). Significantly, all these patronymics are of Mande origin, though none came directly from Mande land. The diversity of their origin indicates the contribution of Muslims of Mande origin to the spread of Islam in all directions.

The three largest Muslim communities in Kotokoli were established at Dedaure (now part of Sokode), near the residence of the *Uro Eso* (the paramount chief), at Bafilo, and at Adjede (known also as Kri-kri). These Muslims came to speak Tem, the language of the Temba (the proper name of the Kotokoli), but they were regarded as strangers by the Temba themselves who called the Muslims *egom*

[1] Studies on the Kotokoli: Froelich, 1961 and 1964; Froelich et Alexandre, 1960; Froelich, Alexandre et Cornevin, 1963; Alexandre, 1964; Cornevin, *NA* 1964 and *CEA* 1964.

In his *Kashf al-Bayān*, Aḥmad Bābā mentioned a people—KTKL. If this reference from 1615/6 is to the Kotokoli of Togo, the date for the foundation of the chiefdoms may need revision (see above, p. 107, n. 5).

[2] Bafilo (GhFL) is mentioned on the route from Salaga to Hausaland over Zabzugu and Djougou (Bowdich, 1819, pp. 490–2, manuscript No. iv; Dupuis, 1824, pp. cxxiv–cxxv, ciii–civ). Cornevin (*NA* 1964, pp. 27–28 and *CEA* 1964, pp. 456–7) says that the name Kotokoli was given to these people by the Dendi, meaning 'to seize and capture', because the Kotokoli used to rob traders. He adds that the name of the town Sokode means in Dendi 'to close', probably because there was some barrier on the route at that place.

('strangers'). As foreigners they had no right to own land, and were allowed to farm only with special permission from the chief.

A change in the Muslims' position came about during the reign of Uro Djobo II, probably in the 1860s. This paramount chief was converted to Islam by his uterine brother al-ḥājj ʿAbdulai Taraore, the imam of Dedaure.[1] Uro Djobo became known as Bukari *Maluam* ('the Muslim'). An ambitious ruler, Uro Djobo embarked on a series of reforms to strengthen the paramountcy (until then regarded as *primus inter pares*) over the other territorial chiefs. He made the trade in salt and slaves a state monopoly, and recruited Muslim mercenaries—Zaberma, Hausa, and Fulani horsemen—against discontented chiefs. It is said that he even tried to impose Islam as a state religion. He granted Muslims the right to own land, as full members of the society. He appointed Muslims as headmen of the Muslim sections with the title of *mal'uro* ('chief of the Muslims').

Uro Djobo Bukari *Maluam* encountered resistance to his reforms, which included also a change in the mode of succession to the paramountcy. He succeeded in confirming his son as his successor, but soon after his death (in the 1870s) reaction gained momentum. The son, Uro Djobo III, renounced all Islamic tendencies, in order to appease the opposition. Relations with the chief of Bafilo had already been strained in the reign of his father, and the mountaineers were in open revolt. Unable to restore order in the chiefdom, Uro Djobo III invited the Germans to intervene in 1888, and a year later a treaty of protection was signed with the Germans. The Germans dispersed the Muslim mercenaries.

An attempt to build a strong, centralized kingdom out of the loose confederation by Uro Djobo II failed, and with it his attempt to make Islam a state religion. Among his successors only two paramount chiefs were Muslims, including the present (1964) *Uro Eso* al-ḥājj Yūsuf Ayeva. The 'Islamic' period in the history of the Kotokoli contributed, however, to the integration of the Muslims; 'it has been since his [Bukari *Maluam*'s] reign that one can speak of "Kotokoli" as distinct from "Temba".'[2] The term Kotokoli covers the Temba and the Muslims who speak Tem, but not the Fulani herdsmen and the Muslims of the *zongo*s, who speak their own languages. Kotokoli

[1] Both had the same mother. She had first been married to a Muslim, and gave birth to the imam. Later she married a member of the Mola clan and gave birth to Uro Djobo (information at Sokode).

[2] Froelich, Alexandre et Cornevin, 1963, p. 53.

became a cultural definition, Temba an ethnic one. Muslims ceased to be ethnically distinct only after the first world war, when young Kotokoli, men and women, who took part in the seasonal migration to the Gold Coast, came back as Muslims. These new converts contributed to the spread of Islam among the local population, and brought closer the Muslim *egom* ('strangers') and the Temba.

CHAPTER XI

Islam in Ashanti

THE study of the history of Islam in the Middle Volta Basin in the pre-colonial period is based mainly on oral traditions and genealogies. The student of this subject examines the past through the prism of his living informants, to which he may add observation of the present scene. Occasionally documentary evidence indicates some milestones, but apart from the Gonja Chronicle all written documents have been recorded either at the very end of the period in the late nineteenth century, or far afield from the area under study. Only for the Muslim community of Kumasi of the early nineteenth century is there contemporary evidence, recorded on the spot. Our main sources are Bowdich and Dupuis, who visited Kumasi as official British envoys, in 1817 and 1820 respectively. Both authors stress the importance of the Muslim community of Kumasi, and bring ample information about its position and its leading personalities. Professor Ivor Wilks was the first to take notice of this rich mine of information, which served him for the study of 'The position of Muslims in Metropolitan Ashanti in the early nineteenth century'.[1]

After Wilks had written his paper, he himself guided the present author to a new contemporary documentary source, Arabic manuscripts from Kumasi of the early nineteenth century preserved at the Royal Library, Copenhagen.[2] These manuscripts, and in particular the correspondence found among them, throw some new light on the Muslims of Kumasi. It is clear from these manuscripts, as had been suggested more vaguely by Bowdich and Dupuis, that the Muslims of Kumasi are representatives of the Muslims further north in Gonja, Dagomba, and Mamprusi. The manuscripts confirm that the pattern of relations between chiefs and Muslims as reconstructed from oral evidence for the Middle Volta states is true also for the relations between the Muslims of Kumasi and their chief, the Asantehene. It is now possible to fit the history of Islam in Ashanti into the wider regional context, at the same time incorporating contemporary

[1] Wilks, 1966; see also Wilks, 1961.
[2] Levtzion, *THSG*, viii.

documentary evidence in an historical comparative study, where otherwise oral evidence only is available.

At the beginning of the nineteenth century the terminus of the large Hausa caravans was at Salaga, where the Ashanti brought the kola.[1] In 1817 Bowdich noted the 'departures of Ashantee caravans' from Kumasi, and the 'arrival in Coomassie of visitors, merchants, and slaves' from the north.[2] This may imply that the bulk of the trade (kola nuts) was indeed carried by the Ashanti themselves (as far as Salaga), but that individual Muslim traders came down to Kumasi. The Asantehene was keenly interested in encouraging trade with the north, and he welcomed Muslim traders in Kumasi, who could then keep direct communication with the court, from where the organized Ashanti state trading was commanded. The resident Muslims in Kumasi could render invaluable service to traders in the north, both in representing them before the Asantehene, and in reporting economic and political conditions.

Muslims in Kumasi represented not only trading but also political interests. At that period both Gonja and Dagomba were tributaries to Ashanti, and Muslims were regarded as representatives of the two. This was described by Dupuis: 'The Moslems of Dagomba and Ghunja, headed by the Bashaw, Abou-Becr, Cantoma, and Shoumo, came in a body to return thanks, in the name of their sovereign, the King of Yandi. . . .'[3] It was probably in this capacity that Baba served as 'a member of the King's council in affairs relating to the believers of Sarem and Dagomba'.[4]

Baba was the son of a Gambaga imam; Kantoma and Suma were members of the Buipe imam's family.[5] The leading personalities in the Muslim community of Kumasi, those who regularly attended the Asantehene, were representatives of Muslim groups, already integrated into the social and political life of the hinterland states. It is likely that following the Ashanti conquest of Gonja and Dagomba, the religious services of Muslims, as seen in the courts of his tributaries, were called for also by the Asantehene. Baba, Kantoma, and Suma did not act on their own only, as is evident from letters they received from Kamshe-Na of Dagomba, and from the imams of Gonja, Buipe, and Kpembe. These letters included instructions for charms to be made for the Asantehene, as well as an assurance that

[1] See above, pp. 31–32.
[2] Bowdich, 1821, p. 2.
[3] Dupuis, 1824, p. 170.
[4] Ibid., p. 97.
[5] See above, pp. 61–62, 126–8.

each of these '*ulamā*' was praying for the king's health and the welfare of his kingdom.[1]

The preoccupation of the Kumasi Muslims with charms and amulets is evident from the fact that over ninety per cent of the nearly thousand folios in the Copenhagen collection are cabalistic formulae, as well as prescriptions for amulets and other charms. These are the same as described by Dupuis:

> The talismanic charms fabricated by the Moslems, it is well known, are esteemed efficacious according to the various powers they are supposed to possess; and here is a source of a great emolument, as the article is in public demand from the palace to the slave's hut; for every man wears them strung around the neck.... Some are accounted efficacious for the cure of gunshot wounds, others for the thrust of laceration of steel weapons, and the poisoned barbs of javelins, or arrows.... Besides this class of charms, they have other cabalistic scraps for averting the evil of natural life; some, for instance, are specific nostrums in certain diseases of the human frame, some for their prevention, and some are calculated either to ward off any impending stroke or fortune, or to raise the proprietor to wealth, happiness and distinction.[2]

Muslims' prayers were demanded, but only to supplement traditional Ashanti rituals. Hutchison, a member of Bowdich's mission, described the preparations for the Ashanti invasion of Gyaman, saying that the king was busy 'making fetish', while 'the Moors came every morning to the palace for prayer and sacrifice'.[3]

Once Islamic influence had reached the Asantehene's court by Muslims of the immediate hinterland, Kumasi came within the reach of itinerant Muslim holy men. One of these was *sharīf* Ibrāhīm whom Bowdich and Hutchison met in Kumasi in 1817. He had been to Mecca and Medina, and came to Kumasi from Busa, on the Niger.[4] 'His great sanctity made the King of Ashantee to send for him to pray and make sacrifice for the success of the war.'[5] The *sharīf*'s relations with the resident Muslims were uneasy, because the former claimed 'the same degree of rank as Baba', which meant practically an equal donation in gold.[6] The resident Muslims, headed by Baba, may have been unhappy to share the king's generosity with the *sharīf*.

[1] Copenhagen manuscripts, vol. i, ff. 3, 73, 107, 146, 169, 188; vol. ii, f. 1. Translations of these letters, in Levtzion, *THSG*, viii.

[2] Dupuis, 1824, p. xi; see also Bowdich, 1819, p. 271.

[3] Hutchison's diary, in Bowdich, 1819, p. 393.

[4] Bowdich, 1819, pp. 92, 397.

[5] Hutchison's diary, in Bowdich, 1819, p. 397.

[6] Ibid., p. 403.

Hutchison says that 'the other Moors here look on him [the *sharīf*] with an evil eye, because he will not wear fetishes as they do, and be present at human sacrifice'.[1] Wilks suggests that *sharīf* Ibrāhīm represented a puritan trend of Islam, which he may have acquired in the Hijaz under the Wahabis' influence or from the Fulani of Sokoto.[2] This is unlikely, because far from revolting against the position of Muslims in pagan states, the *sharīf* himself took advantage of this situation. He wandered about visiting non-Muslim chiefs, from whom he accepted generous presents in return for his prayers. His visit to Kumasi was part of an itinerary through royal capitals; from Kumasi he proceeded to Abomey and Nikki, capitals of the pagan rulers of Dahomey and Borgu.[3] Though he himself probably did not wear amulets, the *sharīf* used to produce these. Among the Copenhagen manuscripts there are two magical formulae said to be given by *Sharīf* Ibrāhīm (*'fī fam sharīf Ibrāhīm'*) to his friend Muḥammad Karamo Toghma, that is Muḥammad Kantoma or Kamaghte of Kumasi.[4] In one of these manuscripts he is referred to as *'sharīf Ibrāhīm Barnawī'*; his *nisba* denotes that he was a native of Bornu.

As a visitor to Kumasi, the *sharīf* was not obliged to be present at royal ceremonies, which included human sacrifice. The resident Muslims, on the other hand, integrated as they had become in the social and political life, had to attend these ceremonies, although they hated the customs, and even tried to abolish human sacrifice by giving the example of sacrificing sheep.[5]

Much of the Muslims' influence at the Ashanti court was due to the religious services they rendered, and to the belief of the king in the power of the Muslims' God and their 'strong Book'.[6] Being literate, Muslims became important also in the Ashanti bureaucracy.[7] Muslims took part in the negotiations of the British envoys in the Ashanti court in 1820. Towards the end of the last century Muslims played an important role in negotiations with Europeans in Mossi, Mamprusi, and elsewhere.[8] Being more articulate, Muslims had easier relations with Europeans than non-Muslims. This could have led European observers to overestimate the Muslims' influence.

The Muslims' influence in Kumasi is said to have diminished

[1] Hutchison's diary, in Bowdich, 1819, p. 397; see also Bowdich, 1819, p. 205.
[2] Wilks, 1966, pp. 323–4.
[3] Dupuis, 1824, p. xv.
[4] Copenhagen manuscripts, vol. ii, ff. 27, 266–7.
[5] Hutchison's diary, in Bowdich, 1819, pp. 393–4.
[6] Bowdich, 1819, p. 272; Dupuis, 1824, pp. 161, 180, 243, 247.
[7] Wilks, 1966, pp. 328–9.
[8] See above, pp. 131, 171–2.

considerably because of the desertion of Baba during the War of 1818 against Gyaman and Kong.[1] Dupuis's mission visited Kumasi after that incident, yet his account suggests that the Muslims were still influential. It is doubtful whether this influence, whatever it might have been, really diminished after the departure of Dupuis and Hutton in 1820.

Following the failure of the Anglo-Ashanti treaty of 1820, communication between the coast and Kumasi became poorer, and information about internal affairs in Kumasi more scanty. Nineteen years after Dupuis's visit, the missionary T. B. Freeman visited Kumasi. As a missionary, he was less sympathetic to the Muslims than Dupuis, who had been on amicable terms with them, and even less than Bowdich who had been somewhat suspicious of the Muslims. A comparison of Freeman's evidence with that of the former visitors is, however, most instructive.

Freeman found the headman of the Muslims in Kumasi 'a prisoner in his own house, chained to a log of wood'.[2] This was taken as an indication of further deterioration in the position of the Muslims. But Freeman noted also that this Muslim had thus been punished for being implicated in a conspiracy together with some Ashanti dignitaries.[3] It can only be suggested, therefore, that Muslims still took part in Ashanti politics in the late 1830s.

Freeman says that 'the king is surrounded by Moors' who 'poison his mind' against the missionaries.[4] This compares well with what Bowdich had to say: 'the impression of the natives that we came to spy the country was sedulously strengthened by the Moors.'[5] Freeman witnessed 'several Moors in the procession' of the king, a scene reported also by Dupuis.[6] Freeman was visited by 'two Moors', who said 'that they came from Mosu [Mossi]'.[7] Foreign Muslim visitors, 'even from Mosee', are described also by Bowdich.[8] Hence, about two decades after Bowdich's and Dupuis's visits, references to Muslims, comparable to the accounts of 1817 and 1820, are on record.

Ramseyer, Kühne, and Bonnat, who were prisoners in Ashanti in

[1] Hutton, 1821, p. 323; Dupuis, 1824, pp. 98–99; Wilks, 1961, pp. 28–29.
[2] Beecham, 1841, p. 93.
[3] Ibid.
[4] Freeman, 1844, p. 43.
[5] Bowdich, 1819, p. 161.
[6] Freeman (1844, p. 48) adds: 'they made by no means a conspicuous appearance.' Dupuis (1824, pp. 70–72), on the other hand, was impressed by the 'dignity and decorum' which 'distinguished the followers of the Prophet' in the king's procession. Both observers were, undoubtedly, influenced by their own attitude to the Muslims.
[7] Freeman, 1844, p. 51.
[8] Bowdich, 1821, p. 2.

1870–4, noticed the extensive use of Muslim amulets by Ashantis of all walks of life, and met Muslims living in Ashanti.[1] Tordoff quotes evidence for the trust in Muslim amulets the Ashanti had during the revolt of 1900.[2] Traditions recorded by Rattray at Juaben, Bekwai, and Nsuta reveal how common it was to refer to Muslims for healing, divination, and charms.[3] A Hausa manuscript records that before the British attack on Kumasi in 1874, the Asantehene sent to Salaga for a Mallam to come and pray for his victory.[4] Is this so different from the situation in 1820?

The late imam of the Asantehene, Imam ʿAbd al-Mu'min (d. 1964), was the grandson of Karamo Tia. Karamo Tia, gifted in working out charms, was brought from Daboya by the Asantehene Kwaku-Dua I (1834–67). He and his successors were known as *Asante Nkramo* ('the Muslims of Ashanti'), and served as the king's imam (*adimem*, in Ashanti).[5] In historical perspective, Karamo Tia continued the service rendered previously by other Muslims from Gonja, such as Muḥammad and Suma. Karamo Tia, however, was created an official imam, which may be regarded as a sign of progress in the introduction of Islam.

Generally speaking, the extent of Islamic religious influence in Ashanti, as observed in 1817 and 1820, was maintained until the end of the last century. No less interesting is the way Muslims had established their influence in the decades preceding the visits of Bowdich and Dupuis. Dupuis recorded information about this earlier period from the Muslims of Kumasi. The Asantehene Osei Kwame (1777–*c.* 1801), in whose reign the Muslim influence began, is said to have been 'a believer at heart', and was deposed because of his 'attachment to the Moslems'.[6] It would seem that under the first impact of Islam chiefs may have been won over, even to the threshold of conversion. But excessive personal inclination caused reaction. In Dagomba, for example, the tradition contrasts the attitudes to Islam of Na Zangina (regarded as a convert) and of his successor Na Andani Zighli (who is said to have put aside the Koran).[7]

[1] Ramseyer and Kühne, 1875, pp. 47, 49, 69; Gros, 1876, p. 54.
[2] Tordoff, Ph.D. London, 1961.
[3] Rattray, 1927, pp. 152, 175, 262.
[4] Krause manuscripts, No. 24; Olderogge, 1960, pp. 170–1.
[5] Information collected by J. Agyeman-Duah of Kumasi, to whom I am grateful for introducing me to the late imam.
[6] Dupuis, 1824, p. 245; Wilks, 1961, p. 22; Wilks, 1966, pp. 334–5.
[7] See above, p. 109.

In this phase of reaction, the next Asantehene, Osei Bonsu (*c.* 1801–24), commenced his reign 'an avowed enemy to the religion of Islam', and even executed several Muslims.[1] It was probably during that period that Baba wrote a letter (dated as pre-1810) to the imams of Gambaga, Buipe, and Daboya, informing them of the calamity which had befallen the Muslims in Kumasi.[2] Later, however, the same ruler changed his attitude to that mild inclination towards the Muslims described by Bowdich and Dupuis. He arrived at a balance, combining traditional local practices with reverence to Islam:

> That monarch is somewhat religiously inclined towards the followers of Mohammed, from a reverential awe of the universal God. . . . Notwithstanding this sovereign chuses to adhere faithfully to his Pagan rites in all their manifold horrors and enormities, he does not neglect to supplicate the Moslems for their prayers, particularly when oppressed with anxiety. . . .[3]

The way Dupuis characterized the middle position of the Asantehene may nearly apply to chiefs in the Middle Volta States. The parallels which one can draw between the early stages in the introduction of Islam into Ashanti and Dagomba do not extend to later developments. The influence of Islam in Ashanti remained marginal; Islamic elements have hardly been incorporated into the Ashanti national culture, as happened in Dagomba; Muslims have not been integrated to the stage of being members of the local society rather than foreign residents; and conversion has been very limited.

A similar process may be traced in the old kingdom of Bono-Mansu, where the presence of Muslims has not left marked traces in the culture.[4] The same is true of the Brong kingdom of Gyaman, where the Muslim community of Bonduku was even more influential than that of Kumasi; yet Islamic influence on the Brong has been arrested. This seems, therefore, to be common to all the Akan states, and we are confronted with the problem of resistance to Islam, which is not easy to explain.

[1] Dupuis, 1824, p. 98; Wilks, 1961, p. 22.

[2] Copenhagen manuscripts, vol. iii, f. 5. On the date of the letter, see above, p. 61, n. 4.

[3] Dupuis, 1824, pp. x–x

[4] See above, p. 8.

CHAPTER XII

Conclusions

'THE forests of the Guinean zone imposed an insuperable barrier to steppe-nurtured peoples.'[1] This is the reason often given to explain why Islam did not penetrate into the forest. Invading horsemen lost their military advantage in the forest, and the Muslim forces had to halt in front of the impenetrable forest. Yet throughout this study it has been reiterated that in this region Islam had not been carried by force, but by peaceful traders. Such traders did reach the courts of forest kingdoms, and built up communication with the rulers. Indeed, the great Muslim caravans usually stopped at the southern end of the savannah, and the number of traders who reached as far south as Kumasi was only a small fraction of the Muslim traders who frequented Dagomba and Gonja. The intensity of Muslims' activities may be one reason for the different impact Islam had on Dagomba and Ashanti. Another reason may be the elaborated religion of the forest people interlocking with a developed political system. Did the matrilineal succession among the Akan, contradicting as it did Islamic law and concepts, strengthen the resistance to Islam? But Dahomey, with patrilineal succession, reacted to Islamic influence in a similar way.[2] On the other hand, Dahomey's eastern neighbours, the Yoruba, came under strong Islamic influence, to the extent that nearly half of the Yoruba-speaking people are now Muslims.

Let us try to look at the position of these forest peoples *vis-à-vis* Islam in an historical perspective. Throughout the eighteenth and nineteenth centuries Ashanti had a definite superiority over the peoples of its northern hinterland. The latter represented Islam, though these states were not really islamized. For Ashanti, therefore, Islam did not represent a serious challenge to their religion. Ashanti was always victorious over those regarded as Muslims. The Ashanti were ready, indeed most willing, to add Muslims' prayers and amulets to their own religious rites. But their religion remained

[1] Trimingham, 1959, p. 24.

[2] On Muslims and Islamic influence in the kingdom of Dahomey, see Dalzel, 1793, pp. xxii-xxiii, 48–49, 132–5; Burton, 1864, i. 258–66, 309–10, 330–5; ii. 45–46, 118, 300.

unshaken; they had no reason to have any doubt in the vitality of their ancestral beliefs, which helped them in expanding their empire to become one of the greatest powers in West Africa. Dahomey had a similar experience. The Yoruba, on the other hand, suffered a humiliating defeat at the hands of Muslims. As the power of Oyo, once the mistress of the Yoruba states, declined, it was overtaken by the Fulani *jihād*. The Fulani had been checked in the forest of Ibadan, but retained control over the fringes of Yorubaland in the open country. Ilorin, a Yoruba province, became a Fulani emirate. The political disintegration of the Yoruba, their defeat by a rising Muslim power, and the inclusion of part of their country within *Dār al-Islām*, must be considered together with other factors in explaining the spread of Islam among the Yoruba.

Confrontation with a Muslim power conditioned the reaction of Mossi and Borgu towards Islam. The aggression of Songhay, in spite of some successful raids, was checked by Mossi and Borgu. Both states rejected Islam which was presented as part of the political and military pressure. To Dagomba Islam was presented in the confrontation with Gonja. The Gbanya invaders, founders of the Gonja state, were not themselves Muslims but recruited the aid of Muslims, and accepted Islamic influence in a way readily adopted by the Dagomba.

Islam in the Middle Volta Basin is characterized by the way it has been integrated into the socio-political system of the states, without risking the survival of this system. As the islamized north threatened the very existence of these states, the integrated form of Islam reached this area by, so to speak, an outflanking manœuvre. The Gbanya invaders, hailing from the Middle Niger, entered the Volta Basin south of the Mossi-Dagomba states. They had already been acquainted with Islam in the service of chiefs in their country of origin. Though an earlier contact between Dagomba chiefs and Muslims cannot altogether be excluded, it is likely that the Gonja example initiated the process of integration. This, it has been shown above, may be explained in the historical context. Similar features in the way Islam has been accommodated in the Middle Volta states make this region a distinct zone of islamization. Yet the pattern differed somewhat from one state to another, conditioned by historical development and social structure.

In Gonja, contact between chiefs and Muslims started before the foundation of the state. Muslims shared the conquest of the land with the chiefs, and developed intimate relations. Yet the two estates remained distinct. As the land was conquered, the local population, formed by several tribal groups speaking different languages, was not moulded to become one nation. The new state was imposed over this heterogeneous population as it existed. The invaders became the chiefly estate, keeping themselves aloof from the conquered, who became the commoners' estate. Hence, following the foundation of the state by conquest, three social estates (chiefs, Muslims, and commoners) became rigidly defined, allowing hardly any social mobility.

Members of the chiefly estate came under Islamic influence, but did not become Muslims. Here as elsewhere in the Middle Volta Basin there is a distinction between being a chief and being a Muslim. Each of the three estates in Gonja had birthright members only. Even among Muslims there was the distinction between the hereditary Muslim community, descendants of the early Muslims whose association with the chiefs goes back to the foundation of the state, and other Muslims who came later to settle in Gonja. The former only enjoyed intimate relations with the chiefs.

Dagomba also was founded by invaders, but there a nation has been moulded through mutual acculturation of the invaders and the conquered. Dagomba history and its social structure suggest an evolutionary development, which brought about a more homogeneous society with a common culture and one language. The development of Islam in Dagomba was gradual but dynamic; Muslims of various ethnic origin, who came in different periods, have all been integrated on the same level. Muslims who had come as late as the mid-nineteenth century were appointed imams at Yendi.

Lines of demarcation among the social estates in Dagomba have not been so boldly engraved as to prevent social mobility. There are clearly defined categories of chiefs, Muslims, and commoners, but individuals often moved from one estate to the other, mainly from the chiefly to the Muslim or commoners' estates. This mobility is inherent in the political system, as it relieves pressure on the limited number of chieftaincies available through a constant process of elimination. The grandson of a chief, whose father was not a chief, had little prospect of getting a chieftaincy. In the next generation, his own son would have been altogether removed from the chiefly estate, i.e. from those eligible for a political office. Almost imperceptibly he would join the ranks of the commoners, unless he became a Muslim as some did.

There is no sign in Dagomba of active resistance to Islam, the attitude being pragmatic. Chiefs have Muslims around them to pray for their welfare and their success. Under the influence of these Muslims, chiefs occasionally pray, but only rarely become genuine Muslims. They go along with Islam as long as it does not interfere with their obligations towards the majority of the non-Muslim subjects. Hence the character of the 'half-islamized' chief.

Chiefs' sons or grandsons were sometimes given to Muslims to be brought up in the faith, a kind of gift on behalf of the chief. Chiefs' descendants with no prospect of chieftaincy may prefer the more privileged status of a Muslim to that of a commoner. Dagomba Muslims of chiefly descent do not renounce their relationship with their non-Muslim kinsmen, either chiefs or commoners. In this way many Dagomba families have Muslim members, so that Islam in Dagomba is not regarded as the religion of strangers only. The naturalization of the stranger Muslims has thus been accelerated, making Muslim a religious rather than an ethnic definition.

Compared with Dagomba, the Mamprusi state was less cohesive, and political tension was higher; there were more disputes over the paramountcy, and less control over divisional chiefs. The involvement of Mamprusi in the affairs of neighbouring stateless peoples, and the part taken by the latter in Mamprusi's internal disputes, brought into the political arena quite a few pressure groups. In these circumstances the Muslims in the two largest communities of Gambaga and Walwale tried to assert a semi-autonomous status, which brought them into some tension with both commoners (e.g. Gambarana) and chiefs.

Islamic influence has been absorbed into customs and ceremonies in Mamprusi, but relations between chiefs and Muslims there have not been as close as in Dagomba. This is well marked by the separate chiefly and Muslim towns: Nalerigu and Gambaga, Wungu and Walwale.

In Wa, chiefs and Muslims share a common interest in the kingdom against the decentralizing tendencies of the commoners; they are, so to speak, in the same boat. The dichotomy between *Wala* (comprising the chiefly lineages and the Muslims) and *Dagaba* (the commoners) may explain why the contribution of the Wala Muslims extended beyond usual religious services to actual political support, and why the Wala chiefs seem to have been inclined towards Islam more than chiefs in other Middle Volta states. The available evidence suggests, however, that genuine islamization of the Wala chiefs started in the second half of the last century only.

Residence in the region of Wa, where a centralized political system overlapped territories of stateless peoples, may explain the background of the Kantosi, a branch of the Wala Muslims, who represent Islam in 'Grunshi' land, the least islamized part of the Middle Volta Basin.

Among all the Muslim groups in the Middle Volta Basin, only the Kantosi were involved in a *jihād*, as an attempt to extend the rule of Islam by force. Muslims in the Middle Volta states became integrated into the social and political system, identifying themselves as members of these states. Though in personal conduct they endeavoured to observe the rules of Islam as much as possible, they presented Islam to their chiefs in mild and diluted forms. In this way they were able to build up communication with the chiefs, winning their sympathy towards Islam, and preparing the way for further Islamic influence. It was these Muslims who carried the burden of spreading Islam and extending its geographical frontiers.

The influence of the Fulani *jihād*, led by ʿUthmān dan Fodio, was carried to this area by Hausa traders and Mallams. It is represented by al-ḥājj ʿUmar of Salaga and Kete-Krachi.[1] Al-ḥājj ʿUmar himself came to Salaga after he had completed his studies in Hausaland. At Salaga, and then at Kete-Krachi, he was surrounded by students, who now rank among the leading Muslim personalities in communities throughout Ghana. Muslims in trading centres were better disposed to accommodate the heritage of the *jihād* movement than were Muslims in chiefs' towns and villages.

The peaceful process of islamization in the Middle Volta Basin has not gone through a revolutionary stage, caused by the *jihād* movements. The study of this process may, therefore, be relevant to the history of Islam in the northern belt of the Sudan until the end of the eighteenth century. There, the *jihād* movements did not only cover earlier patterns of islamization but also changed the ideas present informants may have on the role of Islam and the extent of its influence before the religious upheaval. In Gonja, Dagomba, or Mamprusi, Islamic influence has not remained static during the last three centuries, but has developed on a pattern which may be detected from historical traditions of the local states as well as from genealogical evidence, and is reflected in the present situation. Knowledge of such a peaceful process of islamization may be helpful in reading the information of al-Bakrī about Islam in ancient Ghana, of Ibn-

[1] See above, p. 44, n. 4.

Faḍl-Allāh al-ʿUmarī and Ibn Baṭṭūṭa on Mali, and of al-Saʿdī and Kaʿti on Songhay. One may also get a better idea of the position of Islam in the eighteenth-century Habe kingdoms in Hausaland, as inferred from the works of the leaders of the Fulani *jihād*.

The present study, based mainly on interpretation of traditional evidence, is by no means conclusive. Statements presented here in the affirmative should now be reformulated in the interrogative for further investigation. More data may be furnished by anthropological studies of the process of islamization in its wider sense: dispersion of Muslims; incorporation of Islamic elements into local customs, ceremonies, and festivals; the integration of Muslims into the sociopolitical system; and aspects of conversion. Linguistic research may throw light on the terminology relating to Islam. Students of comparative religion may tell us more about factors of resistance and acceptance inherent in the traditional religions. More evidence on all these aspects is wanted from other parts of Africa, because it is only by a comparative study that nuances in the patterns of islamization become clear. The study of patterns of islamization is important not only for the understanding of a dynamic process of acculturation in Africa, but also for its significance in the context of the spread of Islam in the wider world, bringing together peoples of diverse civilizations.

APPENDIX

Notes on the Chronology of the Middle Volta States

THE dates suggested here for the foundation of these states are by no means new. Y. Person pointed, in passing, to the probability that Bono-Mansu was founded in the fifteenth century.[1] J. Goody maintains that the Gonja invasion occurred in the second half of the sixteenth century.[2] J. D. Fage suggested a date in the second half of the fifteenth century for the foundation of Mossi and Dagomba.[3]

These notes are intended to explore the possibility of dating by calculating the average length of a generation and/or of a reign. Most of the events I had to date in this study were in the eighteenth and nineteenth centuries, for which genealogies are more reliable. Hence, the average length of a generation provided me with an indispensable tool.

(*a*) *Bono-Mansu*

Mrs. Meyerowitz reconstructed the chronology of Bono-Mansu back from 1740, the date she suggests for the destruction of Bono-Mansu by the Asantehene Opoku-Ware (1720–50).[4] The Gonja Chronicle records the coming of the Ashanti army to Takyiman in A.H. 1135 (1723). This date for the conquest of Takyiman is confirmed by two Dutch documents from 1724 and 1726.[5] According to the traditions of Bono, Takyiman, once the second largest town in the Bono-Mansu state, was occupied by the Ashanti during the liquidation of the state.[6] Ameyaw Kwaakye, the last king of Bono-Mansu, died therefore in 1723 (and not in 1740 as suggested by Mrs. Meyerowitz).

Berempon Katakyira, the thirteenth ruler back from 1723, committed suicide after the first defeat of Bono-Mansu by the Gbanya invaders, in 1595 according to Mrs. Meyerowitz.[7] The chronology of Gonja which follows suggests that this invasion occurred in the last quarter of the sixteenth century. So the last twelve rulers of Bono-Mansu reigned a little less than a hundred and fifty years, or an average of about twelve years per reign. On the other hand, the first eight rulers of Bono reigned, according to Mrs. Meyerowitz's dates, from 1295 to 1595, or an average of 37·5 years per reign. The rather short average in the later period may be explained by

[1] Person, 1964, p. 331.
[2] Goody, 1964, p. 200.
[3] Fage, 1964.
[4] On the method of recording the length of reigns in Bono-Mansu, see Meyerowitz, 1952, pp. 29–30. This, as shown below, is probably unreliable, at least for the earlier period.
[5] J. K. Fynn, Ph.D. London, 1964, p. 124.
[6] Meyerowitz, 1958, p. 126.
[7] Ibid., p. 115.

the difficulties Bono's rulers may have had at that period with the emergence of new powers, Gonja to the north and Ashanti to the south. But the very long average for the earlier period is inexplicable and unacceptable.

The destruction of Bono-Mansu was followed by years of chaos. Then Ameyaw Gyamfi, a prince of the Bono royal lineage, renewed the dynasty in Takyiman as vassal of Ashanti. From this chief to Gyako II, who died in 1899, there were eight rulers in Takyiman.[1] The average length of reign for this period is about twenty years (subject to the number of years allowed for the period of chaos after 1723). This average compares quite well with the average reign which may be calculated for Ashanti in about the same period.[2]

If one takes this average, of about twenty years, for the eight reigns before the last quarter of the sixteenth century, a date in the middle of the fifteenth century may be suggested for the foundation of Bono-Mansu.

(*b*) *Gonja*

For the chronology of Gonja one has the eighteenth-century Gonja Chronicle and chief-lists recorded from oral traditions. Corroboration of these two sources is difficult, sometimes impossible. Names in chief-lists do not agree with names in the Gonja Chronicle, because chiefs have a Muslim name besides their Gonja one, and a third may be adopted by a chief on his accession. The Chronicle usually mentions chiefs by their Muslim names, but even where non-Muslim names are mentioned, these cannot be found on available chief-lists.

The earliest *certain* date in the Chronicle is 15th Rabīʿ al-Awwal 1121, i.e. May 1709, for the death of King ʿAbbās. A period of twelve years of civil war before that date interferes with calculating back by lengths of reign. Yet a *probable* date may lead us further: 'we have heard that he [Thaʿara Sulaymān son of Lāta] was deposed at the very end of the eleventh century [of the hijra].' From an earlier reference to the death of his father Lāta in A.H. 1083 (1672/3), sixteen years before, the date A.H. 1099 may be taken for the deposition of Thaʿara. If the reigns of the five kings who ruled before Thaʿara are added—122 years—a notional A.H. 961–91 (1554–83) may be suggested for the reign of Wādih or Nābaʿ, the first king mentioned by the Chronicle.

It was while King Nābaʿ was fighting at Kapuasi that Ismāʿīl, the Muslim from Beʿo, came to the king of Gonja. Ismāʿīl died on his way home. Nābaʿ died about the same time, because when Ismāʿīl's son, Muḥammad al-Abyaḍ, went to greet the Gonja king he met Maʿūra, Nābaʿ's successor.

The Chronicle records the genealogies of three descendants of Muḥammad al-Abyaḍ; his grandson died in 1691 (A.H. 1102), his great-grandson

[1] Ibid., pp. 127–8.

[2] From Osei Tutu (*c.* 1700–12) to Prempeh I (d. 1931) there were eleven kings in Ashanti, or an average of twenty-one years. Wilks (1964*a*) reached an average of fifteen years only for Akwapim.

in 1730/1 (A.H. 1143), and another great-grandson was appointed imam in 1747 (A.H. 1160). Even without speculating an average length of generation among Muslims (and this may reach forty years and more), it would be quite acceptable that Ismāʿīl, father of Muḥammad al-Abyaḍ, died in the last quarter of the sixteenth century. It was at that period that Ismāʿīl met the Gonja king, Nābaʿ, when the Gbanya had already been fighting within the territory of their future state.

Lāta, it has been suggested, is the consolidator of the state, who divided it into the divisional chiefdoms, and in this respect he may be identified with Jakpa of the oral traditions.[1] We may count, therefore, the beginning of the present constitution of Gonja from Lāta's reign (1623/4–1666/7), or the middle of the seventeenth century.

From the Gonja Chronicle it is possible to reconstruct a genealogical list of the paramount chiefs of Gonja from Lāta's son, Thaʿāra (1666/7–1687/8) to Sulaymān, son of ʿAbbās (1742–63). In this period of about a century there were twelve rulers in three generations, or an average of about thirty-three years per generation and over eight years per reign.

Turning to chief-lists: only those of Kpembe and Daboya are probably complete. The Kpembe chief-list, recorded in an Arabic manuscript in possession of the imam of Kpembe, comprises twenty-two chiefs from the first ruler after Jakpa (about the middle of the seventeenth century) to Yissifa (d. 1897), or an average of about eleven years per reign. The four chiefs of Kpembe mentioned in the Chronicle ruled from 1711 to 1751, or an average reign of ten years.

Two Arabic manuscripts record twenty-four or twenty-five chiefs in Daboya, from Chanchanku Beima (*c.* 1900) back to the first ruler at Daboya.[2] The latter came to Daboya from Wasipe (south of Bole). The former residence of the Daboya chiefs is still remembered in their title Wasipe-wura, which suggests that they had stayed there for some time before they moved to Daboya. It is clear that the Wasipe-wuras mentioned in the Chronicle (of whom the earliest died in 1719) had already been at Daboya. According to Dagomba chronology the conquest of Daboya occurred one generation before *c.* 1700. All this evidence points to a notional *c.* 1670–80 for the foundation of the Gonja chiefdom at Daboya. The twenty-four or twenty-five chiefs of Daboya, recorded in the manuscripts, ruled for over two hundred and twenty years, or an average of about nine years per reign.

Calculations based on contemporary evidence (the Gonja Chronicle) and oral traditions (chief-lists) suggest between eight and eleven years as the average length of a reign. In Gonja a rather short average per reign seems common, and may be explained by the mode of succession. Rotation among different branches of the chiefly family, both in the divisions and to the paramountcy, brings a chief to the skin at an advanced age.

[1] See above, pp. 52–53.

[2] IAS/AR-41 and 42.

(*c*) *Dagomba*

Of all the Middle Volta states, Dagomba had the most coherent traditions. The genealogy of the Dagomba chiefs may be established from the Drum History, which recites the names of each Ya-Na's sons, among them, of course, future Ya-Nas. Further, the history of Dagomba may be dated by documentary evidence corroborated by oral traditions. In the last six generations before *c.* 1900 at least one date in each generation is fairly reliable.

In the sixth generation before *c.* 1900, Na Dariziegu faced a fierce attack of the Gonja, who crossed the White Volta after they had conquered Daboya. The conquest of Daboya may, tentatively, be dated *c.* 1670.

In the fifth generation before *c.* 1900, Na Zangina's reign may be dated *c.* 1700–14 by inference from the Gonja Chronicle. The Chronicle recorded the death of Na Atabia of Mamprusi in A.H. 1154 (1741/2), adding that he had a long reign of fifty odd years. Na Atabia probably began his long reign in the late seventeenth century. Na Zangina was installed Ya-Na after he had been chosen by the chief of Mamprusi.[1] That Mamprusi chief, it is said, was Na Atabia. Indeed, both Zangina of Dagomba and Atabia of Mamprusi are of the fifth generation back from *c.* 1900, both are associated with the introduction of Islam, and it is very likely that they were contemporaneous. The Gonja Chronicle records in A.H. 1125 (1713) that a Gonja army was defeated in *Tunuma*, probably *Tuma*, i.e. western Dagomba. No later wars between Gonja and Dagomba are mentioned in the Chronicle which records events year by year. We may therefore assume that this was the last war between the two nations. According to the traditions of Dagomba, the last Gonja attack on Dagomba was repulsed towards the end of Na Zangina's reign.[2] This was probably the War of 1713 recorded by the Chronicle. A year later, A.H. 1126 (1714), the Chronicle records the death of the 'king of Yāni', in all probability the king of Yendi, Na Zangina.

In the fourth generation back from *c.* 1900, Na Gariba, son of Na Zangina, became tributary to Ashanti. Roemer, a Danish trader on the coast, reported an Ashanti expedition against a Muslim nation to the north-east of Kumasi in 1744.[3] This may refer to the Ashanti conquest of Dagomba in the reign of Na Gariba, i.e. *floruit* 1744.

In the third generation before *c.* 1900, Na Andani (Aldāni), son of Na Gariba, is mentioned as the king of Yendi in a letter sent by Kamshe-Na to Kumasi in the 1810s.[4]

Na Andani's son, Na Ziblim Kulunku, may safely be identified with Kirgangu, the name of the Dagomba king known to Barth in 1853.[5]

[1] See above, p. 88.
[2] See above, p. 89.
[3] Quoted in Bowdich, 1821, p. 18; see also Fynn, Ph.D. London, 1964.
[4] Copenhagen manuscripts, vol. i, f. 107. See above, pp. 96–97.
[5] Barth, 1857, iv. 556.

Towards the end of the reign of Na Ya'qūba, another son of Na Andani, a Civil War broke out between Ya'qūba's son Abdulai and his uncles. Soon after the war, the Dagomba were informed that 'Kwaku Dua was no more and Karikari had taken over'.[1] The Asantehene Kwaka Dua I died in 1867. About the same time Na Abdulai succeeded his father as Ya-Na. During Na Abdulai's reign Dagomba became independent of Ashanti after the latter's defeat by the British in 1874. Na Abdulai died in April or May 1876, a date indicated by R. Johnson, who visited Yendi as part of Dr. Gouldsbury's expedition. Johnson commenced his way back to the coast in July 1876, after he had been detained for six weeks, as the roads had been closed because of the death of the king of Yendi.[2] Na Andani II, Abdulai's brother, reigned 1876–99.

The dates established above offer quite a solid chronology for Dagomba history in the eighteenth and nineteenth centuries. From Na Zangina to Na Andani II, a period of about two hundred years, there were five generations of rulers in Dagomba, or an average of about forty years per generation. The same average is true for Mamprusi at the same period, from Na Atabia to Na Berega (d. 1902). A test of this average shows that if a period of forty years is assigned to each of the last six generations before *c.* 1900, all the dates suggested above fall within the assigned periods.

The genealogical list of Dagomba chiefs, based on the traditions recorded by Tamakloe and for Tait, appears quite reliable back to Na Nyaghse. If one calculates back forty years for a generation, Na Nyaghse, the consolidator of the Dagomba state, may have reigned in the second half of the fifteenth century. The same period was suggested also by J. D. Fage.[3] Professor Fage, however, reached this date by correcting an error of sixty years in Tamakloe's chronology. But the dates suggested above for Dagomba rulers show that Tamakloe's error of sixty years is inconsistent, and his chronology seems rather arbitrary.

In the two hundred years from Na Zangina to Na Andani II, there were thirteen rulers in Dagomba, or an average of fifteen and a half years per reign. This average, or indeed any other average length of reign, is inconsistent with dates suggested for individual rulers. Individual reigns fluctuate while lengths of generation seems more consistent; shorter reigns are regulated by a higher number of rulers per generation (e.g. Yatenga). But if the average of fifteen and a half years is taken for the whole list of Dagomba chiefs—twenty-nine rulers back from *c.* 1900—Na Nyaghse's reign will fall in the middle of the fifteenth century, about the same date reached by calculating an average length of generation. King-lists seem to have been better preserved than genealogies; the latter call for further information on parental relationships within an accepted king-list. Hence, where genealogy is absent or unreliable a king-list may give the principal data for chronology.

[1] Tait's manuscripts, text B.

[2] D.C. Accra to Ag. colonial secretary, enclosure in a dispatch to Lord Carnarvon, 6 September 1876, PRO, CO. 96/118, No. 186.

[3] Fage, 1964, p. 182.

(*d*) *Mamprusi*

Dagomba traditions know Na Bawa, or Na Gbewa, the legendary common ancestor of Dagomba and Mamprusi, but in reciting the names and deeds of the Dagomba chiefs, the drummers begin with Na Nyaghse, who may be regarded as the first historical, as distinguished from mythical, ruler. Indeed, Namo-Na, the chief drummer in Dagomba, traces his own genealogy, always an overture to the chanting of the official Drum History, back to Na Nyaghse.[1]

Mamprusi traditional history, it seems, has no historical figure comparable to Na Nyaghse, after Na Bawa/Gbewa. Mamprusi chiefs continue the senior line of chiefs from the common ancestor. This smooth continuity, without a clear break between the mythical origin and the historical development, may have contributed to the weakness of Mamprusi traditions compared with those of Dagomba.[2]

Mamprusi and Dagomba have a similar, collateral, mode of succession. One would expect also about the same number of rulers and generations for the same period. Yet from Na Gbewa/Bawa to *c.* 1900 Mamprusi had twenty-one rulers in ten generations, compared with thirty-two rulers in thirteen generations in Dagomba. Na Atabia of Mamprusi and Na Zangina of Dagomba were probably contemporaneous. Both are of the fifth generation, and the twelfth and thirteenth rulers respectively, back from *c.* 1900. If one takes the period before Na Atabia and Na Zangina, i.e. before *c.* 1700, Mamprusi had nine rulers in five generations compared with nineteen rulers in eight generations in Dagomba. The weakness of Mamprusi traditions before Na Atabia is shown also by the fact that independent recordings of the Mamprusi chief-list agree on the chiefs' names and order in the period after Na Atabia, but differ considerably for the pre-Atabia period.[3]

No sound chronology may therefore be suggested for Mamprusi before *c.* 1700. The dates suggested from the Gonja Chronicle for Na Atabia (late seventeenth century to 1741/2) are of crucial importance, but no other dates in the eighteenth and nineteenth centuries are suggested by documentary evidence. But since Mamprusi and Dagomba had the same number of generations (five) and a similar number of rulers (twelve and thirteen, respectively) in that period, Dagomba's chronology may be helpful also for Mamprusi. Thus, Na Kuligaba (or Kulba) of Mamprusi was the sixth ruler of the third generation back from *c.* 1900, and it would be fair to suggest that he reigned at about the same time as Na Andani I of Dagomba, the seventh ruler of the third generation back from *c.* 1900, who, we know, reigned at the beginning of the nineteenth century.

[1] I was present at such a recital of the Drum History at Yendi on the eve of *ʿId al-Fiṭr*, February 1964.

[2] On the weakness of Mamprusi tradition, see also Fage, 1964, pp. 182–3.

[3] The chief-lists recorded by Rattray and Mackay have probably been corroborated. An independent recording of the Mamprusi chief-list was made by R. A. Irvine in 1898 (NAG, Accra, 1371/53). See also IAS/AR-249.

(*e*) *Mossi*

The chronology of Mossi has occupied many scholars, but a new approach was offered by Professor Fage when he first worked out this chronology in the context of the Mossi-Dagomba group of states.[1] The Mossi chiefs trace their origin back to Nedega, chief of Gambaga, father of Yennega, mother of Widraogo, father of Zungrana, father of Wubri, the founder of the Mossi state of Wagadugu.

It is unnecessary to seek identification of Nedega of the Mossi traditions with Na Bawa/Gbewa of the Dagomba and Mamprusi traditions, or with any other Mamprusi chief. R. A. Prost's investigation of the traditions on the origin of Mossi concludes that Zungrana and Widraogo, father and grandfather of Wubri, never existed, and that Wubri was in fact son of Yennega, daughter of Nedega, king of Gambaga.[2] But Prost's note reminds us also that in the pre-Wubri period we enter the realm of myths of origin, when time can hardly be measured, and names of ancestors may represent more than one concrete personality. In Mossi we are on a more solid historical ground with Wubri, the founder of the state, who is comparable in this respect with Na Nyaghse of Dagomba.[3]

From Naba Wubri to *c.* 1900 eighteen generations are recorded in the Mossi state of Wagadugu, compared with twelve or thirteen generations in the Mossi state of Yatenga. The latter figure compares favourably with the figure of eleven generations in Dagomba since Na Nyaghse. Yatenga had forty-four rulers from Naba Wubri to *c.* 1900, Wagadugu thirty rulers, and Dagomba twenty-nine rulers (from Na Nyaghse). The high number of rulers in Yatenga is explicable by both internal and external wars. On the other hand, the almost equal number of rulers in Wagadugu and Dagomba does imply what may be suggested in terms of generations for Yatenga, namely, that Naba Wubri and Na Nyaghse may have been contemporaneous.

By correlating traditions of Yatenga and Bambara, Tauxier dates the reign of Naba Kango of Yatenga in 1754–87.[4] Naba Kango was the last ruler of the four generations back from *c.* 1900. The following three generations ruled for about a hundred and fifteen years, or an average of thirty-eight years per generation, compared with forty years in Dagomba and Mamprusi. If one calculates thirty-eight years for a generation, Naba Wubri reigned about the middle of the fifteenth century.[5]

It is more difficult to fit into this chronology the Mossi state of Wagadugu with its high number of generations; eighteen compared with twelve or thirteen in Yatenga. This is explicable by the fact that for many generations the genealogy of the Wagadugu chiefs shows a filial succession, from

[1] Fage, 1964, p. 177.
[2] Prost, 1953, pp. 1336–7.
[3] Fage, 1964, pp. 185–6.
[4] Tauxier, 1917, pp. 667–8.
[5] If the Mossi state was consolidated only in the middle of the fifteenth century, references in Ta'rīkh al-Sūdān to earlier raids of Mossi on Mali need a new critical revision. See also Fage, 1964, pp. 178–9.

father to son. A filial succession is unusual in this group of states, because Yatenga, Mamprusi, and Dagomba all have a collateral mode of succession. Indeed, this is true also of inheritance of property and family leadership among the Mossi of Wagadugu themselves.[1] That relationships within the regnal genealogical list between successive rulers are not established beyond doubt is shown also by the fact that various lists do not agree.[2] Genealogies tend to be more reliable both at the earlier and recent periods, while distortions are more often in between, in the long middle period. In the genealogical list of the Moro-Nabas of Wagadugu, the first three generations after Naba Wubri and the last three generations before 1905 clearly show a collateral succession.[3] It could be argued that collateral succession was more common in Wagadugu than is revealed by the available genealogy, but for the purpose of the present study we will have to deal mainly with the two periods for which collateral succession was certainly the rule, because these are the crucial periods in the history of Islam in Mossi.

The first group of Yarse is said to have come to Wagadugu in the reign of Naba Kundumie, grandson of Naba Wubri. Wubri was succeeded by four of his sons. The split between Wagadugu and Yatenga occurred in the time of Naba Kundumie, whose brother Naba Yadega was the first ruler of Yatenga. We can date Yadega, and therefore also Kundumie, by using the average length of a generation suggested for Yatenga, thirty-eight years. Hence, Naba Kundumie may have reigned at the beginning of the sixteenth century.

After Na Kundumie the genealogy narrows to a filial line of succession until Naba Dulugu, the eighth ruler back from 1905. The seven following rulers were of three generations, i.e. in a collateral succession. Naba Dulugu, who appointed the first imam in Wagadugu, was of the fourth generation back from *c.* 1905, and may be dated to the late eighteenth century. His grandson, Naba Kutu, died in 1870.[4]

(*f*) *Wa*

The rulers of Buna and Wa claim origin from Dagomba. Y. Person suggests a date at the beginning of the seventeenth century for the foundation of Buna. Buna traditions, he says, remember the passing of the Gbanya invaders (in the second half of the sixteenth century) before the establishment of the present dynasty.[5]

A tradition recorded by Tamakloe says that Na Dariguyomda of Dagomba (second half of the sixteenth century) led an expedition to Buna. He left behind a son by a local woman, Bunkani, who became the founder of the Buna dynasty.[6] This tradition is not supported by traditions from Buna and Wa. In Buna it is said that Bunkani was the son of a Dagomba

[1] Tauxier, 1912, p. 545; Skinner, 1964, p. 19.
[2] Compare Tauxier (1912, pp. 461–2) with Tiendrebeogo, 1963.
[3] Cf. Skinner, 1964, pp. 36–37.
[4] Binger, 1892, i. 460.
[5] Person, 1962, p. 473.
[6] Tamakloe, 1931, pp. 19–20.

hunter who lived on the eastern bank of the Black Volta, namely in the region of Wa.[1] The History of Wa says that Bunkani was the son of a Dagomba man from the invasion which preceded that of the Wala chiefs.[2]

The History of Wa implies that the dynasty of Wa was established after that of Buna. Dagomba traditions do not mention the creation of the Wa dynasty. In Wa several Dagomba chiefs are mentioned as responsible for the foundation of the dynasty, but none is certain. The available information about the Wala chiefs does not help us in reconstructing genealogy, and therefore an average length of generation is of no help. The only datable ruler is Wa-Na Gangumi, the sixth ruler back from 1896, who reigned at the beginning of the Zaberma raids, in *c.* 1870.[3] The last quarter of the nineteenth century was a troubled period in the history of Wa (three successive conquerors: Babatu, Samori, and the British), and the very short average reign which may be suggested for the last six rulers (four or five years) does not necessarily apply to earlier reigns.

The chief-list of Wa is therefore of little help for the chronology of the kingdom. Fortunately, the genealogical list of imams may lead us to some conclusion. Names of the imams of Wa are preserved in several manuscripts, arranged in the form of a litany. Four such manuscripts consulted end each with a different imam.[4] Perhaps on the death of an imam his name was added, and with it another invocation. The oldest available manuscript ends with Imam Ṣāliḥ, who officiated in the 1910s.[5] The unique form of these lists, and the fact that there has been a continuous tradition, suggest that names of imams may have been so recorded for quite a long time, although one cannot tell when it started.

In one list some imams are mentioned with their fathers' names.[6] In another manuscript, marginal notes add the father of each imam.[7] The additions may be recent, but with an established list of imams, all of the same family, the genealogy reconstructed from its information is not without value.[8]

[1] Labouret, 1931, pp. 21–22.
[2] IAS/AR-152; see above, pp. 141–2.
[3] IAS/AR-22.
[4] IAS/AR-17, 61, 296, and a manuscript in possession of the present imam, Saʿīd. A fifth manuscript, IAS/AR-46, is in the same form but the text of the litany is different. The form is:
'For the sake of imam [name], Oh Allāh [against the name of each imam one of the holy names of Allāh is called] give us . . .'
[5] IAS/AR-17. Imam Ṣāliḥ was the nineteenth imam. The seventeenth imam, Mūsā, officiated during the British conquest (1896), whereas the twenty-first imam, Mahama, died in 1936 (Wa District Record Book, 1922–46, NAG, Accra, 136/54).
[6] IAS/AR 61. The fathers' names may have been added by the scribe of this manuscript, for these names do not appear in the other manuscripts.
[7] IAS/AR-296. This copy ends with Imam Muhammad (the twenty-third imam), probably of the 1940s. The marginal notes are in the same hand as the text.
[8] The genealogy reconstructed from this information has been corroborated by several genealogies of informants in Wa and its region, all of the same family.

The present imam, Saʿīd, is the twenty-seventh imam of Wa, and he is of the seventh generation after Yaʿumaru, the first imam. The seventeenth imam, of the fifth generation, lived in 1894.[1] Imam Ṣiḍḍīq, who held office in *c.* 1870,[2] was of the fourth generation, but one imam who preceded him belonged to the fifth generation. This makes it somewhat complicated, but if we take the period of imams of the fifth and sixth generations (the latter ends with the previous imam of the 1950s), these two generations extended over more than eighty years, or an average of about forty years per generation.[3]

If one calculates back according to this average, the first Imam Yaʿumaru may have come to Wa in the late seventeenth or early eighteenth century. The history of Wa says that Yaʿumaru came in the reign of the third Wa-Na, Pilpu, son of Sorliya the founder of the dynasty. Hence, the foundation of the kingdom of Wa may be dated early in the second half of the seventeenth century, about half a century later than the kingdom of Buna.

[1] 'Chief Priest-Alimami Gamusa' is one of the signatories on a treaty in Wa, dated 4 May 1894 (enclosure 1 in No. 6, *African* (*West*), No. 479, PRO, CO. 879/41.

[2] IAS/AR-22. See above, p. 155.

[3] Twenty-seven imams in seven generations, or three to five imams in each generation, indicate a relatively short average tenure of office, but a rather high average length of generation.

BIBLIOGRAPHY

LIST OF ABBREVIATIONS

BCEHSAOF	*Bulletin du Comité d'Études historiques et scientifiques de l'Afrique Occidentale Française* (Dakar)
Bull. IFAN	*Bulletin de l'Institut Français de l'Afrique Noire* (Dakar)
CEA	*Cahiers d'Études Africaines* (Paris)
CHEAM	Centre de Hautes Études sur l'Afrique et l'Asie modernes (Paris)
GNQ	*Ghana Notes and Queries* (Accra)
IAS	Institute of African Studies (Legon–Accra)
JAH	*Journal of African History* (London)
JAS	*Journal of the African Society* (London)
JSA	*Journal de la Société des Africanistes* (Paris)
JHSN	*Journal of the Historical Society of Nigeria* (Ibadan)
MSOS	*Mitteilungen des Seminars für Orientalische Sprachen* (*Afrikanische Sprachen*, III. Abt.) (Berlin)
NA	*Notes Africaines* (Dakar)
NAG	National Archives of Ghana
PRO	Public Record Office (London)
RGS	Royal Geographical Society (London)
RMM	*Revue du Monde Musulman* (Paris)
TGCTHS	*Transactions of the Gold Coast and Togoland Historical Society* (Accra)
THSG	*Transactions of the Historical Society of Ghana* (Accra)

1. PUBLISHED WORKS

ABRAHAM, R. C., 1962. *Dictionary of the Hausa Language*, London.

AGYEMAN-DUAH, J., 1960. 'Mampong Ashanti: a Traditional History to the Reign of Nana Safo Kantaka', *THSG*, iv. 2, 21–25,

ALEXANDRE, PIERRE, 1964. 'Organisation politique des Kotokoli du Nord-Togo', *CEA*, xiv. 228–74.

—— et FROELICH, J. C., 1960. 'Histoire traditionnelle des Kotokoli et des Bi-Tchambi du Nord-Togo', *Bull. IFAN*, xxii. 211–75.

ALEXANDRE, P. G., 1953. *La Langue More*, 2 vols., IFAN, Dakar.

ANDERSON, J. N. D., 1954. *Islamic Law in Africa*, London.

ANONYMOUS, 1950. 'Note sur les "Pila-Pila" et les "Taneka"', *Études Dahoméennes*, iii. 39–74.

ARHIN, K., 1965. 'Kintampo', *Supplement No. 1 to Research Review*, IAS, Legon.

ARMITAGE, C. H., 1924. *The Tribal Markings and Marks of Adornment of the Natives in the Northern Territories of the Gold Coast Colony*, London.

ASMIS, R., 1912. 'Die Stammesrechte des Bezirkes Sansanne Mangu', *Zeitschrift für vergleichende Rechtswissenschaft*, Berlin, xxvii. 73–89.

AL-BAKRĪ, 1911. *Kitāb al-Masālik wa'l-Mamālik*, pub. par M. G. De Slane, Alger.

—— 1913. *Description de l'Afrique Septentrionale*, trad. par M. G. De Slane, Alger.

BARTH, H., 1957. *Travels and Discoveries in North and Central Africa*, 5 vols., London.

BECK, 1880–1. 'Eine neu Route nach dem obern Niger und dem Sudan', *Jahresbericht des Geographischen Gesellschaft in Bern*, pp. 35–53.

BEECHAM, J., 1841. *Ashantee and the Gold Coast*, London.

BELLO, MUḤAMMAD, 1951. *Infāq al-Maysūr*, ed. by C. E. J. Whitting, Kano.

BELLOT, F., 1949. 'Étude sur la toponomie des quartiers de Ouagadougou', *NA*, xlii. 61–64.

BENQUEY, 1921. 'Considérations sur l'Islam africain (Haute Côte d'Ivoire)', *BCEHSAOF*, pp. 678–88.

BERNUS, E., 1960. 'Kong et sa région', *Études Éburnéennes*, pp. 239–323.

BERTHO, P., 1949. 'Notice sur les Pila-Pila du Dahomey', *NA*, xliii. 74.

BICHON, B., 1963. 'Les Musulmans de la Subdivision de Kombissiry (Haute Volta)', *Notes et Études sur l'Islam en Afrique Noire*, CHEAM, Paris.

BINGER, L. G., 1889. 'Transactions, objets de commerce, monnaie des contrées entre le Niger et la Côte de l'Or', *Bull. Soc. Géogr. Commer.*, Paris, xii. 77–90.

—— 1892. *Du Niger au Golfe de Guinée*, 2 vols., Paris.

BOAHEN, A. ADU, 1961. 'The Ghana Kola Trade', *GNQ*, i. 8–10.

—— 1964. *Britain, the Sahara and the Western Sudan*, Oxford.

BOATENG, E. A., 1960. *A Geography of Ghana*, Cambridge (reprint).

BONNAT, J., 1875*a*. 'A letter from J. Bonnat to Governor Straham', *L'Explorateur*, 1875, pp. 556–8.

—— 1875*b*. 'Le pays des Ashantis et le fleuve Volta', *L'Explorateur*, pp. 58–59.

BOWDICH, T. E., 1819. *A Mission from Cape Coast Castle to Ashantee*, London.

—— 1821. *An Essay on the Geography of North-Western Africa*, Paris.

—— 1821*a*. *An Essay on the Superstitions, Customs and Arts, common to the Ancient Egyptians, Abyssinians and Ashantees*, Paris.

—— 1821*b*. *The British and French Expeditions to Teemboo*, Paris.

BURTON, R. F., 1864. *A Mission to Gelele*, 2 vols., London.

CA DA MOSTO, A. DE, 1895. *Relations des voyages à la Côte Occidentale d'Afrique, 1455–7*, pub. par Ch. Schefer, Paris.

Caillié, R., 1830. *Journal d'un voyage à Tombouctou et à Jenné dans l'Afrique centrale*, Paris.

Cardinall, A. W., 1925. *The Natives of the Northern Territories of the Gold Coast*, London.

—— 1927. *In Ashanti and Beyond*, London.

—— 1929. 'The State of our Present Ethnographical Knowledge of the Gold Coast Peoples', *Africa*, ii. 405–12.

—— 1931. *Tales told in Togoland*, London.

Chanoine, Lieutenant, 1898. 'Le Gourounsi', *Bull. de la Soc. de Géogr. de Lille*, février.

Cheron, G., 1924. 'Contribution à l'histoire du Mossi. Traditions relatives au cercle du Kaya (Haute Volta)', *BCEHSAOF*, viii. 304–12.

—— 1925. 'La cour du Boussuma Naba', *BCEHSAOF*, viii. 3.

Chudeau, R., 1910. 'Le grand commerce indigène de l'Afrique Occidentale', *Bull. de la Soc. Géogr. Commer.*, xxxii. 398–412.

Clapperton, H., 1829. *Journal of a Second Expedition into the Interior of Africa*, London.

Claridge, W. W., 1915. *A History of the Gold Coast and Ashanti*, 2 vols., London.

Cornevin, R., 1959. 'Exploration de von François et du Dr Wolf au Togo (1888)', *NA*, lxxxiv. 106–7.

—— 1962*a*. *Histoire du Togo*, Paris.

—— 1962*b*. *Histoire du Dahomey*, Paris.

—— 1962*c*. *Les Bassari du Nord-Togo*, Paris.

—— 1964. 'Contribution à l'étude des populations parlant des langues Gouang au Togo et au Dahomey', *Journal of African Languages*, iii. 226–30.

—— 1964. 'A propos des Cotokoli du Moyen-Togo', *NA*, ci. 27–28.

—— 1964. 'Contribution à l'histoire de la Chefferie Cotokoli', *CEA*, xv. 456–60.

Dalzel, A., 1793. *The History of Dahomey*, London.

Davies, O., 1961. 'The Invaders of Northern Ghana: What Archaeologists are Teaching the Historians', *Universitas* (Legon), iv. 134–6.

Delafosse, M., 1904. *Vocabulaires comparatifs de plus de 60 langues ou dialectes parlés à la Côte d'Ivoire et dans les régions limitrophes*, Paris.

—— 1908. *Les frontières de la Côte d'Ivoire, de la Côte de l'Or et du Soudan*, Paris.

—— 1910*a*. 'Le clergé musulman de l'Afrique occidentale', *RMM*, xi. 177–206.

—— 1910*b*. 'Les noms des noirs musulmans du Soudan occidental', *RMM*, xii. 257–61.

—— 1912. *Haut-Sénégal-Niger*, 3 vols., Paris.

—— 1921. 'L'animisme nègre et sa résistance à l'islamisation en Afrique occidentale', *RMM*, xlix. 121–64.

DELAFOSSE, M., 1955. *La langue Mandingue et ses dialectes* (*Malinke, Bambara, Dioula*), Paris, vol. ii.

DELBOSOM, A. A. DIM, 1932. *L'empire du Mogho-Naba. Coutumes des Mossi de la Haute Volta*, Paris.

—— 1934. 'Note sur les Yarce au Mossi', *Revue Anthropologique*, xliv. 326–33.

DELMONT, P., 1949. 'Esquisse géographique du Gourma central: le cercle de Dori', *NA*, xlii. 57–60.

DENHAM, D., and CLAPPERTON, H., 1826. *Narrative of Travels and Discoveries in Northern and Central Africa, in the Years 1822, 1823 and 1824*, London.

DOUTTÉ, E., 1909. *Magie et religion dans l'Afrique du Nord*, Alger.

DUNCAN-JOHNSTONE, A. C., 1927. 'Diary of an Overland Journey from Lorha, Northern Territories of the Gold Coast to Dakar, Senegal', *Gold Coast Review*, iii. 269–93.

—— and BLAIR, H. A., 1932. *Enquiry into the Constitution and Organisation of the Dagbon Kingdom*, Accra.

DUPUIS, J., 1824. *Journal of a Residence in Ashanti*, London.

EYRE-SMITH, ST.-J., 1933. *A Brief Review of the History and Social Organisation of the Peoples of the Northern Territories of the Gold Coast*, Accra.

FAGE, J. D., 1955. 'Some Problems of Gold Coast History', *Universitas*, i. 5–9.

—— 1956. 'The Investigation of Oral Tradition in the Northern Territories of the Gold Coast', *JHSN*, i. 1.

—— 1957. 'Ancient Ghana: a Review of the Evidence', *THSG*, iii. 2.

—— 1958. 'The Use of Oral Evidence in West African History', *Bull. of the Inst. of Historical Research*, xxxi.

—— 1959. *Ghana: A Historical Interpretation*, Madison.

—— 1964. 'Reflections on the Early History of the Mossi-Dagomba Group of States', in *The Historian in Tropical Africa*, ed. by Vansina, Mauny, and Thomas, London, pp. 177–91.

—— 1964*a*. 'Some thoughts on State-formation in the Western Sudan before the Seventeenth Century', *Boston University Papers in African History*, vol. i, ed. by J. Butler, Boston, pp. 19–34.

FERNANDES, V., 1938. *Description de la Côte d'Afrique de Ceuta au Sénégal*, ed. par P. de Cenival et Th. Monod, Paris.

—— 1951. *Description de la Côte occidentale d'Afrique* (*Sénégal au Cap de Monte, Archipels*), ed. par Th. Monod, A. Teixeira da Mota, et R. Mauny, Bissau.

FISCH, R., 1911. *Nord Togo und seine westliche Nachbarschaft*, Basle.

FISHER, H. J., 1963. *Ahmadiyyah. A Study in Contemporary Islam on the West African Coast*, London.

FORTES, M., 1940. 'The Political System of the Tallensi', in *African Political Systems*, ed. by Fortes and Evans-Pritchard, London.

FORTES, M., 1944. 'The Significance of Descent in Tale Social Structure', *Africa*, xiv. 362–85.

—— 1945. *The Dynamics of Clanship among the Tallensi*, London.

—— 1945. *The Web of Kinship among the Tallensi*, London.

FREEMAN, A., 1898. *Travels and Life in Ashanti and Jaman*, London.

FREEMAN, T. B., 1844. *Journal of Various Visits to the Kingdoms of Ashanti, Aku and Dahome in Western Africa*, London.

FROBENIUS, L., 1913. *The Voice of Africa*, 2 vols., London.

FROELICH, J. C., 1954. *La tribu Konkomba du Nord-Togo*, IFAN, Dakar.

—— 1962. *Les Musulmans d'Afrique Noire*, Paris.

—— 1962*a*. 'Le nom des Kotokoli du Moyen-Togo', *NA*, xcv. 92–93.

—— ALEXANDRE, P. et CORNEVIN, R., 1963. *Les Populations du Nord-Togo*, Paris.

GARLICK, P. C., 1960. *African Traders in Kumasi*, Accra.

GOODY, J., 1953. 'A Note on the Penetration of Islam into the West of the Northern Territories of the Gold Coast', *TGCTHS*, i. 45–46.

—— 1954. *The Ethnography of the Northern Territories of the Gold Coast, West of the White Volta*, London.

—— 1956. *The Social Organisation of the Lo-Willi*, London.

—— 1959. 'Ethnohistory and the Akan of Ghana', *Africa*, xxix. 67–81.

—— 1963. 'Ethnological Notes on the Distribution of the Guang Languages', *Jour. of African Languages*, ii. 173–89.

—— 1964. 'The Mande and the Akan Hinterland', in *The Historian in Tropical Africa*, ed. by Vansina, Mauny, and Thomas, London, pp. 193–218.

—— 1965. 'Ashanti and the North-West', Supplement No. 1 to *Research Review*, IAS, Legon.

——1967. 'The Over-kingdom of Gonja' in *West African Kingdoms in the Nineteenth Century*, ed. by D. Forde and P. M. Kaberry, London.

GREENBERG, J. H., 1946. *The Influence of Islam on a Sudanese Religion*, New York.

—— 1960. 'Linguistic Evidence for the Influence of the Kanuri on the Hausa', *JAH*, i. 205–12.

GROS, 1876. 'Les Ashantis d'après les relations de M. Bonnat', *L'Explorateur*.

HALLET, R., 1964. *Records of the African Association, 1788–1831*, London.

HÉBERT, P., 1961. 'Samory en Haute Volta', *Études Voltaiques*, ii. 5–55.

HILTON, T. E., 1960. *Population Atlas of Ghana*, London.

—— 1963. 'Notes on the History of Kusasi', *THSG*, vi. 79–81.

HODGKIN, TH., 1966. 'The Islamic Literary Tradition in Ghana', *Islam in Tropical Africa*, ed. by I. M. Lewis, London, pp. 442–60.

HOGBEN, S. J., and KIRK-GREENE, A. M. H., 1966. *The Emirates of Northern Nigeria*, London.

HUTTON, W., 1821. *Voyage to Africa*, London.

IBN BAṬṬŪṬA, 1922. *Voyages*, texte arabe accompagné d'une traduction par C. Defremery et le Dr B. R. Sanguinetti, Paris.

AL-IDRĪSĪ, 1866. *Kitāb Nuzhat al-Mushtāq fī Ikhtirāq al-Āfāk* (*Description de l'Afrique et de l'Espagne*), pub. et trad. par R. Dozy et M. J. De Goeje, Leyde.

ILBOUDO, P., 1966. *Croyances et pratiques religieuses traditionnelles des Mossi*, Paris.

JONES, D. H., 1963. 'Jakpa and the Foundation of Gonja', *THSG*, vi. 1–30.

KABORE, V. K., 1966. *Organisation politique traditionnelle et évolution politique des Mossi de Ouagadougou*, Paris.

KA'TI, MAḤMŪD, 1913. *Ta'rīkh al-Fattāsh*, texte arabe et traduction française par O. Houdas et M. Delafosse, Paris.

KIMBLE, D., 1963. *Political History of Ghana*, London.

KIRBY, B., 1884. 'A Journey into the Interior of Ashanti', *Proceedings of the RGS*, vi.

KOELLE, S., 1854. *Polyglotta Africana*, London.

KRAUSE, G. A., 1887. 'Lettre à M. Duverpier', *C.R. des Séances de la Soc. de Géogr.*, p. 356.

KRIEGER, G., 1954. 'Kola Karawanen. Ein Beitrag zur Geschichte des Hausahandlers', *Mitteil. Institut Orientforschung*, ii. 289–324.

LABOURET, H., 1931. *Les tribus du rameau Lobi*, Paris.

—— 1938. *Nouvelles notes sur les tribus du rameau Lobi*, Dakar.

LANDER, R. L., 1830. *Records of Captain Clapperton's Last Expedition*, London.

—— and LANDER, J., 1832. *Journal of an Expedition to explore the Course and Termination of the Niger*, London.

LAST, M. D., and AL-HAJJ, M. A., 1965. 'Attempts at defining a Muslim in 19th century Hausaland and Bornu', *JHSN*, iii. 231–40.

LE CHATELIER, A., 1899. *L'Islam dans l'Afrique Occidentale*, Paris.

LEO AFRICANUS, 1956. *Description de l'Afrique*, nouvelle édition, trad. par A. Épaulard et annotée par E. Épaulard, Th. Monod, H. Lhote et R. Mauny, Paris.

LEVTZION, N., 1966. 'Salaga—A Nineteenth Century Trading Town in Ghana', *Asian and African Studies*, Jerusalem, ii. 207–44.

—— 'Arabic Manuscripts from Kumasi of the Early Nineteenth Century', *THSG*, viii.

LHOTE, H., 1955 and 1956. 'Contribution à l'étude du Touareg Soudanais', *Bull. IFAN*, B, 1955, 334–70; 1956, 391–407.

LIPPERT, J., 1907. 'Über die Bedeutung der Hausanation für unsere Togo- und Kamerunkolonien', *MSOS*, 193–226.

LOMBARD, J., 1957. 'Un système politique traditionnel de type féodal: les Bariba du Nord Dahomey. Aperçu sur l'organisation sociale et le pouvoir central', *Bull. IFAN*, xix. 464–506.

—— 1960. 'La vie politique dans une ancienne société de type féodal: les Bariba du Dahomey', *CEA*, iii. 5–45.

—— 1965. *Structures de type 'Féodal' en Afrique Noire: Études des dynamismes internes et des relations sociales chez les Bariba du Dahomey*, Paris.

LONSDALE, R. LA T., 1882. 'Report, 24 March 1882', *Parliamentary Papers*, 1882, xlvi, C. 3386, enclosure 2 in No. 42.

MANOUKIAN, M., 1951. *Tribes of the Northern Territories of the Gold Coast*, London.

MARC, L., 1909. *Le Pays Mossi*, Paris.

MARTY, P., 1920. *Études sur l'islam et les tribus du Soudan*, 4 vols., Paris.

—— 1922. *Études sur l'Islam en Côte d'Ivoire*, Paris.

—— 1926. *Études sur l'Islam au Dahomey*, Paris.

AL-MAS'ŪDĪ, 1861–77. *Kitāb Murūj al-Dhahab wa Ma'ādin al-Jawhar*, pub. par C. Barbier de Meynard et Pavet de Courteille, Paris.

MAUNY, R., 1961. *Tableau Géographique de l'Ouest Africain au Moyen Âge*, IFAN, Dakar.

MENJAUD, H., 1932. 'Documents ethnographiques sur le Gourma recueillis en 1907 par Maubert', *JSA*, ii. 35–47.

METCALFE, G. E., 1964. *Great Britain and Ghana (Documents of Ghana History), 1807–1957*, London.

MEYEROWITZ, E. L. R., 1951. *The Sacred State of the Akan*, London.

—— 1952. *Akan Traditions of Origin*, London.

—— 1958. *The Akan of Ghana*, London.

—— 1962. 'Akan Oral Historical Traditions', *Universitas*, v, 2, pp. 44–49.

MONTEIL, LIEUTENANT, 1894. *De Saint-Louis à Tripoli par le Tchad*, Paris.

MONTEIL, CH., 1924. *Les Bambara de Ségou et du Kaarta*, Paris.

—— 1927. *Le coton chez les noirs*, Paris.

—— 1932. *Une cité soudanaise—Djenné*, Paris.

MONTEIL, V., 1963. 'Sur l'arabisation des langues négro-africaines', *Acta Africana*, ii. 12–19.

—— 1964. *L'Islam Noir*, Paris.

NADEL, S. F., 1946. *A Black Byzantium. The Kingdom of Nupe in Nigeria*, London.

—— 1954. *Nupe Religion*, London.

NICHOLAS, F. J., 1952. 'La question de l'ethnique "Gourounsi" en Haute-Volta', *Africa*, xxii. 170–2.

NORTHCOTT, H. P., 1899. *Report on the Northern Territories of the Gold Coast*, London.

OLDEROGGE, D. A., 1960. *Zapadnuy Sudan v xv–xix* (Western Sudan in the fifteenth–nineteenth centuries), Moscva.

OZANNE, P., 1962. 'An Earthware Oil-lamp from near Nsawam', *THSG*, v. 72–77.

PAGUCKI, R., 1955. *A Survey of Land Tenure in Customary Law of the Protectorate of the Northern Territories*, Accra.

PALMER, H. R., 1908. 'The Kano Chronicle', *Journal of the Anthropological Institute*, xxxviii. 58–98.

—— 1927. 'History of Katsina', *JAS*, xxvi. 216–36.

—— 1928. *Sudanese Memoirs*, 3 vols., Lagos.

—— 1936. *The Bornu Sahara and Sudan*, London.

PÉRIE, J., et SELLIER, M., 1950. 'Histoire des populations du cercle de Dosso (Niger)', *Bull. IFAN*, xii. 1015–74.

PARK, MUNGO, 1799. *Travels in the Interior Districts of Africa*, London.

PERRON, M., 1924. 'Le pays Dendi', *BCEHSAOF*, pp. 51–83.

PERSON, Y., 1956. 'Esquisse sociale et historique des Gbabatse de Samle (Semere)', *Bull. IFAN*, xviii. 202–27.

—— 1962. 'Tradition orale et chronologie', *CEA*, vii. 462–76.

—— 1963. 'Les ancêtres de Samori', *CEA*, xiii. 125–56.

—— 1964. 'En quête d'une chronologie ivorienne', in *The Historian in Tropical Africa*, ed. by Vansina, Mauny, and Thomas, London, pp. 322–38.

PRIESTLEY, M., and WILKS, I., 1960. 'The Ashanti Kings in the Eighteenth Century: a Revised Chronology', *JAH*, i. 83–96.

PROCEEDINGS, 1790, 1810. *Proceedings of the Association for Promoting the Discovery of the Interior Parts of Africa*, London.

PROST, P. A., 1945. 'Notes sur les Boussanse', *Bull. IFAN*, vii. 47–53.

—— 1953. 'Notes sur l'origine des Mossi', *Bull. IFAN*, xv. 1933–8.

PROUTEAUX, M., 1925. 'Divertissements de Kong', *BCEHSAOF*, 606–50.

RAMSEYER, F. A., and KÜHNE, J., 1875. *Four Years in Ashantee*, ed. by Weitbrecht, London.

RANDAU, R., 1934. 'Les Yarce', *Revue Anthropologique*, lxiv. 324–5.

RATTRAY, R. S., 1913. *Hausa Folk-lore*, London.

—— 1923. *Ashanti*, London.

—— 1927. *Religion and Art in Ashanti*, London.

—— 1929. *Ashanti Law and Constitution*, London.

—— 1932. *Tribes of the Ashanti Hinterland*, 2 vols., London.

RENOUARD, G. C., 1836. 'Routes in North Africa', *Journal of the RGS*, vi. 102–13.

ROUCH, J., 1953. *Contribution à l'histoire des Songhay*, IFAN, Dakar.

—— 1956. 'Migrations au Ghana', *JSA*, pp. 33–126.

—— et BERNUS, E., 1959. 'Notes sur une communauté "Nigérienne" ancienne en Côte d'Ivoire: Marabadiassa', *NA*, lxxxiv. 107–10.

AL-SA'DĪ, ʿABD AL-RAḤMAN, 1900. *Ta'rīkh al-Sūdān* (éd. et trad. par O. Houdas), Paris.

SAVONNET, G., 1956. 'Notes sur quelques ruines situées dans la région de Léo (Haute Volta)', *NA*, lxxi. 65–67.

SEEFRIED, VON, 1913. 'Beitrage zur Geschichte des Mangovolkes in Togo', *Zeitschrift für Ethnologie*, xlv. 421–35.

SHIELDS, C. B., 1926. 'The Western Gonja (Bole) District', *Geographical Journal*, lxvii. 421–31.

SHINNIE, P. L., 1961. 'Yendi Dabari', *GNQ*, iii. 4.

—— and OZANNE, P., 1963. 'Excavation at Yendi Dabari', *THSG*, vi. 87–118.

SKINNER, E. P., 1958. 'Christianity and Islam among the Mossi', *American Anthropologist*, lx. 1102–19.

—— 1963. 'Strangers in West African Societies', *Africa*, xxxiii, 307–20.

—— 1964. *The Mossi of Upper Volta*, Stanford.

—— 1966. 'Islam in Mossi Society', in *Islam in Tropical Africa*, ed. by I. M. Lewis, London, pp. 350–73.

SMITH, H. F. C., 1961. 'A Neglected Theme of West African History: The Islamic Revolutions of the Nineteenth Century', *JHSN*, ii. 169–85.

STEVENS, P. D., 1955. 'Konkomba or Dagomba?', *TGCTHS*, i. 211–16.

TAIT, D., 1961. *The Konkomba of Northern Ghana*, London.

—— 1963. 'A Sorcery Hunt in Dagomba', *Africa*, xxxiii. 136–47.

—— and STEVENS, P. D., 1955. 'History and Social Organisation', *TGCTHS*, i. 5, pp. 193–209.

TAMAKLOE, E. F., 1931. *Brief History of the Dagbamba People*, Accra.

TAUXIER, L., 1912. *Le Noir du Soudan. Pays Mossi et Gourounsi*, Paris.

—— 1917. *Le Noir du Yatenga*, Paris.

—— 1921. *Le Noir de Bondoukou*, Paris.

—— 1924. *Nouvelles Notes sur le Mossi et le Gourounsi*, Paris.

TIENDREBEOGO, Y., 1963. 'Histoire traditionnelle des Mossi de Ouagadougou', ed. par R. Pageard, *JSA*, xxxiii. 7–46.

TORDOFF, W., 1965. *Ashanti under the Prempehs, 1888–1935*, London.

TRANAKIDES, G., 1953. 'Observations on the History of Some Gold Coast Peoples', *TGCTHS*, i. 2, pp. 33–44.

TRIERENBERG, G., 1914. *Togo: Die Erschliessung des Landes*, Berlin.

TRIMINGHAM, J. S., 1959. *Islam in West Africa*, London.

—— 1962. *History of Islam in West Africa*, London.

URVOY, Y., 1936. *Histoire des populations du Soudan central* (*Colonie du Niger*), Paris.

—— 1949. *Histoire de l'empire de Bornou*, IFAN, Dakar.

VANSINA, J., 1965. *Oral Tradition*, Chicago.

VOULET, 1897. 'Au Mossi et au Gourounsi', *Bull. de la Soc. de Géogr.*, xix. 720–51.

WADDY, B. B., 1897. 'Some Reminiscences of the Western Northern Territories of the Gold Coast', *The Nigerian Field*, xxii. 70–85.

EL-WAKKAD, M., and WILKS, I., 1961–2. 'The Story of Salaga and the History of Gonja', *GNQ*, iii. 8–31; iv. 6–25.

WATHERSON, A. M. C., 1908. 'The Northern Territories of the Gold Coast', *JAS*, vii. 344–73.

WESTERMANN, D., 1914. *Die Verbreitung des Islam in Togo und Kamerun*, Berlin.

WILKS, IVOR, 1960. 'A Note on the Traditional History of Mampong', *THSG*, iv. 2, 26–29.

—— 1961. *The Northern Factor in Ashanti History*, Legon.

—— 1962. 'A Medieval Trade Route from the Niger to the Gulf of Guinea', *JAH*, iii. 337–41.

—— 1964. 'The Growth of the Akwapim State: a Study in the Control of Evidence', in *The Historian in Tropical Africa*, ed. by Vansina, Mauny, and Thomas, London, pp. 390–411.

—— 1964*a*. 'The Growth of Islamic Learning in Ghana', *JHSN*, ii. 409–17.

—— 1965. 'Ghana', *The Encyclopaedia of Islam* (new ed.), ii. 1003–4.

—— 1966. 'The Position of Muslims in Metropolitan Ashanti in the Early 19th Century', in *Islam in Tropical Africa*, ed. by I. M. Lewis, London, pp. 318–41.

—— 1966*a*. 'Aspects of Bureaucratization in Ashanti in the Nineteenth Century', *JAH*, vii. 215–32.

—— 1967. 'Ashanti Government', in *West African Kingdoms in the Nineteenth Century*, ed. by D. Forde and P. M. Kaberry, London.

WITHERS-GILL, J., 1924. *The Moshi Tribe*, Accra.

WOLFSON, F., 1958. *Pageant of Ghana*, London.

ZAHAN, D., 1961. 'Pour une histoire des Mossi du Yatenga', *L'Homme*, i. 5–22.

ZECH, VON, 1949. 'Land und Leute an der Nordwest Grenze von Togo', recueilli et trad. par Froelich et Neth, *Études Dahoméennes*.

ZWERNEMANN, J., 1958. 'Shall we use the word "Gurunsi"?', *Africa*, xxviii. 123–5.

2. UNPUBLISHED MANUSCRIPTS

(*a*) *Theses*

ALEXANDRE, P., Dipl. 1959, 'The political Institutions of the Kotokoli, a tribe of Northern Togo'. University of London. Diploma in Anthropology.

DRY, D.PHIL., 'The Position of Islam in Hausa Society'. Oxford University.

FYNN, J. K., PH.D. 1964, 'Ashanti and her neighbours, *c.* 1700–1807'. University of London.

HILTON, T. E., PH.D. 1956, 'The Distribution and Density of Population in the Gold Coast and Togoland'. University of London.

LAVERS, J. H., M.SC. 1964, 'The Organisation and Distribution of Trade in Central Sudan'. University of London.

TORDOFF, W., PH.D. 1961, 'The Political History of Ashanti, 1888–1935'. University of London.

(*b*) *Notes and Reports*

ANGELIER, M., 'Essai de Monographie d'un canton Gourmantche. Le Canton de Diapangou (Haute-Volta)' (1958). CHEAM, no. 2836.

ARMSTRONG, J. A., 'Essays on the Peoples of Nandom and Lambussie' (1933). NAG, Tamale, C. 430.

BEYRIES (GOUVERNEUR), 'L'Islam au Soudan Français' (1956). CHEAM, no. 2940.

BRAIMA, J. A., 'A History of Gonja'. Consulted at IAS, Legon.

CARDINALL, A. W., 'Correlative Report on Native Customs' (1927). NAG, Tamale, C. 2.

CHAILLEY, M., 'L'Islam au Dahomey' (1959/60). CHEAM, no. 3241.

DAVIES, A. W., 'The History and Organisation of the "Kambonse" in Dagomba', NAG, Tamale, C. 459.

DICKSON, J. R., 'A Short History of Atebubu' (1933). NAG, Kumasi, B. 538.

DUNCAN-JOHNSTONE, A. C., 'Enquiry into the Constitution and Organisation of the Gbanya Kingdom' (1930). NAG, Tamale.

EYRE-SMITH, 'Comments on "Interim Report on the people of Nandom and Lambussie Divisions of the Lawra District" ' (1933). NAG, Tamale, C. 431.

FELL, T. E., 'Notes on the History of Banda' (1913). NAG, Kumasi, D. 216.

GILBERT, 'Report on the Constitution, Organisation and Customs of the Nanumba People' (probably 1930s). NAG, Tamale, C. 470.

GOULDSBURY, DR. V. S., 'Report of his Journey into the Interior of the Gold Coast' (27. 3. 1876). PRO, Enclosure in no. 5162/5 CO. 96/119.

GROSHENRY, 'Les migrations dans le Haut Dahomey' (1950). CHEAM, no. 1665.

GUINNESS, J., 'A Report on the Origins and Journeys of the People of Tumu' (1933). NAG, Tamale, C. 471.

——, 'Interim Report on the Peoples of the Nandom and Lambussie Divisions of the Lawra District' (1933). NAG, Tamale, C. 430.

HOBBS, H. J., 'Notes on the History of Mo' (1919). NAG, Kumasi, D. 216.

—— 'Notes on the History of Banda' (1926). NAG, Kumasi, D. 216.

LECOMTE, R., 'L'Islamisation du cercle de Séguela' (1953). CHEAM, no. 2178.

MACKAY, C. F., 'A Short Essay on the History and Customs of the Mamprusi Tribe'. NAG, acc. no. 1521.

MATHIEU, M., 'Notes sur l'Islam et le christianisme dans la subdivision centrale d'Ouagadougou' (1956) CHEAM, no. 2619.

MATTEI, R., 'L'Empire du Mogho-Naba, les chefferies, contribution à la connaissance de l'Islam en pays Mossi' (1960). CHEAM, no. 3326.

PITT, W. J., 'The Mfantra' (1925). NAG, Kumasi, D. 216.

PUJOL, 'Christianisme et colonisation en pays Mossi' (1956). CHEAM, no. 2684.

RATTRAY, CAPT. R. S., 'Annual Report, April 1929–April 1930'. NAG, Tamale, C.1.

READ, MAJOR M., 'Essay on the Peoples of the North-Western Province' (n.d., probably in the 1910s). NAG, Tamale, C. 437.

RICHARD-MOLARD, J., 'L'Islam comme ferment cyclique en Afrique Noire' (1950). CHEAM, no. 1682.

SYME, J. K. G., 'The Kusasis, a Short History' (1932). NAG, Tamale, C. 406.

TAMAKLOE, E. F., 'A Brief History of the Nanumba People'. (Obtained from a teacher in Yendi, now at IAS.)

TOMLINSON, H. H., 'The Customs, Constitution and History of the Gonja People' (1954). Reproduced in mimeograph by IAS, Legon.

WHITTALL, P. E., 'A Short History of Tumu District' (1912). NAG, 135/54.

(*c*) *Hausa and Arabic Manuscripts*

S.O.A.S. Library, 'History of Babatu, Samori, and Others by Mallam Abu', acc. No. Hausa, 98017.

University of Ibadan, *Bayān ujūb al-hijra 'alā 'l-'ibād*, by Shaykh 'Uthmān b. Fūdī, acc. No. 82/53.

—— *Rawḍ al-jinān fī dhikr manāqib 'sh-shaykh 'Uthmān*, by Wazir Gidadu b. Layma. 82/28.

Krause manuscripts, 'Gottlob Adolf Krauses Haussa-Handschriften in der Preussischen Staatsbibliothek Berlin', *MSOS*, 1928, pp. 105–7, xxviii–lxxx. (Several manuscripts translated by Mr. T. Moustapha at Legon.)

Royal Library, Copenhagen, 'Arabic MSS. from the Guinea Coast', Cod. Arab. CCCII.

IAS, Legon, Collection of Arabic manuscripts: IAS/AR- . . .

3. ARCHIVES

Public Record Office, London.

National Archives of Ghana (NAG), Accra, Kumasi, Tamale.

District Offices in Ghana.

Archives Nationales, section d'Outre Mer, Paris.

Ministère de l'Intérieur, Ouagadougou.

Bureaux de Cercles, Haute Volta (Boromo, Bobo-Dyulaso, Leo).

INDEX

Figures in italics refer to pages where the subject concerned is specially treated.

PRINTED IN GREAT BRITAIN
AT THE UNIVERSITY PRESS, OXFORD
BY VIVIAN RIDLER
PRINTER TO THE UNIVERSITY